T0245659

Scott Ryder served for 22 years with the Australian Army, including sixteen years as an operator with the 2nd Commando Regiment. He served in East Timor and on multiple tours of Afghanistan and Iraq. He holds numerous commendations and a Masters of Business, and he works with veteran charities to improve the lives of veterans and their families.

PRAISE FOR *FORGED IN FIRE*

'Prepare to be riveted by this extraordinary account from one of Australia's elite warriors. In this gripping narrative, Scott Ryder takes readers deep into the heart of combat, sharing not only the intensity and challenges of special forces operations but also the camaraderie and resilience that define the men and women of the Australian defence force. His firsthand experiences, vividly recounted, offer an unparalleled glimpse into the courage, strategy and sacrifice required to be the best. This book is not just an account of battles fought and won; it's a testament to the human spirit when faced with extreme pressure under enemy fire. It is an absolute must-read for anyone seeking an authentic, powerful and unflinching look at modern warfare.'

Daniel Keighran EMBA, VC

'Scott is not famous; his chest is not bedecked with the grandest tin and ribbon. His voice is from among us rather than up on high. And his account of the DNA of the commando, the lesser sung super-soldier, is all the better for it.'

From the foreword by Chris Masters, author of
Flawed Hero* and *No Front Line

FORGED IN FIRE

AN AUSTRALIAN COMMANDO'S STORY OF
LIFE AND DEATH ON THE FRONTLINE

SCOTT RYDER

ALLEN&UNWIN
SYDNEY•MELBOURNE•AUCKLAND•LONDON

Allen and Unwin
Cammeraygal Country
83 Alexander Street
Crows Nest NSW 2065
Australia
Phone: (61 2) 8425 0100
Email: info@allenandunwin.com
Web: www.allenandunwin.com

Allen and Unwin acknowledges the Traditional Owners of the Country on which we live and work. We pay our respects to all Aboriginal and Torres Strait Islander Elders, past and present.

 A catalogue record for this book is available from the National Library of Australia

ISBN 978 1 76147 141 4

Set in 13/16.7 pt Minion Pro by Midland Typesetters, Australia

10 9 8 7 6 5 4 3 2 1

To my daughter.
I hope this makes you proud one day.

'Out of every one hundred men, ten shouldn't even be there, eighty are just targets, nine are the real fighters, and we are lucky to have them, for they make the battle. Ah, but the one, one is a warrior, and he will bring the others back.'

Heraclitus

CONTENTS

ABBREVIATIONS

1 Cdo Regt	1st Commando Regiment (Reserve)
1 SAS Sqn	1st Squadron, Special Air Service Regiment
2 Cdo Regt	2nd Commando Regiment
2ic	second-in-command
2 RAR	2nd Battalion, Royal Australian Regiment
2 SAS Sqn	2nd Squadron, Special Air Service Regiment
3 RAR	3rd Battalion, Royal Australian Regiment
3 SAS Sqn	3rd Squadron, Special Air Service Regiment
4 RAR (Cdo)	4th Battalion, Royal Australian Regiment (Commando) (later 2 Cdo Regt)
6 Avn Regt	6th Aviation Regiment
ACQB	advanced close-quarter battle
ADF	Australian Defence Force
ADFSSO	Australian Defence Force School of Special Operations
AFP	Australian Federal Police
AH-64	Apache attack helicopter
AME	aeromedical evacuation

ANA	Afghan National Army
APC	armoured personnel carriers
ATV	all-terrain vehicle
CFA	combat first-aider
CHQ	company headquarters
CO	commanding officer
CPP	close personal protection
CQB	close-quarter battle
BCQ	basic close-quarter battle
CRTC	commando reinforcement and training cycle
CSM	company sergeant major
DA	direct action
DS	directing staff (military instructors)
DSM	Distinguished Service Medal
FE	force element
FE-A	Force Element Alpha—SASR
FE-B	Force Element Bravo—2 Cdo Regt
FE-E	Force Element Echo—SOER
HR	hostage rescue
HQ SOCOMD	Headquarters Special Operations Command (previously SOHQ)
HR	hostage rescue
IED	improvised explosive device
INTERFET	International Force East Timor
IRR	Incident Response Regiment (later SOER)
ISR	Intelligence, Surveillance and Reconnaissance
JTAC	joint terminal attack air controller
KIA	killed in action
MARSOC	(US) Marine Special Operations Command
MG	Medal for Gallantry
MRE	mission rehearsal exercise

ABBREVIATIONS

NCO	non-commissioned officer
ND	negligent discharge (of a weapon)
NVG	night-vision goggles
OC	officer commanding
OIC	officer in charge
OP	observation post
Operator	generic term for special forces soldiers from 1 Cdo Regt, SASR, 2 Cdo Regt or SOER
PKM	(Russian-made) Pulemyot Kalashnikova machine gun
PMV	protected mobility vehicle
POD	period of darkness
PRC	provincial response unit
PSD	personal security detachment
PT	physical training
RAAF	Royal Australian Air Force
RAN	Royal Australian Navy
RAPSL	ram-air parachute static line
RAR	Royal Australian Regiment
RMO	regimental medical officer
ROE	rules of engagement
RPG	rocket-propelled grenade
RSM	regimental sergeant major
RW	rotary wing (usually helicopter)
SASR	Special Air Service Regiment
SF	special forces
SFTF	Special Forces Training Facility
SNCO	senior non-commissioned officer
SOCOMD	Australian Special Operations Command
SOER	Special Operations Engineer Regiment (formerly IRR)

SOG	Special Operations Group, Victoria
SOHQ	Special Operations Headquarters (later HQ SOCOMD)
SOTG	Special Operations Task Group
SRV	special reconnaissance vehicle
STU	Special Tactics Unit, Iraq
TAG-E	Tactical Assault Group–East
TAG-W	Tactical Assault Group–West
TF66	Task Force 66
TF632	Task Force 632
TIC	troops in contact
TK	Tarin Kowt, Afghanistan (also spelled Tarinkot)
TL	team leader
UAE	United Arab Emirates
UD	unauthorised discharge (of a weapon)
UH-60	Black Hawk utility helicopter
UNTAET	United Nations Transitional Administration East Timor
VC	Victoria Cross/Victoria Cross for Australia
VDO	vehicle drop-off
WO	warrant officer

FOREWORD
FROM CHRIS MASTERS

It is a rare boast to claim friendship with operators at all points of the ultra-competitive special forces trident. The special operations engineers were the most welcoming—less elitist and more engaged with civilian values and skill sets. The Special Air Service Regiment (SASR) was the hardest, given its enhanced exclusivity and that it is an established brand in need of no publicity. And in the middle, the 2nd Commando Regiment (2 Cdo Regt). While not exactly media-friendly, it had a story to tell that had so far failed to reach the Australian public.

Those of 2 Cdo Regt, badged in 2009 and formed from an infantry battalion, 4 RAR (Cdo), were commonly disparaged as upstarts by the rival SASR, which drew on a deeper history (it was formed in 1957) and the heritage of its famed British namesake.

To those unfamiliar with inter-unit rivalry, the depth of animosity between these big dogs of special forces (which is reflected in these pages) might come as a surprise. I know I struggled when embedded in Afghanistan with the combined yet fractious task force. The 'dos' (commandos) and 'cats' (SASR), as they termed each other, stood determinedly apart, mirroring the continental divide: the sandy-bereted SASR based in Perth, and green-bereted 2 Cdo Regt in Sydney.

When they were herded together at Camp Russell in Afghanistan's Uruzgan province, the commando lament was that when special forces attracted bad publicity, it was their fault, but when the news was good, SASR got the credit. Given that my job was to tell the story, cooperation, which was a touch more forthcoming from the 'dos', was welcome. And I was persuaded. It soon became apparent that recognition was deserved.

2 Cdo Regt, operating with larger numbers than SASR, and with greater combat power, was regularly engaged in heavy fighting. The raids on the heroin facilities that helped finance the insurgency took them deep into neighbouring Helmand and the furnace of battle.

One such raid, south into Kandahar, brought the author of this book close to death. Indeed, three of his comrades did not survive that helicopter crash, which also claimed the life of the US crew chief as well as seriously injuring all other occupants.

Of the many tales that will be told of Afghanistan, among the most inspirational is the fight for life by the seven surviving commandos of that crash. Their families were in it too, and somewhere in the middle of a tortuous recovery period I met Scott and his wife, Sarah.

I was struck by both their difference and their similarity. Scott is cocky and charmingly irreverent. Sarah is shy with a reserved selflessness familiar among civilian partners. But what they had in common was a striking indomitability. They were not going to be beaten.

A common feature of the special forces persona is the pursuit of excellence. High performance is less an objective than a norm. For Scott, after all that training, being put out to pasture was unthinkable. And against all odds, he not only recovered from the catastrophic injuries he sustained in that helicopter crash, but was able to pass a series of exacting combat fitness tests that returned him to a cherished and unbroken brotherhood.

We connected from time to time. I liked his company. Scott has an innate capacity for reflection, and this too can be a soldierly trait. They spend a lot of time thinking and yarning. The interior self can be on show with other soldiers, but rarely with outsiders. And for plenty of soldiers, it remains entirely concealed. Seeing too much can make the processing too grim a challenge.

When writing about the Afghanistan conflict and interviewing veterans for the Australian War Memorial, I came to appreciate the rawness of accounting from the common—or, if you like, uncommon—soldier. While the officers choose their words with care, the other ranks, if you can get them to talk, gush forth unfiltered. While their respect for superiors is sparsely rationed, and their appreciation of command responsibility scant and grudging, right or wrong they tell it as they see it.

And there you have Sergeant Scott Ryder. Here is a book from a soldier who not only lives and breathes 'on the tools', as he puts it, but knows how to describe it from the inside out. Scott is not famous; his chest is not bedecked with the grandest tin and ribbon. His voice is from among us rather than up on high. And his account of the DNA of the commando, the lesser sung super-soldier, is all the better for it.

PROLOGUE

I'm getting frustrated at the overburdened internet, waiting for my search results for 'how to write an autobiography', while sitting beside my bunk bed on my third deployment to Afghanistan. This is how this book started—as a way for me to capture my thoughts, jotting down memories and stories over a decade, and culminating in a year-long labour of love to get it written. As I wrote, I was unsure if this would ever be seen by a publisher or would simply become a collection of memories shoved away in a drawer. Either way, it has been a challenging, rewarding and cathartic experience.

Everyone has a story to tell. I have met so many extraordinary people, from all walks of life, who have faced significant challenges to survive, and whose stories inspire and motivate their readers. My story is unique, but it doesn't compare to many people's daily hardships, losses and sufferings, a fact of which I am acutely aware.

I didn't write this book to feed my ego or promote myself—there are enough titles in the military genre doing that. Nor is this book designed to be a historical account of Australian military operations—other authors have done a far better job of that than I ever would. This book aims to give you an honest, insightful look into a young man who joined the Australian Army at seventeen and dedicated 22 and a half years of his life to doing a job he loved with a passion.

Australia's primary war-fighting special forces (SF) unit, the 2nd Commando Regiment (2 Cdo Regt), has a short but proud history in which I played a small part. Although the regiment's achievements over the past few decades could not fit in one book, writers such as Chris Masters have done an exceptional job of capturing its involvement in Afghanistan. Masters' book *No Front Line*, which every Australian should read, has a level of research and detail that I cannot fathom.

By telling my story, I do not wish to minimise or discount the experiences of other operators in Australia's longest war, who have all fought with enormous courage in some of the fiercest combat Australian soldiers have seen since the Vietnam War. The events in this book are accurate as far as I can remember them. Others may remember some dates, places and events differently, but I can only tell my story from my eyes and memory.

Where I am describing events I didn't witness myself, I have done my best to capture the accounts of those willing to share them with me. For others, it was just too painful. Countless more stories could fill multiple books, and I hope one day they will. In the Australian participation in the Global War on Terror, 2 Cdo Regt has seen the most casualties—the physical scars are evident when you walk past the companies at Tobruk Lines, the commando barracks in Sydney, while the emotional scars, kept hidden for so long, are slowly starting to surface, increasing each year since the war ended.

I want the sacrifices of the partners and families to be recognised. Without their love and unwavering support, our job would be impossible. This book could never have been written without the love and support of my beautiful wife, Sarah, who has also been through so much with me. She willingly took a back seat to my career, and her devotion and support will never be forgotten.

As the war in Afghanistan recedes into the past, and stories of combat and sacrifice are replaced with reports of SF war crimes allegations, I hope this book serves as a counter-narrative—a small glimpse behind the curtain of a secretive world that has taken so much from so few.

Additionally, I want to give injured soldiers hope and show them that sometimes doctors can get it wrong. It's a long road, but there is light at the end of the tunnel, and willpower knows no bounds. For many of us, the battle doesn't end with the flight back home.

This book is dedicated to the fallen heroes of modern Australia and the current generation of operators holding the torch until they are again called into the fray. This is for all those broken men whose lives will never be the same, and their families, who are left to pick up the pieces.

Always remembered. Without Warning.

CHAPTER 1

BOY SOLDIER

I was born in Nepal, and my family returned to Australia to live when I was twelve years old.

Starting over is a big deal for any child, but it seemed worse than death for a kid who was used to being the odd one out—not many blonds in Nepal. With time, though, I warmed to the idea. I took solace from the fact that I would be the top dog at my new school in Australia. Despite being half Nepalese, I figured I would look like everyone else, and I assumed that I sounded like everyone else when I spoke, so I saw no reason not to be accepted straight away. In fact, I was confident that within a few weeks I would be running the show. How wrong I was.

My parents were starting again, well into their thirties. They were building up their lives from scratch, a stage most people go through in their twenties, as we flew to Australia with the bags we had and nothing else. I cannot even begin to comprehend how difficult or stressful that must have been for them.

When we arrived, we initially lived with my mother's parents in the Hills district in north-western Sydney, in the suburb of Kellyville, which at the time could still be categorised as semi-rural. My grand-parents had built the house, pool and granny flat with their bare hands, and after we moved in, my granddad made an additional bedroom for me and my sister.

It wasn't ideal, but it was a godsend for a family making a fresh start. The granny flat was a simple demountable building with a kitchenette and lounge room, and an outdoor laundry and toilet. With the typical naivety of a child, it wasn't until I started to visit my friends' houses in early high school that I realised my family was a bit different from the rest.

My granddad, Jim, was a good old-fashioned, hardworking Aussie larrikin who worked for years for the local council and an engineering company as a fitter and turner, among many other jobs. Growing up in his house meant following all the rules my mother and her sister had had to follow when they were young—keeping elbows off the table, using manners, helping with the chores, and so on. Jim was also a keen amateur radioman, and had a huge radio mast.

He spent most nights in his radio room speaking to his mates, other radio aficionados, worldwide via voice or Morse code. I would spend countless hours talking on the radio and watching him fix things, and I eagerly practised Morse code to follow in his footsteps. Jim also had a shed where he would build his projects and repair almost anything that had broken, even building a fully certified mini steam engine from scratch—every piston, chamber and wheel was handcrafted on his lathe. He would often take me under his wing and try to teach me carpentry or welding—which I learned with moderate enthusiasm but have yet to take to.

Outside of that, my teens are a blur. I was a late bloomer, a skinny kid with floppy hair and no strengths to speak of at school. I enjoyed history, particularly modern history, and English, but most classes during my high school years were spent attention-seeking and being disruptive. I always seemed to be on the fringes of groups in my year, always accepted but never the first pick—in sports or for dates.

As a child, my inability to concentrate for any significant period and my never-ending energy were a double-edged sword. On the one hand, these things made me extraordinarily productive and proactive, and on the other they made it difficult to immerse myself in complex tasks and be present. It was not until I was considering discharge from the army that I realised I had almost all the signs and symptoms of ADHD, and I am sure this would come as no surprise to anyone who has spent even five minutes talking to me.

There were simple things, like my inability to relax at a restaurant or enjoy family holidays. I could never be calm, and was constantly fidgeting. If I had attended primary school in Australia, it's likely that my issue would have been identified early on and remedied, but I am also thankful that it wasn't, as I would have had no chance at all to make a career in the military with diagnosed ADHD.

Still, there were some things I took to. I played soccer for the local club for a few years, and also began taking taekwondo classes in my area. I loved the intensity and agility of the sport and attained my black belt when I was sixteen. I also competed in tournaments, including the state championship, and for a time there, I aspired to represent Australia in the Olympics. Still, I lacked the prerequisite talent—and I was too focused on army cadets.

Over time, violence became the primary method by which I attempted to find acceptance. At my new Australian school, I was bullied by a bunch of local kids. I suppose my slight accent and the fact that I was thrown into the mix with kids who had known each other since kindergarten didn't help. My mother, whose advice centred on 'Sticks and stones may break your bones, but words will never hurt you', always counselled me to turn the other cheek and be the bigger person.

Advice that seems sound for an adult, however, doesn't necessarily resonate with a twelve-year-old in the playground. I had been training in taekwondo for a while by then, so one day, when I'd had a gutful of the bullying and insults, I turned around and punched my antagonist square in the face. Stunned, the kid, who was much bigger than me, squirmed away holding his nose, crying and embarrassed. A few months later, another kid pushed me down the stairs, so again, I punched him in the face. This time, however, my aim was off and I hit him in the ear. He too scurried away. I waited for the inevitable reprimand from the teachers, but I heard nothing. Then something interesting happened. More people started talking to me and asking me if I wanted to go for bike rides after school.

In the mind of a twelve-year-old seeking acceptance, therefore, the modus operandi was sealed: throwing fists and spinning heel kicks. Unfortunately for me, however, my MO didn't change until I was well into my twenties. My pride could not handle the fact that people thought they could bully or intimidate me at bars and clubs due to my small frame. I refused to walk away and, much to the admiration and bewilderment of my mates, my fists would fly.

I started to gain a reputation as a fighter, and I think that made a part of me proud, to follow in the footsteps of my father, who had also been known to throw a punch or two in his younger days. I am baffled and thankful that the countless bar and street fights I was in did not land me in serious trouble with the law, and that I didn't get hurt myself or hurt someone else. Years later, when Sydney's nightlife was decimated after a string of 'coward punches' that killed a bunch of young men, I used to breathe a sigh of relief that I hadn't killed anyone. But I came close to facing charges once, when I was about 22.

A bunch of army mates and I were drinking in George Street in Sydney's Rocks area when a group of people sitting near us started getting rowdy. One chap, whom I guessed to be in his mid-thirties, decided to throw the old, 'What are you staring at, cunt?' What I was staring at was his missus, a stunning blonde in a short black dress. I didn't bother with a response, but jumped on the table and started throwing my fists at his head and, for good measure, his mate's as well. Security was soon dragging me out in an armlock, which I presume was not much of a challenge with a 174-centimetre, 62-kilogram lad. It was then that I saw what I thought was a familiar face advancing towards me.

I thought the bloke was friends with the group I had just done battle with, which left me with no option but to fight him. My arms were still being held behind my back, but as the threat approached, I kicked him square in the face. As it turned out, though, the kid was familiar to me because he worked at the pub as a glassie, and the only reason he was walking in my direction was to clean up the broken glass after my game of fisticuffs in the corner.

I was arrested and taken to the Rocks police station to await my fate. Thankfully, nobody was willing to press charges and I was released with a firm warning.

Don't allow me to delude you about my fighting prowess. I lost just as many fights as I won, and regularly came home with black eyes, a broken nose and a mild concussion. As I said, I'm amazed I was never seriously hurt.

I joined the army cadets in Year 7. Public schools did not have cadet units, which in Sydney were typically left to prestigious private schools, but my parents drove me to a cadet unit based out of North Sydney

Boys High School. At twelve years old, I sat there while older teenagers from the 206 Regional Cadet Unit addressed us in their immaculately pressed camouflage uniforms, and I was hooked. That day I knew my fate was to be a soldier, and I held that belief for another 28 years until my discharge in 2023.

When I reflect on my time as a cadet, I realise that the training and activities we participated in would not happen these days. All I see cadets do now is drill on the parade ground and receive many PowerPoint presentations. My time as a cadet at the 206 Regional Cadet Unit, however, must have been a window of unprecedented autonomy for the adult cadet officers who oversaw us. Our Tuesday nights were spent learning how to use the 7.62mm Fabrique Nationale self-loading rifle (L1A1 SLR), which I knew from reading all my war books was the standard-issue rifle for foot soldiers during Australia's involvement in the Vietnam War.

We abseiled off the high school's roof and learned first aid, minor craft handling and how to use and talk on radios. The unit was run by an ex–British Army reservist paratrooper and an ex–Australian Army Reserve commando, and the team had a distinct special operations flavour to it. The unit headdress was the maroon beret I knew was the beret for airborne infantry worldwide, and it made me immensely proud.

I attended every single training night and weekend bivouac. I climbed quickly through the ranks, leading teams on weekends of minor craft handling, learning how to drive and maintain zodiac inflatable craft, navigating through the bush with a map and compass, and spending many nights in the rain sleeping under 'hootchies' (plastic sheets that you anchor and angle to create a hasty, low-visibility rain cover) while getting eaten alive by mosquitoes.

I learned at a young age that my blood must be cocaine for mosquitoes, as every time I was in the field I would be attacked mercilessly, while the man beside me barely got a bite. It was a torture that I would endure for my entire army career.

One experience that sticks in my mind was a week-long field activity in Wisemans Ferry, north-west of Sydney on the Hawkesbury River. We were camped on a private property, where we were training in minor craft handling and field craft. It had been a long day, and when we were finally told to move onto a steep hill and set up our hootchies, torrential rain began to fall. The officer commanding (OC), an ex-commando, wanted us to experience sleeping in rugged terrain—this is a typical tactic for training reconnaissance and SF patrols, as it minimises their chances of compromise by the enemy. When we finally got settled into our sleeping bags, cold and soaked through, the OC's parting words were, 'Welcome to the infantry.' The other kids groaned, muttered under their breath and swore; I had a smile from ear to ear.

When I was sixteen, I was allowed to attend the cadet parachute course at the civilian skydiving centre in Nowra, a few hours south of Sydney. After a weekend's ground training, we had to jump out of a Cessna aircraft on a static line (which opened the parachute automatically) with a square parachute. Naturally I found it exhilarating, and I caught the parachute bug. Later, when I joined the recon/snipers platoon in 3 RAR, I learned that this was a version of the ram-air parachute static line (RAPSL) that I would repeat frequently in my career.

Cadets is also where I fell in love with shooting. Our unit would ask volunteers to go out to Hornsby Rifle Range, where we would work in the butts[1] party, lifting targets for the old blokes from the different rifle clubs. Ultimately, we would be given a few hours to shoot all their guns, where I learned I was a natural. I spent even more time at the range during the week.

I was subsequently selected to attend the Australian Army Skill at Arms Meeting in the cadet division, where I took out the top three positions in the shooting matches I competed in. Little did I know that I was forming the building blocks of a mastery of arms I would draw upon numerous times as an adult in Australia's longest war.

After a few suspensions from school, I was advised to enrol in the Duke of Edinburgh award program to earn back some brownie points. I agreed, as many of my mates in cadets were also completing the program. This international youth development program designed for 14- to 24-year-olds included volunteering, skills and physical recreation, and I eagerly signed up for an upcoming hike in the New South Wales Snowy Mountains.

The hike was from Guthega Power Station through to Mount Kosciusko, and we would do it over three days. As soon as we began, a mate and I stormed off, eager to get to every stop first. For some reason, the two teachers stayed at the back of the group, which allowed me to get further down the track. Around Mount Tate, fog and heavy rain set in, reducing visibility on the slippery path, leading the teachers to turn the group around. Of course, my mate and I, who had already summited and were waiting for the rest of the group, needed to be made aware.

Rain and fog consumed us while we waited on top of the hill. After an hour or so, I decided we needed to get off the mountain, as the rain and freezing wind were cutting straight through our clothes. My mate was beginning to show signs of hypothermia, so we cut a track off the mountain and into a creek line that offered some shelter from the wind.

We came across two adult hikers who were also seeking refuge from the wind, and they allowed us into their tent to wait out the storm. Meanwhile, the teachers, now frantic, spent the night walking up and down the track, desperately looking but unable to find us, as the tent we were in was on low ground and not visible from the trail, even in good weather.

My grandmother was in the kitchen preparing lunch when she heard a broadcast on ABC Radio about two high school kids from Sydney who had gone missing in the Snowy Mountains. She called my mother immediately, and my mum knew that if any kids were missing, I would be one of them. The school had failed to contact our families, in the hope of finding us first, which only added to the panic and fear of our parents. New South Wales police, ambulance and rescue services had been activated to find these missing kids, and the media were beginning to gather at the rescue centres to tell this familiar national story.

Safe in the tent, we got a few hours' sleep. When I woke up in the morning, I walked to the top of the mountain where I could get some mobile reception and called my mum to tell her where we were, which she passed on to emergency services.

We were found a few hours later, much to the disappointment of the media, who must have been hoping for a juicer news story.

CHAPTER 2

SIGN HERE

I had always had a keen interest in the army and wanted to join, but the desire became even stronger as I grew older. I was around fifteen years old and riding my bike on the road where we lived. It was a warm summer afternoon, and as I glided down the road towards home, I looked up at a spectacular red sky. I stopped, sat on my bike and looked up, and had an incredible yearning to be in the clouds.

The thought of flying around in the sky and jumping out of the big green Hercules plane I used to see flying from the Richmond Royal Australian Air Force (RAAF) base on the outskirts of Sydney—and getting paid to do it—seemed like a dream career. I had spent countless hours talking with my cadet mates about what a job in the 'regs' (jargon among cadets and reservists for permanent full-time soldiers) would look like. I also viewed the army as able to provide me with a cashflow I'd never had.

We had moved from my grandparents' place a year or so after coming to Australia and were now renting a modest three-bedroom house a few minutes away. It was hardly a palace, yet it seemed like Versailles compared to the two-room granny flat.

My father worked for years as a painter before switching to working in a factory, placing labels on bottles of product. It was mind-numbing, low-paying work, but he never complained.

My mother was working at a bank, also on a modest income, so there was not much money to throw around on stuff all my other friends seemed to have at my age. Joining the army at seventeen would give me income for the things I wanted. In addition, the unit that I desperately wanted to join, the 3rd Battalion of the Royal Australian Regiment (3 RAR), was based at Holsworthy Barracks in Sydney. It was an ideal situation; I could be a soldier, and still see all my friends and family, *and* flaunt my newfound wealth—perfect.

I used my time in cadets to seek as much information as possible about the army, the infantry, and particularly 3 RAR, and as I approached seventeen, I became obsessed. Everything I read was about the military, wars and the army. I studied army recruiting brochures cover to cover and religiously read the army magazine that was still publicly circulating. I asked questions of anyone who would give me the time of day about the job, the hours, life on exercises, anything.

It sounded like an exciting life. I could not fathom why a fit young man would opt for a mundane office job or work in finance or marketing. The youthful exuberance that would give me my first career has also cost me a lot over the years. Still, I have zero regrets.

I still did all the things typical teenage boys did. I chased after girls, drank too much beer, went to parties and smoked cigarettes, but it was almost as if I was playing along until I could start my life correctly, as a soldier. All my friends were happy just waiting to turn eighteen and going to a few parties; I can only recall a few of my schoolmates speaking of career aspirations or even moving out of home. And if I was already sure about my career path, the events in Timor in 1999 cemented my life's trajectory for good.

Around this time the Australian Defence Force (ADF) was deployed as part of International Force East Timor (INTERFET). I watched with enthusiasm the news of the army's involvement, particularly when it touched on 2 RAR and 3 RAR. I cut out every article from the papers on the operation. I recorded on VHS every clip I found on the news, watched them on repeat and cursed the universe for not allowing me to have been born a few years earlier so I could be on the nightly news too, kicking in doors in Dili with 3 RAR soldiers, who, for me, took on godlike status. I could not wait to join their ranks.

Before I knew it, I was sixteen and nine months and, with my parents' blessing, I booked into the ADF recruiting office in Parramatta in Sydney's west. When I arrived, I introduced myself to the sergeant I was meeting, and before waiting for any more nonsense, informed him my name was Scott Ryder, that I wished to join the Australian Regular Army as an infantryman, and that I wanted to be posted to 3 RAR.

The plump Ordnance Corps sergeant (I recognised the badge on his polyester uniform), with all the charisma of the door I'd just opened, sat back in his chair and responded with, 'Hang on, young fella, there's a whole lot more to do before we get to that stage. Do you know all the other available jobs?'

I was baffled. What did this fat fuck not understand? I was a paratrooper in waiting, and all I needed for him to do was to start the paperwork.

'We have no positions available for infantry right now, mate. How does artillery or transport sound to you?' he asked.

I was crushed. My dreams were shattered in an instant, and I was speechless.

The sergeant must have seen my look of panic and despair. 'Okay then, Scott, what do you know about the infantry and 3 RAR?' he asked.

This was my moment to shine. I had been preparing for this for a long time. I took a deep breath, and then, in a three-minute burst, told him about basic training at Kapooka, infantry training at Singleton and the introductory parachute course at Nowra, as well as the role of the infantry. I didn't stop there, however. I continued with a breakdown of 3 RAR by subunit, and talked about recent operations in Timor, which platoons made up Support Company, what a day in the life of an infanteer in the battalion looked like, and typical infantry weapons systems and their main uses.

With a slight grin, the sergeant sat back in his chair and folded his arms.

'Look, mate,' I blurted out, 'I'm not some kid who's seen too many movies and wants to be Rambo; I know I'm young, but this is what I'm supposed to do for the rest of my life. The only reason I wasn't in here sooner is that I wasn't old enough.'

His grin widened. 'Well, Mr Ryder,' he responded, 'you've certainly done your homework, haven't you?'

I got a letter of offer in the mail the following week.

My birthday is in December, so I had to wait until April to start my basic soldier course at Kapooka near Wagga Wagga in southern New South Wales the following year. I had left school at the end of Year 10 on the advice of my teacher, who knew I wished to join the army and was tired of my constant disruptions and lack of interest in schooling. So, at sixteen, I decided to begin building my wealth and looked for a job.

First I worked at Pizza Hut, where I was sacked after three weeks. I worked at a video shop for another few weeks, which was easy enough, although I did get a warning after I put adult videos in the kids' section for my own amusement. Their willingness to endure my immaturity met its limits at their Christmas party, held at the chain owner's home. I can't recall what I told my parents to be allowed to attend a party with 60 adults, nor do I know how the owner thought it would be okay to invite underage kids to a party filled with booze, but there I was. So I dutifully did what any other sixteen-year-old kid would do: I got blind drunk. So much so that I passed out in the owner's bedroom, covered in my own vomit, where his wife found me. That ended my entertainment sales career.

I then got a job with a painter and decorator, who took me on as a painter's labourer and, after a few weeks, began teaching me how to paint. I was only paid a measly $200 a week, but it was enough to cover the cost of cigarettes and clothes, and, more importantly, it taught me the value of hard work.

One afternoon I was standing in a garage doorframe near the RAAF base in Richmond, when a C-130 Hercules roared above us. I had hurriedly climbed up the ladder and stood on the roof to get a better view of the plane when paratroopers started spewing out the side doors. I stood and watched in amazement, unable to get enough of the marvellous sight of the airborne invasion, as the parachutes disappeared behind the row of houses between me and the drop zone. A few minutes later, I was back on the ground, looking at a nowhere-near-complete doorframe, and the stark contrast between paratroopers jumping from planes and my reality of sanding doorframes sank in. I vowed I would never have another dull job like this and yearned for the time when I'd be jumping out of those stallions of the sky. I counted down every day till I was old enough to join the army, consumed by the anticipation and excitement of starting my dream career.

After my oath of allegiance to the Queen at the Sydney recruiting office in front of friends and family, I hopped on a bus at seventeen, bound for the army. My first day was Anzac Day 2001, and after the dawn service we kicked off the first week.

I recall looking around and thinking how much older and bigger all the other men were, and a tiny seed of inadequacy was planted. These feelings stayed with me my entire military career, and aside from making me doubt my abilities, they motivated me to try harder. To my surprise, however, some of the oldest and biggest men quit the training, which gave me my first lesson of the army: size does not equate to competence.

My section commander, an artillery bombardier, disliked me and was always at me about wishing to join the infantry, constantly urging me to pursue a more 'worthy' career, such as artillery. 'Don't call me Corporal, I don't wear a skirt,' was his favourite saying, implying that all other corporals in the army were below the artillery corporals. He was also encouraging: 'Recruit Ryder, you're a piss-ant. You'll make a terrible grunt. Why are you bothering?' was one classic. I certainly hope Kapooka instructors have improved their mentorship since I was there.

This wasn't the last time I saw my favourite artilleryman. Years later, in 2008, on my first tour of Afghanistan with the Special Operations Task Group (SOTG), we were returning to our base at Tarin Kowt (TK) after conducting a night-time raid on a Taliban medium-value individual and taking more than a dozen fighting-aged males we believed to be Taliban for further interviews and processing. I was escorting two of the fighters off the back of the Chinook helicopter to the waiting area, where regular army members would often fill the role of escort to the on-base detention facility. It had been a long night—my hair was dishevelled and curling under my helmet and I was covered in mud and sweat from the long foot infiltration, a stark contrast to the other escorts, who were clean, uniformed, shaven and fresh.

The two detainees I was charged with became belligerent and refused to walk, so I grabbed them by the backs of their necks and moved them along, barking at them to comply. As I approached the first escort at the gate near where the chopper had stopped, I saw that it was none other than my favourite bombardier, who was now a warrant officer (WO). He recognised me instantly. 'Not a bad day's work for a bunch of blokes in skirts, is it?' I asked smugly as I handed the Taliban prisoners over to him. He just stared at me with his mouth wide open. It's the small wins that count.

The morning routine in Kapooka always began the same way. We were accommodated in small adjoining rooms that had two bunkbeds, a small wardrobe space per person and a locker under each bottom bunk. Every bed space had to be set out the same way, with zero room for personal style or flair. At some ungodly hour, the instructors would turn all the lights on and violently rattle a broomstick on the inside of a steel garbage bin, to startle us and reinforce the importance of urgency. It didn't matter how fast we moved in army training; it was just never fast enough.

Each platoon lived on its own floor, with three platoons making up a company. We were 42 platoon, Delta Company. 'Hallway 42,' the instructors would bark at us as we leapt out of bed. 'Hallway 42!' we would scream out in response. We would then grab the bottom sheet from our beds and sprint into the hallway, where we would stand to attention and await the command to 'number', ensuring all recruits were out of bed and accounted for. Once instructors were satisfied with the count, we were given a few minutes to commence our 'morning routine', which involved changing out of our issued pyjamas, making the bed, and taking care of our 'ablutions': shit, shower, shave. This is where it got interesting.

Everything that is done in army training is tailored towards preparation for combat, irrespective of whether the role the recruit will go into after training will be fighting-oriented or not. Dental assistants, infantry and clerks all go through the same program. This form of cultural indoctrination ensures that all roles in the army can operate in conflict zones and, if needed, function at a base level and survive. For example, the reasoning behind repeating all commands given by the instructors, colloquially known as the 'echo' system, is to ensure that orders given to subordinates in the heat of combat are heard, acknowledged and understood.

Americans take this further and physically sound out 'HUA' (heard, understood, acknowledged) to confirm their directions, which I always found quite amusing. Similarly, the emphasis on ensuring tasks are completed on time relates to the cohesive nature of combat, where all participants are required to stick to critical timings in support of each other, and where failure to do so places others at risk. This is the beginning of the chasm that forms between civilians and soldiers and continues to grow with each day. Tardiness is not something you accept as a soldier, however things might work in society. But the gradual breaking down of individuality in place of a team orientation has stood the test of time since professional armies were formed thousands of years ago.

Kapooka was the first time I shaved. During the morning routine on our first day, we were instructed to go shit, shower and shave, and to complete those tasks in the shortest time possible. Being seventeen, and half Nepalese, I had a baby face that had never felt a razor because I grew almost no facial hair. In my mind, that seemed to be a minor obstacle when attempting to shave, and as I stood in front of the mirror, my face covered in shaving cream, I looked to the man next to me for some guidance.

It seemed simple: slap on some shaving cream and slide a razor around my face—too easy. I grabbed my razor while the corporal burst into the bathroom and yelled at us to hurry up—our shit, shower and shave activity seemed to be taking too long. Feeling panicked due to his proximity, I slid the razor all over my face as fast as I could, trying to ignore the numerous spots of blood that began oozing through the cream.

Satisfied I had shaved sufficiently, I wiped my face with my towel and began marching back to my room, quite pleased with myself. The recruit instructor was yelling some orders to people behind me as I marched towards him, and as I got close, he looked at me and stopped mid-sentence.

'Recruit, what the fuck happened to your face?' he asked.

'Nothing, Corporal, just finished shaving,' I replied, trying to ignore the warm streams of blood that I could feel dripping off my face and onto the floor.

'Is that your first time shaving?' he asked. I thought about lying, as I didn't want to look like a helpless kid, but I realised it would be a hard sell—my face looked like it had just fought with Edward Scissorhands.

'Yes, Corporal,' I responded sheepishly.

'Follow me,' he ordered.

The recruit instructor then spent five minutes teaching me how to hold a razor and shave properly, negotiating the various contours of my face to avoid cuts—the advice I needed. Although initially humiliated, I slowly started feeling a sense of belonging. In the army people look out for each other, regardless of rank or title. At that moment, I looked up to that recruit instructor like the big brother I never had.

After basic training, we hopped on a bus and drove to the Hunter Valley, approximately two hours north of Sydney, to the School of Infantry at Lone Pine Barracks. The ten-week course was designed to qualify army recruits to become infantry in the Royal Australian Infantry Corps, the full-time units of which belonged to the Royal Australian Regiment (RAR). All the instructors were infantrymen, most veterans of INTERFET, and I eagerly awaited the training they delivered.

The infantry's initial employment training courses have changed significantly over the last couple of decades, driven by the RAR's experience in Afghanistan and other world events. When I went through in 2001, however, there was probably very little that had changed since Vietnam, aside from the introduction of a few technological developments such as night vision goggles (NVG).

We did significantly harder physical training (PT) than anything we had done at Kapooka, mainly based on weekly pack marches or 'stomps' that increased in pack weight and distance travelled each time. Despite being one of the smallest members of my platoon, I had no difficulty keeping pace.

We learned how to patrol, conduct section attacks, and build defensive positions by digging with our hands into the ground. My section commander for these outfield exercises was a corporal from 3 RAR called Tate. In his late twenties, he was a charismatic and energetic instructor who always seemed to inspire and motivate the trainees in his section. He was a veteran of 3 RAR's direct fire support weapons platoon, and a well-respected non-commissioned officer (NCO), both at Lone Pine Barracks and in 3 RAR, as competent as he was tough. Thanks to my massive frame, the nickname Tate conjured up for me was 'Changi', the infamous Second World War prison camp.

One day towards the end of the course, we were outfield, and Tate was delivering a set of orders for an upcoming activity. Realising I hadn't eaten all morning, I grabbed a muesli bar. Mid-sentence, Tate stopped and rested his eyes on the hapless kid slowly eating his muesli bar.

'Changi, what the fuck are you doing?' he barked. Everyone froze and turned to look at me.

'Eating a muesli bar, Corporal,' I responded.

My answer seemed to infuriate him even further. Now thoroughly enraged, he addressed the whole platoon: 'If I find any of you cunts eating during a set of orders again, I will take you down the creek line and punch your fucking heads in. If any of you fucks manage to beat me, I'll come down here, grab a star picket, and put it through your fucking head!'

From that day till my last day in the army, I always hesitated to eat whenever someone was addressing a group of soldiers. Sometimes the old ways of teaching diggers do work.

I thoroughly enjoyed the training at the School of Infantry, otherwise known as 'the school of cool', and before I knew it, we were eagerly awaiting news of which battalion of the RAR we were to be posted to. Most of the battalions in 2001 were up north, at either Townsville, Brisbane or Darwin. I had zero interest in going to any of them, as they were not airborne infantry and I would not be jumping out of planes. Tate knew how badly I wanted to join his battalion, 3 RAR, and after the last day of the course, when we were clearing up and packing our gear, the platoon sergeant lined us up for the news.

Names were called out in no order and each soldier's new unit read out. The last name was called, and then the sergeant asked if anyone had been missed. Anxiously, I stuck my arm in the air, with the sergeant and Tate unable to contain themselves.

Tate looked at me and nodded.

'Ah, yeah, Ryder, you're going to 3 RAR, mate.'

I was going to be a paratrooper and stay in Sydney. I was elated.

We spent our last day at Lone Pine at the boozer on base, telling lies to the platoons a few weeks behind us. We were veterans of the school now, so we had plenty of words of wisdom for the nervous kids waiting to complete the course. That day was also significant for another reason: it was 11 September 2001. I was fast asleep in my bunk when one of my mates from the platoon, Sionne, shook me awake. 'Ryder, come to the rec room; someone flew a plane into the World Trade Center,' he whispered breathlessly.

I leapt out of bed and ran to the recreation room, where a crowd of trainees and instructors slowly began building. Moments later, we watched live as the second plane flew into a tower. We all sat there stunned, unable to believe what we'd just seen. Aside from utter surprise, however, was another feeling I would get every single time a terrorist attack or another significant event occurred in any part of the world that had a link to Australia—excitement.

In Washington DC, Prime Minister John Howard, who had arrived a few days earlier for talks with President George Bush, began his day, as always, with a brisk walk, followed by his Secret Service entourage. Little could he have known that the events of the following few hours would plunge Australia into a prolonged war in the Middle East that would scar the national consciousness for decades to come. At a press conference the following day, Howard, without consulting his cabinet, announced Australia's commitment to and solidarity with the United States:

> My personal thoughts and prayers are very much with those left bereaved by these despicable attacks on the American people and the American nation. Words aren't very adequate, but they are a sign that we feel for our American friends, that we stand by them, we will help them, we will support action they take to properly retaliate in relation to these acts of bastardry against their citizens and against what they stand for.

Despite the tragedy unfolding in the United States, only one thing consumed my thoughts: we were going to war, and I had just completed my infantry training. My timing was ideal. My only reason for concern, however, was that it might happen too quickly, as I wouldn't turn eighteen for another couple of months; thus is the frame of mind of a teenage soldier. But as it turned out, my time contributing to the Global War on Terror that spanned more than two decades would not begin for another seven years. When I did finally take part, it was with the Australian Special Operations Command (SOCOMD) as a commando.[2]

CHAPTER 3

OLD FAITHFUL

Only later did I realise how much the six years I spent in 3 RAR shaped a large portion of my adult life, and not always in a good way. The stories I tell about this period are pretty colourful, and the looks of shock, horror and disbelief on people's faces have convinced me that we were generally out of touch with the rest of civilised Australian society.

The battalion, known colloquially as the Boon, was in Kapyong Lines at Holsworthy Barracks in Sydney's south-west. Holsworthy had been home to the battalion since it had moved from Woodside Barracks in South Australia in 1981, making it the southernmost infantry battalion of the RAR at the time. Part of the army's 3rd Brigade, which also included 1 RAR and 2 RAR, the battalion included Parachute Company and the Parachute Battalion Group. Designed to insert via parachute to secure a point of entry for follow-on forces, 3 RAR was the only military unit to use this as a primary method of entry. Special Operations was the other organisation that employed this insertion option.

Holding the nickname Old Faithful, the battalion had a proud history, particularly during the Korean War, most notably its actions at Kapyong and Maryang San, which the battalion commemorates annually. 3 RAR was also the red-headed stepchild of the 3rd Brigade—we were often left to our own devices in Sydney, due to the head shed of the brigade's location being in Townsville and the distinctly different insertion method our unit employed.

As I said earlier, at the time, 3 RAR was the only unit in the RAR that wore a beret as its primary headdress. Proudly we wore that maroon beret, which was a staple for paratroopers around the globe. With it, however, came the attitude of elitism typical of airborne infantry globally, much to the disgust of the rest of the RAR. We indeed were special, but maybe not entirely in the way that we believed. The battalion comprised four rifle companies, Alpha, Bravo, Charlie and Delta companies, and Support Company. The latter included the direct fire support weapons platoon, which focused on anti-armour and heavy weapons; the signals platoon, which ensured the unit could always communicate in the field; the assault pioneer platoon, which focused on demolitions, construction and water mobility; the mortar platoon, which operated the indirect fires with the 81mm mortar; and the reconnaissance and sniper platoon, which was the eyes and ears of the unit, the snipers providing precision fires when needed. The battalion also included Administration Company, which managed the logistics and administrative functions; the battalion was run through Regimental Headquarters, comprising the commanding officer (CO), regimental sergeant major (RSM), and other executive positions.

Each company had its own parade ground, offices and living quarters in Kapyong Lines. Our living quarters was a three-storey, red-brick building with a shared laundry room and toilet block known as the SAL (showers and latrines). Each level of the building had nine rooms, which was the exact number required for an infantry rifle section, and unless blokes were married, most of the men 'lived on'. The battalion was placed on a slight slope with the area canteen and on-base shop at the top of the hill, and the unit carpark at the bottom.

What I'm about to tell you has been watered down considerably, as I don't want to tarnish the unit's reputation. This was a different time. Safe spaces, inclusive pronouns, gender quotas, diversity and inclusion were non-existent. Things seemed more straightforward then. Not only was a culture of hard drinking accepted by the hierarchy, but it was ingrained in the rest of Australian society too.

I laugh when I see senior officers who are ex-3 RAR, most of whom not only permitted the behaviour of my degenerate colleagues but probably took part, preach morals and behaviour standards in their messaging. There was an unwritten rule: any officers still drinking past a certain time would be removed so they wouldn't witness any bad behaviour. Hapless lieutenants were 'escorted' out a few times while I was there.

For an officer, it was better to pretend these things didn't happen and head to the officers' mess for sandwiches and brandy. Any ORs (other ranks) who had a semblance of sanity and tried to stop the repugnant behaviour from spiralling out of control were instantly made persona non grata, which was career suicide in the battalion and studiously avoided by anyone who wished to retain social capital in this pressure cooker of testosterone and egos.

I don't think I can sufficiently convey to the average member of society just how stellar our tolerance for alcohol was. Looking back, I am amazed at how much alcohol a skinny kid could put away in one sitting. In one of the epic piss-ups we regularly hosted, I threw up six times in one night. Regardless, I continued drinking, as my wish to stop drowning my body in more alcohol was outweighed by my desire not to be labelled a weak cunt for failing to consume my own body weight of beer and Bundaberg rum.

The centre of gravity for the battalion was the notorious unit boozer called the Shat. Nobody knows precisely where the name came from, but I can say that our esteemed establishment was light on aesthetics and heavy on debauchery. The walls inside were covered in memorabilia displaying the long, proud tradition of the battalion, and it contained a TV room and a toilet. All the furniture was bolted to the floor; if it wasn't, it would eventually have been thrown into a fire. Yes, we used to burn our furniture.

What is now known in the hospitality industry as 'the responsible service of alcohol' was unheard of. The bar staff of the Shat were injured diggers and junior NCOs undergoing rehab, who were regularly threatened, abused and sometimes bashed for no reason. There was also no age limit, and a large portion of new march-ins were underage. Beer and cigarettes were cheap, and all civilian and military rules of law seemed to stop at the door. One night, I watched the eight-year-old son of a WO walk up to the bar and return with an armful of Bundy and cokes. When the kid put in his order, the eighteen-year-old barman had looked nervously towards the WO, who glared and pointed at him to comply.

My first day in 3 RAR was 12 September 2001, and I was nearly jumping out of my skin as we drove through the gates of Kapyong Lines to start our careers. After a brief introduction from the on-duty guard commander, we grabbed our gear and were directed to the transit rooms above the famed Shat. I shared a room with Jamie Clark, whom I had befriended at Singleton. The same age as me, Jamie was from Perth and was as obsessed with being a soldier as I was. Our main topic of conversation was still 9/11, and we spent the rest of the day shooting the shit and nervously awaiting our first duties in the unit.

Unbeknown to us, momentum was slowly building below us down in the Shat as the crowd assembled and the music got louder.

Somehow I fell asleep, and a few hours later, I was woken by a bottle shattering downstairs. Jamie and I both leapt out of bed to see what was happening, and the scene I witnessed below shocked me.

The first thing I saw was a bloke standing on a table drinking out of a helmet with the whole bar heckling and abusing him, followed by a crowd throwing their bottles at him in unison. To the right of that was a bloke getting the shit belted out of him by a much larger, fully naked man, with another bunch of blokes yelling and cheering him on. All this chaos was occurring amidst a thick blanket of smoke from some plastic chairs burning at the back fence.

My experience of the army thus far had only been in training institutions where this sort of behaviour would be severely repri-manded. I recall thinking how much these diggers would be in the shit when the corporals and sergeants got hold of them. My shock intensified when, as I watched one of the main antagonists now holding a digger up against the fence by his collar, I saw three stripes on his arm. He *was* a sergeant! I turned and caught Jamie's eye, and I knew we were both thinking the same thing: 'What have we gotten ourselves into?'

An hour or so later (we still hadn't had a moment's sleep), we heard yelling in the corridor outside our room and sat up in our beds. 'Where are you, lid cunts?' a figure bellowed outside our door. We didn't say a word. The figure had zeroed in on our room and was repeatedly kicking the door. 'Open up, cunts!' he screamed. Jamie jumped out of bed, turned the light on and obeyed.

A massive man with thick black hair towered in our doorway, taking a few seconds to settle his gaze on the two pathetic seventeen-year-olds staring back at him.

'You some of the lids that just marched in?' he asked.

'Yep,' I replied sheepishly, still unsure what a lid was.

'Get downstairs and buy some beers, cunts,' he asked politely. Jamie and I ran back to our gear, threw on shorts and T-shirts, and followed our new friend down the stairs.

We walked meekly into the beer garden in brown shirts with our surnames printed across the front, looking like absolute lids. From there, the large man who herded us downstairs pointed to the bar. 'Carton of Bundy rum,' he directed. Jamie and I walked over to the bar and bought the carton, then followed our new friend to a table of soldiers looking at us with disdain. I placed the carton on the table and took a seat—and everyone turned their glare to me without saying a word.

'What the fuck are you doing, cunt?' one soldier asked.

'Having a rum,' I replied.

'Fuck off, cunt, we don't drink with lid cunts,' another para-trooper informed me.

So Jamie and I walked back upstairs, looked at each other and jumped into bed. This was my introduction to the Shat.

Each company of 3 RAR had around 100 men, and certain stereo-types would be conformed to while drinking at the Shat.

Diggers from the rifle companies would typically sit anywhere Support Company soldiers didn't. Support Company was where the senior specialist soldiers were, and naturally the diggers spent their time trying to network into a place on a 'support course' so they too could get into the senior company.

Assault pioneers, known as 'pies and beers', were typically less fit, slightly overweight rum addicts and they were tight with mortar platoon, known affectionately as 'mortards'.

Recon/snipers were the 'leg shavers' who always drank in their PT kit. The black 3 RAR recon/sniper PT shirts were a status symbol, and entering the platoon was not easy. The stereotype was therefore that the platoon only drank Powerade and watched from the sidelines.

The guys in direct fire support weapons platoon, known as 'bellies', were the meatheads of the unit, their culture stemming from the neo-Nazi era of the late 1980s. Their bizarre and degenerate antics persisted for decades. For example, irrespective if it was in the Shat or out in public, one of them would randomly scream 'Who are we?!' the response being a unanimous 'Heavy fucking weapons'. Another gem was when they would stand around in a circle and take turns punching each other in the face in a clockwise direction. Pack marching—carrying heavy weights across long distances—was a staple in the infantry. In every story heavy weapons told of how much weight they had to carry in the field, the measurements seemed to go up at least 20 per cent.

At the time I arrived at Holsworthy, 3 RAR was in preparation for its next deployment to East Timor after INTERFET. Support Company was being re-roled as a rifle company, so my cohort of brand-new march-ins was being posted to each of its platoons. Jamie and I were assigned to the mortar platoon and were directed to our new living quarters.

During that period in 3 RAR, unless you had been part of INTERFET, your opinions were worthless, and there was a distinct dichotomy between those veterans and the rest of the unit. And the only thing worse than not being an INTERFET veteran was not yet being a qualified paratrooper; having never been to Timor, and still yet to do our introductory parachute course, we were both.

As if life wasn't hard enough, we were thrown into the most senior company of the unit, where we were destined for misery from our first day. Today, in the post-Afghanistan army, infantry soldiers become section commanders after only four or five years, with most battalions offering specialist support courses in the first year. But back in those days, people seemed to stay in the army for a lot longer. Even to get a look-in to a support course took at least four or five years, with promotion from private to the next rank of lance corporal not even a possibility for another few years after that.

The system in play in 3 RAR in the early 2000s created a level of exclusivity where even the opportunity to *attempt* a support course was something you had to earn based on merit and performance in the rifle companies. So, having a bunch of seventeen-year-olds march straight into Support Company was unprecedented, and we were hated by the senior soldiers, who did not hesitate to express their disdain.

Our new home, the mortar platoon of Support Company, was now re-roled as 11 platoon, Delta Company. Recon/snipers was the only platoon to maintain its specialist role for the next East Timor deployment. The lines for Support Company were across the road from the famed 3 RAR Guard Room, and comprised a dozen or so demountable buildings with four small, cramped bedrooms and a shared toilet, shower and external laundry. Very modest. When 3 RAR moved to Townsville many years later, these exact buildings would be repurposed as training buildings and relocated to the Special Forces Training Facility (SFTF) at the back of Holsworthy Barracks.

A typical day for us was waking up around 6.30 a.m. and meeting the rest of the platoon for morning duties, which involved cleaning your room, common areas, the toilets and laundry. Years later, the cleaning of defence buildings would be outsourced to civilian contractors, but back then, it was left to the soldiers to maintain their own barracks blocks. In my opinion, this is just one of many factors that has changed the expectations and work ethic of young soldiers for the worse. In his fantastic book *Legacy*,[3] about the New Zealand All Blacks, James Kerr makes clear that a key ingredient in their success was remaining humble and completing basic tasks, such as 'sweeping the sheds', which ensured strong team cohesion both on and off the field.

Our morning cleaning would be typically followed by an 'emu bob', which involved everyone coming together in a line to pick up rubbish and cigarette butts. No matter how much the lines were destroyed with smashed beer bottles, burnt furniture and millions of cigarette butts, the culprits would always get up in the morning and clean up before starting work, or 'first parade'. The platoon sergeant would then inspect the lines, giving out 'extras': extra duties for areas not up to standard.

Cleaning was followed by an hour of PT, almost always involving running or pack marching, with pull-ups and push-ups. Compared to the current climate of Human Performance Optimisation and other science-based training programs, the PT in 3 RAR seems archaic. Still, we didn't know any better, and it was most certainly adequate for the hard infantry work expected of paratroopers.

I was incapable of staying out of the spotlight, for all the wrong reasons. Before moving to Support Company, we had paraded with Bravo Company while Regimental Headquarters sorted out the positions in preparation for the deployment. It was my third or fourth day in the unit, and a bunch of us hit the city for a night on the cans, only getting on the train back at well past two in the morning. Naturally, I fell asleep and woke up alone, unable to recall who else I got on the train with and not knowing where they were.

I looked at my watch and panicked; it was 5 a.m. and I was on a train carriage alone. Frantic, I searched for a signpost to see where I was and saw a sign for Campbelltown station, which was multiple stops past Holsworthy on the train line. I dashed out of the carriage and hailed a taxi, yelling at him to get to Holsworthy Barracks as fast as possible.

Seconds felt like hours, before finally the cab stopped at the front of the base. As this was still the weeks after 9/11, the protocols at the front gate were changing, which caused significant delays for the morning traffic into the base, so I paid the driver, flashed my ID at the checkpoint and sprinted towards 3 RAR.

As I approached the lines, I stopped to look at the time: 0724. I had six minutes to be on parade. Knowing I had missed the morning routine and fearing being called a 'jack cunt', I agonised over what to do next. To maintain discipline, the army has its law book, whose punishments range from a few extra duties to loss of pay and even imprisonment. One of those charges is AWOL (absent without leave), which was common enough but still attracted a loss of income and a mark on your conduct record. I was a seventeen-year-old lid, but I assessed that being out of dress must attract a lesser punishment than not being there, so I sprinted for the Bravo Company parade ground, where the platoon was lining up for roll call.

This was my first actual day in the unit, and God knows what the platoon must have been thinking when they saw this skinny, nervous, dishevelled kid march onto the parade ground and take up a spot in the rear rank in his jeans and collared shirt, reeking of piss from the night before.

'Listen in, and answer your name when called,' the sergeant directed.

When my name was finally called, I came to attention. 'Sir,' I responded in a loud, clear voice.

The platoon sergeant looked up, saw me in the rear rank and immediately scowled.

'Ryder, come out the fucking front,' he commanded. All eyes in the platoon fell on me. 'Why the fuck are you not in PT gear?' he asked.

I thought about lying through my teeth for a split second, then thought better of it. 'I was on the cans and was running late, Sergeant, and I thought it would be better to be here on time out of dress than not to be here at all,' I responded.

The sergeant's scowl slowly turned into a grin, then a chuckle, followed by a full belly laugh, with the platoon following suit. 'Fall in, cunt, welcome to Bravo Company.'

So went my first day at Bravo Company; I didn't even make it to the first meal break without half the unit talking about me. Classic Scott.

While I was finding my feet in 3 RAR, the Howard government deployed a contingent of SASR to Uruzgan province, Afghanistan, on 26 October 2001. Another two rotations would occur before they returned to Australia on 5 November 2002.

Australia would largely withdraw all troops within a year, with efforts being weighted towards the war in Iraq. But while the 'Coalition of the Willing' was focused on toppling Saddam Hussein, the security situation in Afghanistan continued to deteriorate, and Prime Minister Howard was under pressure from US President George Bush to again stand alongside the US for a potential increase in the Afghanistan war commitment.

In June 2005, a submission was made to Australia's National Security Committee to draw down troops in Iraq and increase the footprint in Afghanistan as a Provincial Reconstruction Team. SF were not included in this initial proposal. When Air Chief Marshal Angus Houston was promoted to Chief of the Defence Force, however, the decision was made to deploy a 190-strong contingent comprising SASR, commandos (4 RAR (Cdo)) and the Incident

Response Regiment (IRR).[4] The SOTG deployed to Afghanistan in September 2005, and would continue there until the Abbott government announced the withdrawal of troops in 2013.

Although Australian Special Operations Command as of 2023 would have a joint selection course and the working relationship between commandos and SASR would improve significantly to enhance the SF capability, it certainly did not start that way.

It was a rocky start to the war for 4 RAR (Cdo). Relegated to base security and being used as a support to SASR, the commandos were underutilised and stonewalled at every turn. In one joint operation to FOB (Forward Operating Base) Cobra, a US SF outpost, commando officers were not even allowed to enter planning rooms, while SASR patrols were accommodated inside the base.

On completion of one task, SASR patrols drove off leaving 4 RAR (Cdo) without a ride home; it fell to the Canadians to give the teams a lift back. Anthony Evans, one of the commandos present on the day, recalled the Canadians' shock at the treatment of the commandos by SASR: 'Even they were disgusted with the SAS . . . they could not believe the way they treated their own countrymen.'[5]

I would find all this out for myself over the next two decades. But for now, I was headed to my first deployment to Timor.

CHAPTER 4

WORLD WAR TIMOR

Unlike a SF unit, regular army units spend up to five months preparing for a deployment. Training starts at the platoon level in their home location, then the entire deploying formation usually gathers up north for validation and further training. As Delta Company members, we built up at Holsworthy, starting at the section, platoon and company levels, before moving to Townsville in North Queensland.

There, the entire 3 RAR Battle Group conducted six weeks of training before returning to Sydney on pre-deployment leave. I had just turned eighteen and was excited to get a taste of actual operations after religiously following 3 RAR's previous deployment to INTERFET.

Timor has a chequered past. East Timor, now known as Timor Leste, is located 2011 kilometres north of the Australian coast and was colonised by the Portuguese in the mid-sixteenth century after they had traded with the island nation for some time. Skirmishes with Dutch traders resulted in an 1859 treaty in which the Portuguese ceded the island's western half, which became part of Indonesia in 1945. The Japanese occupied the whole island of Timor during the Second World War; however, the Portuguese resumed colonial authority of East Timor after the Japanese surrender.

East Timor declared independence from the Portuguese on 28 November 1975, but was invaded by neighbouring Indonesia nine days later and incorporated as a province of Indonesia. During the two-decade occupation, Indonesia made substantial investments in infrastructure, but dissatisfaction grew. Between 1975 and 1999, 102,800 conflict-related deaths (approximately 18,600 killings and 84,200 deaths from hunger and illness) occurred.

On 30 August 1999, in a UN-sponsored referendum, an over-whelming majority of East Timorese voted for independence from Indonesia. Immediately following the referendum, anti-independence Timorese militias—organised and supported by the Indonesian military—commenced a punitive scorched-earth campaign.

The militias killed approximately 1400 Timorese and forcibly pushed 300,000 people into West Timor as refugees. Most of the country's infrastructure was destroyed during this punitive attack. On 20 September 1999, INTERFET was deployed to the area, ending the violence.

Following a United Nations–administered transition period, East Timor was internationally recognised as an independent nation on 20 May 2002. INTERFET was followed by the United Nations Transitional Administration East Timor (UNTAET), during which battle groups continued rotations of six months or more. And early 2002 saw the 3 RAR Battle Group 'Old Faithful', of which I would be a part, return to Timor.[6]

The regiment was in battle long before it landed in Timor. Army activities, particularly back then, always seemed to be led by a senior officer who would ban drinking to minimise or outright avoid alcohol-related incidents. For every activity we would receive the typical brief indicating it was a 'dry' camp, and everyone would nod in agreement. Then, ten minutes later, we would all be changing into jeans to hit the town—officers included.

This culture of communicating and disregarding these rules persisted throughout my entire army career, and I always found the whole ritual quite strange. Midway through the training trip to Townsville, every single member of 3 RAR decided to go batshit crazy in the main strip in town, known as 'The Strand'. To this day, it must be the most insane night out I have ever been part of—and I cut my drinking teeth in Sydney's Kings Cross in my twenties, so that's saying a lot.

I can't recall how it started, but there had already been a few punch-ups between 3 RAR and our rivals from 1 RAR and 2 RAR earlier in the night. I was in a bar when some of the lads from Alpha Company burst through the door and informed us that some bouncers had bashed one of the assault pioneers, and we were all heading to the bar to fill the bouncers in, which in the army means beat them up.

The bar was a nightclub called the Bank, and as we approached, I got my first look at the carnage. Approximately 60 metres from the entrance, I watched Jeremy, a large soldier of Papua New Guinean descent, chase one of the bouncers down the road, then eventually catch him with a punch to the back of the head, before finishing him off once he fell—all to the clapping and cheers of every 3 RAR lad watching.

Closer to the Bank, another Support Company soldier threw punches at two cops, eventually being restrained and arrested. All this occurred while 3 RAR lads sprinted down the street and civilians ran the other way. At the Bank's steps, about 50 3 RAR guys tried to force their way into the bar while a small group of security and bar staff attempted to stop the stampede.

Not wanting to miss out, I joined the group trying to gain entry, where I fell and was spat out to the side. When I stood up, I got a better view down the other side of the street, where the chaos at the Bank was being replicated at three or four other venues. Somehow, the fear of missing out on the Bank assault had made every other subunit of 3 RAR decided to storm a bar. All of this was occurring against the backdrop of a steady stream of approaching police sirens and ambulances, breaking glass and screaming civilians.

Eventually, I entered the Bank, where one hapless young waitress pleaded in vain for us to stop this senseless assault—before one of the lads jumped the bar and attempted to kiss her, at which point she ran for the exit. We now had the bar to ourselves. Half a dozen of us jumped over and started serving ourselves top-shelf spirits amidst howling and cheering, which eventually turned into the 3 RAR song, 'We're a Pack of Bastards'.

After the Bank stopped resisting us, we moved up the street to see how the other companies had gone in their battles, and were pleased to learn we had secured key terrain up the road. Then reality hit as a dozen police cars screeched to a halt at the front of the Bank. The police didn't even ask questions, just arrested anyone who hadn't got away.

When one 3 RAR guy was pinned to the ground by an over-weight cop, three or four full-sized bottles of Bundaberg rum were hurled at the cop and his car, narrowly missing his head, to shouts of, 'Let him go, ya fat cunt!'

Even the kebab shop wasn't spared. Its workers stood where the customers typically would, while a bunch of 3 RAR lads jumped the counter and wildly carved at the legs of beef and chicken, beer in hand, as other lads rolled around the floor in fits of laughter—wild times. Finally, the excitement waned, and we went back to base to get some sleep, oblivious to the severity of what had just occurred.

The following day, we were woken around 0500 and told to get in cams (Auscam[7] uniforms) and form up on parade. The CO stormed to the front of the formed battalion and informed us that this was by far the worst behaviour he had ever seen in his time in the army, and that the premier of Queensland had been made aware of last night's events and had informed the chief of army that nobody from the 3 RAR Battle Group was to leave the barracks for the remainder of our time in Queensland. Moreover, numerous unit members had been arrested, with another handful in hospital. Half a dozen security and bar staff had also been to an emergency department, and Queensland Police and the military police would be on base to continue their investigation.

I am unsure what the CO thought our response would be, but we tried not to burst out laughing every time he informed us of each event; everyone still thought it was a colossal joke.

Then came the final nail in the coffin. 'The brigade commander has informed me that 3 RAR are not to wear their berets while on this mission rehearsal and will instead wear bush hats,' he informed us. That was not on. Whispers of anger and shock rippled through the ranks, with 'That's fucking bullshit' and 'Is this cunt serious' being typical responses. The brigade commander was a wise man who knew the worst thing you could do to an airborne infantry unit was to take away their identity well played, sir.

The culture in 3 RAR and the army overall would soon undergo significant change. Previously overlooked issues were addressed, holding leadership accountable. The culture gradually aligned more with broader society, though some resisted the perceived 'soft' approach. For many, it had no impact on soldiering; instead, leaders were expected to earn respect rather than rely on fear.

*

We spent most of our time training at the High Range Training Area on the outskirts of sunny Townsville and lived at the 2 RAR transit accommodation for the duration. We slept on green stretcher cots, surrounded by zip-up, dome-shaped netted structures called 'mozzie domes', which would be necessary for the tropics where we were headed. One weeknight, after another night of 'no drinking', we woke up to find that at least 30 of the mozzie domes in the shed we were living in had been sliced open with a knife.

One of the heavy weapons guys had got a gutful of beers and decided to go on a clandestine attack on mozzie domes, leaving many men slapping at their faces all night under frenzied mosquito attack. The culprit was a senior, so nobody was game enough to confront him; the fact that nobody awoke during his slasher campaign was also impressive.

We spent much time in the field and walked to prepare for the trip. The training covered a spectrum, including how to deal with crowds, patrolling different types of urban sprawl, and actions of contact and attacks. To replicate operating within a civilian population, we flew to Scottsville in regional Queensland, where we lived and worked among the local population.

We would patrol, sleep for the night, and then deal with multiple scenarios that were likely to arise in Timor, all done with blank rounds. When soldiers go into the field and sleep at night, one or two people are always awake to stand guard and watch for the enemy. More practically, however, this also stops civilians from entering the position and stealing equipment.

Falling asleep while on guard, known as 'on piquet', is not taken lightly. But not sleeping is easy when patrolling or doing anything physical; it is a different game when you are lying still after a day of arduous activity, particularly in training when there is no real threat.

One night at High Range, our section commander ordered a

single staggered piquet, which was always preferred as everyone got more sleep. The downside was, though, that you didn't have anyone to keep you awake. Being woken from a deep sleep to get up, then getting your gear on and then sitting or lying down somewhere for hours, staring into the bush, is something you never get used to, and you certainly can't get better at 'not being tired'.

After a long day of patrolling in the heat with heavy packs, I was woken from a deep sleep and told I was on piquet. You always know your place in the food chain by how you are woken up. Section commanders were usually woken gently with, 'Hey Dave, you're on piquet, mate.' As lids, we would get shaken awake with, 'Ryder, get up,' or 'You're up, cunt.' I got up, grabbed my gear, and followed the soldier to my spot. I lay down, made myself as comfortable as possible, and studied the piquet list, which had everyone's times, duration, and who would be woken up next. It was 0130, and I had an hour and a half before I was to wake up Danny, the section second-in-command (2ic), so I sat back against a tree, put my night vision goggles (NVGs) down, and diligently kept watch.

The next thing I knew, the sun was up, and I realised immediately that I had fucked up. I panicked, looked at the list, and saw Reveille was at 0500; it was now 0540. I rushed around the section position and woke everyone up, who quickly worked out that I must have fallen asleep. I saw the 2ic and section commander whispering near the command pit, and I didn't have to guess what they were talking about. After cooking my breakfast, I got a whistle from Dave, the section commander, with a field signal for 'come here'.

As I approached, he gestured for me to sit beside him.

'What happened on piquet last night?' he asked.

I hesitated and thought about being honest but decided against it.

'Wasn't tired, so I decided to do the rest of the night's piquet,' I replied.

He stared at me with the look of a disappointed father. 'Do you think I'm a fuckwit?' he asked.

Unsure how to respond, I shook my head to indicate that I didn't think that.

'I'll ask you again, what happened on piquet last night?'

I decided to spill the beans. 'I fell asleep,' I replied sheepishly.

'I don't want to bang on about how important it is to stay awake on piquet,' Dave said, 'so I won't. But to emphasise how important it is that you get it right, you have double piquet tonight.'

My entire career, I have faced a predicament in these scenarios. One part of me knows I should just shut the fuck up, but the other side needs answers and simply cannot accept the status quo, no matter what the consequences. As a senior NCO in SOCOMD, this aspect of my personality was earned and, at times, appreciated. As a seventeen-year-old lid, however, it certainly wasn't. Dave must have seen the puzzled look on my face.

'Do you have an issue with this, Ryder?' he asked.

I didn't mean to sound like a smartarse, but I wanted to know the logic behind punishing a tired and sleep-deprived guy with even less sleep. 'Well, I couldn't stay awake for one piquet, so how will giving me two help? I'll probably just fall asleep again.'

I had double piquet for the next four nights. Some lessons take me a while to learn.

After an eventful pre-deployment, we said our goodbyes and boarded a flight for Dili, East Timor's capital. All the companies of the battalion would rotate positions around the different bases every couple of months, and Delta Company's first post was the northern coastal town of Aidabalaten. The first thing I remember thinking when we stepped onto Komoro Airstrip in Dili was how hot and humid it was. The sort of humidity that has you constantly sweating from head to toe, even without massive packs and helmets. I wondered how on earth I was going to be able to patrol the jungles and mountains in a few weeks when I was covered in sweat from just walking off the aircraft to the reception area.

After finding a spot for our stretchers and mozzie domes, we began a few days of intelligence briefs and preparation for the first lot of patrols. Under the UNTAET mission, patrols were either deemed 'blue hat', meaning we would wear our blue UN hats and brassards on our arms to identify us as peacekeepers, or 'green hat', which saw us patrol clandestinely with camouflage on our faces. Blue hat patrols were typically conducted in areas of urban sprawl, low-visibility green hat patrols in the jungle and mountainous regions. As it takes a few weeks to acclimatise correctly, the first few patrols were in 'patrol order', which meant we just carried ammunition, water and a few section stores for short durations. Still, the heat was oppressive and covered me in constant perspiration, but it was good preparation for the upcoming longer-duration patrols.

Finally, after months of preparation, we stepped off on our first patrol in the coastal town of Aidabalaten. I wasn't quite sure what to expect; I knew we wouldn't be getting ambushed every day and getting stuck in prolonged gunfights, as that didn't even happen during INTERFET for the most part. Regardless, a part of me would take every step wondering if this would be the moment I would finally get shot at.

We also patrolled a lot in vehicles. The base in Aidabalaten also had a squadron of M113 armoured personnel carriers (APCs), which hadn't advanced since their use in Vietnam. Vehicle-mounted patrols in the APCs saw us sitting inside, inhaling exhaust fumes and feeling car-sick for hours before the ramp would come down and we would walk around a town before getting back in for another few hours' torture. APCs had no air conditioning, so we sat there covered in sweat, feeling sick, trying to hydrate. To make this worse, we were required to wear our helmets.

The six-wheel infantry mobility vehicles were not as bad due to having open sides and fresh air, but weeks of spending hours a day facing a wall of green as we wound our way up and down mountain ranges had us all taking air-sickness tablets. I am confident the 40 Winfield cigarettes we were each smoking a day didn't help either.

The locals were very interested in our activities. Sitting down and having a meal while dozens of local kids hovered around, asking for water or chocolate, was a novelty at first, but grew old very quickly. Nevertheless, the people were always friendly; the kids always had a smile on their faces.

The most challenging work was the green hat patrols in the densely vegetated area called the Atabai jungle. Thick secondary growth made movement difficult, and we often took turns as lead scouts cutting our path into the forest with machetes, which was challenging work. We would typically carry no less than 48 hours' worth of water and food, which was hard work for a 68-kilogram eighteen-year-old. Due to the heat, we weren't eating much, but trying not to guzzle all our water at once when wearing long-sleeved clothing and gloves, and carrying 50 kilograms or so of gear, took a good deal of discipline.

Water discipline was strictly monitored by the section 2ic to ensure we managed the balance between staying hydrated and not consuming too much. Water is also heavy, and the men often didn't carry enough. This is when I first started to see men much larger than me go down with heat conditions. Each section had a combat first-aider (CFA) who carried drugs and litres of intravenous fluid for heat conditions, and on one patrol, he had to get resupplied with IVs as we had three members of the section succumb to heat-related issues. The team 'tough guys', typically the biggest 'lid haters', often went down first. Jamie and I, the new guys, didn't go down once, and I am proud to say that I never did in my 22-year career.

Every combat soldier hopes for a gunfight or 'contact' in their career, and at eighteen, on my first deployment, I was no exception. But even though our operation was classified as 'warlike operations', not a single round was fired in anger in the entire Battle Group, and I soon realised that all the hype around the trip was just hubris. Nonetheless, this didn't stop me from continually wondering when my day would come. For the entire deployment, I imagined what being shot at would sound like and how I would react. This was not just wishful thinking; as every foot soldier knows, you continually look for fire positions and rehearse your actions on contact as you patrol.

I did this more than most. Around this time, the movie *Black Hawk Down* had come out, and in our new position as the Battle Group's quick reaction force, we had much downtime to watch movies. We repeatedly watched this particular movie, imagining what it would be like to be one of the soldiers in that disastrous operation in Somalia.

After quick reaction force tasking, we moved to the mountainous region of Bobonaro. If the pack work was hard in the jungles of Atabai, it was even worse in Bobonaro. Our patrol routes were all over mountain ranges that never seemed to end; the backbreaking weight of our packs never seemed to lighten, no matter how much water and food we consumed. We worked in isolation as infantry sections, where young section commanders, or seccos, enjoyed a level of autonomy never repeated in my time in the regular army.

We would patrol as a section for weeks, calling in water and ration resupply by chopper as needed. I remember how much

I couldn't wait to be a secco and wondered if I would ever get the chance. But years later, when I was a secco, the level of autonomy on operations had dissipated. A peacetime army culture saw responsibility diminish, only to grow again when the RAR battalions began their rotations to Afghanistan.

On our tour, we also visited other companies' base locations, including Bravo Company's patrol base on the border with Indonesia, known as the Tactical Coordination Line. One of these bases was in Balibo, where five Australian journalists were murdered before the Indonesian invasion in 1975. The Indonesians claimed the 'Balibo five' died in the crossfire. This version of events was never officially challenged by the Australian government and the AFP investigation would be eventually abandoned in 2014.

The murders occurred in a building known as 'the kissing house', and the story of the events surrounding them gives a small insight into the violence and horrors faced by the Timorese at the hands of the Indonesians. On the walls of one of the rooms inside the house there are clear lip marks, where the Indonesian soldiers would force the young Timorese girls they raped to kiss the walls before they were murdered. Standing in that house and looking at the blood-stained lip marks on the walls, I imagined the fear and suffering the people killed there must have experienced.

We saw out the rest of our time in Timor on a high mountain hilltop, suitably named 'Everest', a radio-communication retransmission site. Our job was to ensure radio communications would work through most active regions, and this involved an infantry section living at the site to secure it. Aside from cleaning, cooking and working out, there was nothing to do there, and the boredom that all soldiers experience on operations soon had us in its grasp. As Jamie and I were the new guys, all the shit tasks came down to us while the remainder of the section played cards and shot the shit. Fairness was not a thing in the pseudo-hierarchy of Delta Company 3 RAR.

The worse task by far was burning human excrement. The toilets were wooden 'thunderboxes', simple toilets in wooden cubicles, with 40-gallon drums cut in half as the catchment systems. The only way to eliminate the waste was to drag the drums out, pour diesel on them, and continually stir them until the excrement shrank to a manageable size.

So our days involved cooking meals, cleaning up, sleeping, doing weights in the prison gym at the back, reading *Ralph* and *Zoo* magazines, and burning shit. This was our life for about six weeks, and I yearned to do something else.

Malaria was a real risk in Timor, and to counter it, we were all given tablets of doxycycline, a broad-spectrum antiviral, which we were to take daily. Our section 2ic was tasked with tracking daily doxy use in a roll book which would be checked later by the platoon sergeant.

Jamie eventually had enough of the bullying and unfair allocation of tasks, and over the weeks spent more and more time in his tent. I had a more pragmatic approach to our treatment and saw it as a rite of passage for the new guys.

One morning, Jamie didn't join me in the kitchen to help with preparing lunch, so I went up to his stretcher to see if he was okay. I found him in his winterweight sleeping bag, shivering while sweating profusely and complaining he was cold. I knew straight away that he had malaria. I ran down to find Chook, the 2ic. Looking startled, Chook jumped up and ran towards Jamie's tent while the secco pulled out his notebook to start writing the report for Jamie to get aeromedical evacuation (AME).

After seeing Chook's reaction, I remember thinking that maybe he wasn't a bad bloke after all. But then I found him kneeling next to Jamie's stretcher while trying to get a pen in Jamie's hand, with his doxy roll book sitting on Jamie's chest. Chook hadn't been filling out the roll book, and knew he would have to send it off with Jamie on the AME, so he was covering his arse! Jamie ended up being fine and re-joined us a few weeks later.

Chook did selection for 4 RAR (Cdo) a few years later and went on to become a WO class one; we often have a good laugh about that day.

After the end of the Vietnam War in 1975, only small contingents of soldiers deploying to Somalia and Rwanda broke up the long stretch of peacetime. The deployment to Timor ended in 2002, when I was eighteen years old. Although we didn't know it then, this would begin a period of unprecedented operational tempo for the Australian Army's SOCOMD.

I was an immature kid forced to grow up very quickly, being surrounded by men who were much older and bigger than me. I was always in the shit for something, constantly being counselled or outright abused for getting something wrong, and never seemed to get off a shit list for longer than a few weeks before getting pinged for another indiscretion.

But the deployment to Timor gave me life lessons that would shape the rest of my career and the man I would become. By doing the shit jobs as the lid, I built my reputation and proved my worth. I learned that sometimes the biggest bullies were the worst soldiers, and that aggression and harsh words did not equate to professionalism and performance. I knew that outside of the gym, size and strength did not correlate with fitness in the field, with some of the strongest and biggest guys being the first to go down with heat exhaustion and dehydration.

Most importantly, however, I started to see that I was a bit different from most of the guys in the battalion; they didn't have the passion I had for improving and being the best soldier they could be. There were some great soldiers in the company, but a lot were going through the motions, knowing they would probably leave the army in a few years. After less than two years in the army, I was already looking for more.

Unbeknown to me at the time, while I was slowly finding my feet as a soldier and working on mastering the basics, back home in Australia, a small group of senior commandos were over in Perth with the Special Air Service Regiment (SASR) learning skills to bring back home to Sydney for the first rotation of the Tactical Assault Group–East (TAG-E)—skills that in my final years in the army I would myself be teaching.

CHAPTER 5

A PACK OF BASTARDS

After our return from Timor, we had some leave, which I spent in Sydney's Hills district with friends and family. I was eighteen and had a whole bunch of deployment money in the bank while most of my friends were still finishing school, so I did what any teenage boy with a high disposable income would do: spent it in pubs and clubs chasing girls.

This was the first time I realised just how different I already was from my schoolfriends, who were doing the same thing they were before I joined the army. Everyone was very interested in my experiences on deployment, which mainly involved patrolling and living among the local population, but I of course had zero stories of combat and valour, much to their disappointment.

For the first time in my life, I was the person who had all the things that everyone else didn't. For an eighteen-year-old, that meant money for drinks, which I was very generous in sharing with anyone I was out with. Seeing the tremendous amounts of money I was spending on my leave, my mother suggested that I put away half of what I had left and continue spending the rest.

Of course, I disregarded this advice and continued to spend money like a rock star. I would go out on a Thursday night, wake up in the morning, go out for a big breakfast, then spend a few hundred dollars on clothes to go out in the next night; I didn't do laundry most of the time. This egregious spending would continue until I was left with only a few hundred dollars, having spent around $42,000 in a few months; in 2002 this was a lot of money, far more disposable income than my parents had ever had.

On my return to work, Delta Company changed back to being a support company, and all the lids were nominated to undertake support courses in the platoons I was with. That meant completing the basic mortar course, which I did in Puckapunyal in Victoria. Even though it was never my ambition to be a mortarman, I did enjoy the pressure of working the dials on the mortar against the clock to get rounds downrange, despite the endless map/protractor work we had to do before live-fire training. Like all grunt work, it was challenging.

We used to 'man-pack' (carry on our backs) the tubes and bombs, which made our packs ridiculously heavy, and I had begun to suffer from pain in my lower back. I had noticed it towards the end of the Timor trip, when I lay down at night. It wasn't surprising given my body weight and the heaviness of the packs we carried around for months on end, but I didn't pay much attention to it or bring it up with anyone at work. The last thing I wanted was to be known as a malingerer: career and social suicide in the battalion.

The modern-day commando reinforcement and training cycle (CRTC), which qualifies new commando operators, spends much time focusing on Human Performance Optimisation programs that teach the trainees how to move, train and recover their bodies. Immediately after selection, all successful trainees begin their

Human Performance Optimisation journey in Canberra at the Australian Institute of Sport.

By the time the qualified operators start their jobs in the commando regiments, they all know how to train specific parts of their bodies to ensure they are not injured carrying weight, which is a large part of the job. Back in 2002, however, none of this existed. I recall Benjamin Chuck, who was my team-mate for my first two SOTG rotations as a commando, being shocked that I was able to bench press my own bodyweight easily but was unable to back squat even close to that. My training as a young, single soldier was for looking good on the beach, not being better at my job.

Finally, we were driven down to Nowra to complete our basic parachute course, after which we would finally be paratroopers. The course was conducted over two weeks, during which, after some physical assessments and ground training, we completed seven static-line descents from 1000 feet to gain our 3 RAR parachute wings. Static-line jumping involves a nylon line attached to an inner cable of the aircraft, which when extended on exit pulls the main parachute out of the container. The jumps increased in complexity, starting from minimal equipment, called clean fatigue, to complete kits, including guns and full packs, known as combat equipment.

Our progression through the course also saw an increase in the speed with which we exited the aircraft. We began with a controlled exit, and built up to running out the side doors on the C-130 Hercules aircraft in a move known as the '3 RAR Shuffle'. Our exit of the aircraft was controlled by jumpmasters, who were either from 3 RAR or the Parachute Training School, later re-named the ADF Parachuting School.

Static-line jumping is designed to get a large body of troops on the ground as quickly as possible; the jumps were all, therefore, typically under 1000 feet, giving the jumpers little time to enjoy the view.

I loved watching the earth rush by as I stood in the doorway, before eventually throwing myself out, waiting for the violent motion of the parachute being ripped open. Non-parachutist members of the military, particularly from the other RAR battalions, always perceived static-line jumping as a high-risk activity; to the untrained observer, the landings could look a lot harder than they were.

If you completed the landings as taught and the wind conditions were moderate, you were almost guaranteed not to get injured. But if you didn't hold the correct body position for landing, broken legs were a real possibility, leading the other RARs to call us 'dirt darts' or 'splat cats'.

When night jumping on an exercise years later, we were given red Cyalume sticks, glowsticks for marking our location if we were seriously injured. High winds in the drop zone led to dozens of soldiers being injured that night. I landed about 2 metres from a barbed-wire fence, and after I landed, I stood up to start packing my parachute. The drop zone looked like a rave, with Cyalume sticks dotted over the entire area. Regardless, I loved the thrill of jumping and would always volunteer for an extra jump scheduled in the unit, much to the bewilderment of some of my brethren, who loved screaming 'airborne' at the pub, but avoided actually jumping at all costs.

After a short time in the mortar platoon, a night of drinking led me to be moved into the rifle companies. It was an epic piss-up, starting with bean bags being ripped open and leading to desk chairs and drawers being thrown from the third-floor balcony. Someone then suggested a fun game to see who could throw bricks of soap from the balcony with enough force to smash the windows of the adjacent building, which belonged to Charlie Company.

We spent the following 30 minutes hurling every bar of soap in the building, smashing a 3-metre-high window of the internal staircase. Bored of the soap world cup, we resorted to more destruction of our property into the early hours of the following day.

Typically, we would all get up at some stage in the morning and clean up the evidence, but for some reason, we all slept in on this occasion. It just so happened that the company sergeant major (CSM) of Charlie Company had decided to drive to work to wrap up some administration in his office and came across the scene of carnage.

He found dozens of drawers and chairs smashed on the ground, hundreds of cans of Bundaberg rum and thousands of pieces of broken glass. Furious, the CSM banged on the door of a ground-floor room of Charlie Company, where he asked one of the brand-new march-ins to identify the individuals responsible for the chaos.

'I don't know everyone who was drinking, sir, but I saw Ryder and McDonald up there,' he responded.

My fate was sealed. I had just woken up mid-morning and walked onto the balcony for a cigarette when I saw the CSM storming towards our building. Naturally, I did the courageous thing and hid in my room.

'Private Ryder and Private McDonald!' he screamed from the ground floor.

I froze, instantly awash with that sick feeling in your stomach that you get in the army when you know you are in a world of shit; it was a feeling I would often get as a digger in Old Faithful. I eventually stepped out of my room to face the music. The CSM had us stand at attention in front of Charlie Company while he gave us one of the best 'face rippings'[8] I ever received in the army. He gave us exactly two hours to clean up all the mess, then we were to report to him on the Charlie Company parade ground at 0730 the following day.

That morning, John McDonald and I were marched onto the parade ground, where the CSM continued to berate us in front of the whole of Charlie Company, at one point sinking so low as to claim we were too junior to even be in Support Company. He would make sure we were removed, which we were a week later. The Charlie Company lads couldn't keep the smirks off their faces; they thought it was hilarious. But I'd never really wanted to be in the mortar platoon, so I was happy to get back to a rifle company.

Kapyong and Anzac days were an annual two-day bender that went back decades. The Battle of Kapyong occurred on 22–25 April 1951, during the Korean War between UN forces, including Australians, Canadians and New Zealanders, and the Chinese People's Volunteer Army. 3 RAR had been instrumental in ensuring the Chinese could not break through the UN front, ultimately stopping their advance to Korea's capital, Seoul.

Preparation for Kapyong Day would begin weeks in advance, with lots of drills on the parade ground and rehearsals of blank-fire attacks, parachuting and displays of military equipment and vehicles, which were always well received by friends and family.

Immediately following the parade, everyone would move to the Shat for beers, which started relatively tamely due to the children and wives who were present. Eventually, however, the Shat would erupt, while 'We're a Pack of Bastards' was sung by old Korean War diggers arm in arm with current 3 RAR lads. It was a great experience that I used to cherish every year, and one not many serving 3 RAR members will experience now, due to the rapidly dwindling numbers of Korea vets attending each year. I always felt such a strong sense of pride and belonging in my time with 3 RAR. I would never again feel the same esprit de corps we experienced in that battalion, even within SOCOMD.

After an all-day-and-night drinking session at the Shat, we would change into our suits or stay in the same polyester dress uniforms we were in from Kapyong Day, and catch the train into the city to begin the bender that was Anzac Day. Some years we would participate in the march. Other years, we would start our descent into chaos with an early morning pub crawl in the Rocks in Sydney—a usual 3 RAR area of operations for the day.

One year, not long after we came back from Timor, a few of us stumbled into the big dawn service at Martin Place in Sydney on the back of a sixteen-hour Kapyong Day drinking session. I already knew on the walk there I was in trouble.

Despite what my body told me, I persevered, as pulling the pin on Anzac Day was not an option—not for a lid anyway. The feeling of nausea grew in step with the slowly strengthening pre-dawn sunlight, and without warning, dark vomit erupted from my mouth. Somehow, I managed to keep most of it off my clothes and shoes as I vomited into my hands and bent over, slowly letting the remnant of black death slip off my fingers and onto the ground in front of me, much to the horror of the group of people nearby. Incredibly, I did all this without making a sound, standing there bent over, wiping tears from my eyes and vomit from my hands, as the bugler sounded the Last Post at the Cenotaph. It was going to be a rough day, Lest We Forget.

A few weeks after Anzac Day, I received my first military charge. One of my boys' field packs had been broken from carrying mortar tubes, and he had tried unsuccessfully to get it replaced at the Q store (quartermaster's store). The storemen had informed him there were none in the system, and he would have to source his own. I was rostered to spend the day at the main store to help the storemen with random jobs, and I came across a small room with dozens of brand-new packs.

Thievery in the army is not tolerated, but 'permanently borrowing' things is okay. As they say, 'If you're not shopping army, you're paying too much.' As I left for my shift, I casually grabbed a pack, slung it over my shoulder, and walked out just as the senior storeman drove into the storage area.

When I returned to my room, the CSM was waiting for me. He asked me where I got the pack, and I admitted I had stolen it from the quartermaster's store. I was charged a week later and, as punishment, was given a seven-day restriction of privileges, which involved working from 5 a.m. to 11 p.m. doing menial tasks such as sweeping and cleaning.

One of my tasks was to sweep leaves off the battalion parade ground, a bitumen area about 200 metres long. It was a windy day, and every leaf I swept with my broom would blow back minutes later. Frustrated, I called a mate in the assault pioneer platoon and got the petrol leaf blower. The on-duty sergeant came storming over when he heard the blower start.

'Private Ryder, what the fuck are you doing with the blower?' he asked, red-faced.

'You told me to remove the leaves from the parade ground, Sergeant,' I replied.

'Did I say you could use a blower?' he asked, almost shouting.

'In all fairness, Sergeant, you didn't specify how to remove the leaves, you just said to get rid of the leaves.'

I was given an extra day of duties. Thinking outside the box is not well received when you are being punished.

Despite always being in trouble, I was starting to develop and mature as a soldier. After being banished from Support Company, I was sent to Alpha Company in a rifle section, where I took the role of the lead scout under a mixture of competent and not-so-competent section commanders. Despite my 'heat-seeking' nature,

I was starting to develop habits and understandings about myself that would continue to serve me well in my career and life.

I was constantly in trouble for being late, so I learned how to set multiple alarms and give myself enough sleep, stressing so much that I would wake well before my alarm. I was frequently losing bits of gear out in the field, so I became methodical in checking and rechecking my gear before, during and after activities. To this day, I don't leave a restaurant or taxi without physically conducting a check of everything I am supposed to have and then rechecking it several times. For this reason, I have never lost a phone or wallet in my illustrious drinking career. I had trouble remembering tasks, numbers and dates, so I started carrying a notebook and pen everywhere I went, later switching to calendars and notes on my smartphone—again, habits I have to this day.

While I was on my first deployment in Timor, Australia's two main fighting SF units, SASR and 4 RAR (Cdo)—later renamed 2nd Commando Regiment (2 Cdo Regt)—started building the commando capability to bolster the Australian special operations arsenal and would soon begin rotations to Afghanistan.

After establishing themselves at Kandahar Airfield, 1 SAS Squadron saw action in Operation Anaconda, a sixteen-day operation in Shah Wali Kot on the border of Pakistan, which involved more than 2000 coalition troops. The new and untested commando unit, 4 RAR (Cdo), was tasked with protecting the home front and raising the TAG-E, but it wasn't long before the commandos got a chance to prove their worth too.

The Tactical Assault Group–West (TAG-W)—at the time the only army domestic counterterrorism subunit—was based out of

SASR in Perth in Western Australia, which hindered their ability to react to domestic incidents on Australia's more populous eastern seaboard. During the 2000 Sydney Olympic Games, SASR was temporarily based in Sydney. After 9/11, and the 2002 Bali bombings in which 88 Australians were killed, the government was forced to review the domestic terrorism response, and the decision was made to raise TAG-E out of the Sydney-based 4 RAR (Cdo).

A small group of senior commandos spent months with SASR undertaking the advanced close-quarter battle (ACQB) course, learning how to drive specialist counterterrorism vehicles and fine-tune their explosive-breaching skills to enter terrorist-held buildings. The SASR instructors didn't take it easy on their students, and rightly so—the first group of TAG-E set the conditions and standards for what would grow to become the best counterterrorist assault force on the planet. Their skills, which trickled down through the TAG-E rotations in Sydney, would build critical capabilities used for years of combat in Afghanistan and Iraq.[9]

CHAPTER 6

JAMIE AND JAKE

On 10 March 2005, we were finishing up a horrendous twelve-day field activity behind Holsworthy Barracks that ended with a 40-kilometre pack march back to Kapyong Lines. Infantry battalions have always been notorious for long trains, and the '40 clicker' was by far the most dreaded, requiring us to walk for six to eight hours, depending on the pace. At the time, the OC, an ex-SASR troop commander who would later become 3 RAR's CO, was big on fitness.

Most of this walk was in torrential rain, and we returned to the Alpha Company lines in the early morning, our backs locked up and skin raw from chafing. As I dumped my pack, a colleague from another company, Christian, walked up to me with a look I had not seen before.

'Mate, did you hear about Jamie?' he asked.

'No, what happened?' I asked, my first instinct to hope that he had not been in contact before me. He had deployed to the Solomon Islands a few weeks earlier, and I had been very envious of his second deployment.

'He's dead,' Christian said bluntly, touching my shoulder.

'What do you mean?' I stammered.

'Jamie's gone, mate. He fell in a hole in the Solomons.'

I stood there blankly, staring at him. I could feel the eyes of the other company members on me. Not knowing what to do, I returned to my field gear and unpacked my kit—a response to somebody dying that I would repeat many times. After a few minutes, my eyes began to well. Not wanting the other lads to see me cry, I walked into the toilets and closed the door, then sobbed uncontrollably as the news sank in.

Jamie had been on patrol around Honiara, the capital, providing security to the police officers from the Australian-led Regional Assistance Mission to the Solomon Islands, when his patrol came across an old mining shaft. Jamie had moved closer to inspect it, looking for military weapons caches, when he'd slipped on the edge and fallen into the shaft.

The following week or so is a blur. But I do remember how that afternoon, I was called into the CO's office, where I was informed I would be one of the pallbearers. This involved rehearsing for the service and then carrying Jamie's body when he was flown into Sydney Airport, and again at his funeral, which was scheduled to take place in Perth the following week.

Feet still blistered and back covered in chafing from the 40-kilometre march, I spent the next few days rehearsing for the ramp ceremony, repeatedly practising the movement and formations, which involved the guard of honour, the army band and Jamie's close mates as pallbearers carrying his coffin.

The day arrived for Jamie's ramp ceremony with full military honours at Sydney Airport. We arrived at a side gate of the airport usually reserved for private airlines, where we conducted one last rehearsal before waiting for the aircraft to touch down. The pallbearers' job was to stand dead still at attention in full ceremonial uniform and then slowly march through the guard of honour to pick up the coffin, before marching the other way to the rear of the hearse.

As we strode through the guard of honour, the aircraft lowered and taxied to a standstill. As with so many military funerals in my career, I tried not to look at the family, as I knew I wouldn't have been able to maintain the solemn, steady gaze required for my duties.

When we picked Jamie's coffin up, I was surprised at the weight. It was a full-sized refrigerated coffin flown from the Solomons, and its edge sat directly on my collarbone. This was, however, a small price to pay, and the other pallbearers had already settled into their positions. As we carried Jamie through the guard of honour, I glanced at his mother, who was wailing loudly.

I stayed staunch; he was not in the car yet. Other family members began crying, the sound getting louder as we approached them. We finally placed Jamie down, folded the Australian national flag over his coffin, and put him in the car. At this stage I was barely holding it together. After the car tailgate closed and we were dismissed, I collapsed onto my knees in tears. Jamie's mother, Avril, walked over to me and hugged me tightly.

It was the first time somebody close to me had died. After the funeral, I packed my emotions away to be dealt with later. I would do this numerous times in my career.

The year after Jamie died, I lost another mate. Jacob 'Jake' Kovco was fatally wounded by a gunshot to the head from his own pistol while on deployment to Iraq in April 2006. Jake was a country boy from Victoria, and despite our different upbringings, we had developed a great friendship during our years together in 3 RAR. I liked the way Jake always had a smile on his face, and he seemed to like my energy and constant storytelling, which I would do a lot of at the Shat.

When Jamie was about to head to the Solomons, I remember I avoided seeing him because I was intensely jealous that he was getting another deployment. I didn't want to see him pack all his kit and talk about the impending trip while I stayed back in Sydney. This was something that I would severely regret after he died, and I told myself that next time, if any of my mates were deployed when I wasn't, I would try to spend time with them.

As Jake's trip to Iraq approached, he texted me asking if I wanted to come over for a beer while he packed his kit in his garage. Once again, envy overcame me, and my first reaction was to make an excuse. But the guilt of not seeing Jamie off was still raw, so I had a beer with Jake and feigned excitement for him, gutted that I wasn't joining him. As it turns out, this would be the last time I would see Jake or hear his voice, and I am grateful that I overcame my jealousy.

Jake's death and repatriation were an absolute disaster. From day one, the information was confusing, contradictory and, for those who knew Jake, did not make sense. Initial reports claimed that Jake had accidentally shot himself in his room, which later changed to his pistol discharging. Jake was a competent soldier and the idea of him accidentally shooting himself just didn't add up.

The two other soldiers in the room were not looking at Jake when his pistol was fired, and Jake's unit was scrutinised in the media and even accused of covering up the shooting.[11] Jake's death was also my first taste of how abhorrent the press could be. Articles were published claiming Jake was having an affair, that his mates killed him, and that the hierarchy was covering up facts. His family was grilled by the media, with constant articles full of fantastical accounts and commentary from 'military experts' on their version of events, all of which were false and misleading.

Jake's body was due to be flown back on 26 April via Kuwait, but it was misplaced, and the body of a Bosnian contractor was returned instead. The ADF blamed the Kuwait mortuary, but this did nothing to stem the shock and anger from the 3 RAR community and Jake's family.[10] The media once again licked their lips, and a string of articles was published about the mysterious death of Private Kovco, with all parties involved doing their best to abrogate responsibility.

The Military Board of Inquiry into Jake's death and the subsequent events identified a process failure, due to the numerous agencies and organisations involved with Australian repatriations. It stopped short of blaming any single person or organisation.[11]

The drama didn't end there. After Jake's funeral in his hometown of Briagolong in Victoria, which we all attended, a CD-ROM containing a confidential Defence Department report into the failed repatriation was left in a Melbourne airport lounge by the investigating officer, an army brigadier. Journalist Derryn Hinch was given the CD by the member of the public who had found it, and subsequently broadcast the damning results of the inquiry.

For a community that had already grown tired of constant media attention and was increasingly frustrated at senior ADF leadership's failure to take any responsibility for the bungle, this latest drama further fuelled the anger and contempt.

A coronial inquest concluded that Jake had died by accidentally shooting himself while mishandling his weapon, which his family found difficult to accept.

Major Kyle Tyrrell, who was the officer commanding the security detachment Jake was part of, explained that despite the tragedy of the whole ordeal, the real unsung heroes were the rest of the 3 RAR soldiers in Jake's group. 'Jake's death had a visceral impact on the entire combat team, which was further complicated by an unforgiving media, multiple investigations, a series of systemic failures and incompetencies within the ADF, and the ongoing complexity and volatility of operating in the most dangerous place in the world . . . and yet, as has quite often been the case, these wonderful Australian soldiers continued to prosecute their mission with extraordinary professionalism until the final moment of their deployment. They did Jake proud!'

Jake's and Jamie's deaths further solidified my bond with 3 RAR. They were the first in a long line of my colleagues who would die over the next two decades. I continued to deal with it the only way I knew how: by burying it and pretending it had never happened.

The remainder of my time in 3 RAR was filled with exercises at Singleton, or in North Queensland for larger-scale army exercises where 3 RAR would always arrive in style by parachute. One exercise, Swift Eagle 2005, which was conducted in the town of Innisfail in North Queensland, started with one of the most significant parachute drops I would do in the battalion.

We took off from RAAF Richmond in Sydney, jammed in the C-130 Hercules like sardines, and commenced our long flight up the coast. The pilots were doing their own training, flying in formation to avoid fictitious enemy formations on the ground. They intermittently performed 'tactical flying', which involved getting the paratroopers laden with the kit in the back as sick as possible.

For this jump, we got dressed in our combat equipment in the aircraft, and got into our parachutes, with reserve parachutes on our chest, webbing, pack and weapons clipped onto our bodies, ready to be checked by the parachute jumpmasters. If you have ever experienced car-sickness, imagine the worst car-sickness possible. Imagine 100 or so blokes dripping with sweat, holding on for dear life as a Hercules is thrown around the sky. Then add the smell and sight of a few dozen blokes' vomit all around you, and you will start to get a pretty good idea of what a tactical jump in 3 RAR was like.

The army has a unique talent for taking an activity that could be perceived as fun, and ruining it to the point where you never want to do it again. Civilian skydiving from 10,000 feet in shorts is enjoyable; jumping from a C-130 in complete tactical kit is not.

I was on the last aircraft and the first to jump off the ramp.

Once we had been checked and hooked onto the static line inside the plane, we held on for dear life as the Hercules hugged the Queensland coastline, banking hard from left to right. More men threw up, some on the floor, some on the parachute of the bloke in front of them. Nobody cared anymore.

The immense weight of our combat equipment mixed with our weapons and parachutes made standing almost unbearable, and the seconds until we could get off the darn plane felt like hours. At the one-minute call, the plane banked sharply to the left, and as I looked out at the ramp, I could see three other C-130 Hercules flying in perfect formation, all with ramps down and laden with paratroopers ready to jump.

This was another of those moments in my life when I felt a feeling of total contentment. I knew there was no place I would rather be than inside this tube of vomit and sweat hurtling through the sky. The plane corrected itself, the ocean below us disappeared, and the ground rushed up beneath us. The green light came on, and I stared at the parachute jumpmaster, waiting for the 'chop'. When it came, he looked at me, slapped me on the back and screamed, 'Go!' as I jumped off the ramp into a brilliant Queensland morning from 1000 feet.

I must have been doing something right, as I was soon panelled for the army junior leadership course, which was to be held in Perth. I attended the course with a mate from Alpha Company, Paul de Gelder. As we headed to the airport, Paul told me that he was using this course as a piss trip, as he had his application in to transfer to the navy as a clearance diver. I had a solid drinking partner from Old Faithful for the next few weeks.

Paul duly joined the navy, and in 2009, when he was conducting dive training in Sydney Harbour, he was attacked by a 3-metre bull shark. He survived the shark attack but lost parts of his left arm and leg. He is now a motivational speaker and a keen shark advocate. I regularly see him on television and social media; he exemplifies resilience and courage, and uses his story to help protect the animal that took his limbs.

During this period, I had more frequent encounters with SF, predominantly with soldiers from across the road at 4 RAR (Cdo). Soon after, training facilities were built near the Army Aviation Regiment, and Black Hawk Helicopters appeared on the airstrip at the back of Holsworthy Barracks. When I returned to Holsworthy, I started seeing the 4 RAR (Cdo) guys around the gym and coffee shop on base, which gave me greater insight into the unit.

4 RAR (Cdo) was only just developing as a world-class SF unit at the time. Where most competent, motivated men in 3 RAR aspired to be was in SASR, which until very recently had been Australia's only full-time special operations unit. The unit was raised in 1957 and was based on the United Kingdom's 22 Special Air Service (SAS) regiment, which it emulated in structure, naming convention and symbology, including the famed flaming sword emblem and sandy-coloured beret. In 1980, when 22 SAS soldiers roped down the Iranian Embassy in London and explosively breached a stronghold on international television with gas masks and Heckler & Koch

MP5 submachine guns, the mystique-building and commercialisation of the 'SAS' brand would begin. Even today, the public and media colloquially use the term 'SAS' to brand all SF units, including commandos.

SASR's reputation was forged through sacrifice and impeccable professionalism during Vietnam. Similarly, 4 RAR (Cdo)'s reputation would slowly grow with each rotation to Afghanistan with Task Force 66 (TF66), the Australian SOTG.

The commercialisation of the SAS brand, especially with books, further drove the public fascination, particularly among young soldiers, who all dreamed of wearing the sandy beret one day. When *Bravo Two Zero* was released in 1993, when I was a young army cadet, I read it from cover to cover, along with any other book I could get my hands on that had 'SAS' or 'SASR' on it. People in the army, particularly in the infantry, all held SASR in high regard. They watched as outsiders as SASR men walked around the base confidently. The SASR men were perceived as infallible, with their non-issued guns and bits of kit that we would never dream of being issued.

Stories would regularly circulate from some bloke who knew a guy in the SASR, or an ex-3 RAR guy who had passed selection, 'gone west' and killed six people in Afghanistan, or an SASR squadron that had been in intense combat for hours. As a young soldier, I would listen to these stories with amazement, jealousy and insecurity. I wanted to be the guy whose heroic feats were circulated among the RAR, and I had a burning desire to make the selection for SASR. That was until I saw the TAG-E training on a range at Holsworthy.

During a training activity with 3 RAR, we were allowed to train at the 4 RAR (Cdo) Method of Entry house, which was situated on Luscombe Airfield, where the 6th Aviation Regiment currently sits.

After TAG-E was raised, three facilities were purpose-built to meet its specialist training needs. The first was a single-storey 'kill house', or room floor combat range; the second was a three-storey structure with a lot of small rooms, windows, doors and balconies, where the operators would train explosive and manual breaching; and the third was a 25-metre outdoor live-fire range, which sat across the road from the Method of Entry house.

We were receiving a brief for our training activity on the roof when we heard shooting occurring on the fire range, drawing our attention. Eight black-clad TAG-E operators with gas masks and MP5 submachine guns were conducting live-fire serials, shooting on the move, constantly changing from their primary weapons to their pistols. I was amazed at the speed with which the operators would draw their guns, change magazines and get their MP5s back up, all while constantly looking around so they knew precisely where their other team-mates were.

They all walked in perfect alignment, firing rapidly at targets, looking like modern ninja warriors. They looked fit, strong and confident in their skills, which provided a stark contrast to the fat sergeant in front of us, his gut hanging over his issued belt-kit, stammering through the brief he hadn't rehearsed. 'Don't look at them; pay attention to the brief. They're too special for us to look at,' he said sarcastically, glancing at the TAG-E operators on the range, then returned to his agonisingly long brief.

I vowed to myself then that I would never be a fat, washed-up sergeant in the regular army. I stared at the TAG-E operators with a sense of jealousy—I wanted to be one of them. My thoughts weren't on being in the SASR anymore—they were firmly set on becoming a commando. That day, the seed was firmly planted in my mind that would set the trajectory for the next seventeen years of my life.

CHAPTER 7

THE EYES AND EARS

In 2005, before I attempted selection for commandos, I wanted to spend time in the premier platoon of the infantry battalions, the reconnaissance and sniper platoon. In 3 RAR, recon/snipers was revered by people who wished to hold a place in the platoon one day and despised by soldiers who knew they would never have a chance at filling its ranks. Although the platoon comprised recons and snipers, both elements typically worked in isolation in the field and barracks.

The critical role of recon/snipers was to be the 'eyes and ears' of the CO, who would use information and intelligence acquired by the platoon to shape and plan operations for the rifle companies. Aside from surveillance, their other tasks included ambushing and path-finding, all conducted in small four-person patrols.

While all 3 RAR was inserted via static-line parachute, recons and snipers were inserted via RAPSL, which were conducted at up to 10,000 feet with steerable square parachutes. The higher altitude and ability to steer with precision made this form of parachuting more prestigious. More importantly, however, recon/snipers got to wear as their regular barracks dress a black PT shirt with 'Recon 3 RAR' printed around a white silhouette of soldiers holding binoculars. The remainder of the battalion was required to wear camouflage uniforms or 'cams'.

One Kapyong Day, we watched the recon/sniper platoon RAPSL from 8000 feet onto the parade ground at 3 RAR. I looked on with envy as the soldiers landed their square canopies gently at the back of the battalion on parade; I had to be one of them. I had played enemy for Jamie's recon course the year before, so I had a pretty good idea of what to expect. I started preparing myself physically for the course and was panelled not long after.

The introductory reconnaissance courses in the RAR, particularly 2 RAR and 3 RAR, were notorious for their difficulty, and my course was no exception. Having said that, nothing was special about anything we were taught in recon; if anything, it was just the basic infantry skills done well. It went for about five weeks, the first two weeks completing theory and practical lessons. We began with how to properly camouflage, patrol and build hides in the bush, known as rural hides. Each day would begin with brutal PT sessions that tested every trainee, and I thanked Christ that I had adequately prepared for the course. It was some of the toughest PT I experienced in the army.

The course initially worked on building trainees' essential skills and pack fitness to ensure we could withstand the last phase, which was fourteen continuous days in the field. We would be in 'marching order'—heavy packs, webbing, boots and weapons—everywhere we went for the first few weeks. We would also have to wear camouflage cream on our faces the entire time. The idea of cam cream was to reduce the shine on the face and disrupt its familiar outlines, all in the name of concealment. Wearing cam cream on your face all day is always uncomfortable; we had to continually reapply it, as sweating would slowly wear it off.

In recon/snipers, applying camouflage symbolised our willingness to do the job, even extending to painting our packs and webbing. Everything was camouflaged, including the snap-lock bags used to waterproof our socks, undies and other items, including food. We would wrap a bag in brown sports strapping tape to minimise noise, then paint the tape to camouflage it.

Toiletries were held in small plastic containers, which would once again be wrapped in tape and painted. For our deployment to Timor in 2006, a member of recon/snipers even painted his brown issued boots; nothing was off limits for camouflage.

The last two weeks of the recon course were the field assessment phase, which to this day remains the most challenging fieldwork I ever did in the army, outside of deployments. For two weeks, we would try to remain hidden in the Mogo State Forest, a few hours south of Sydney, and be assessed on everything we had learned so far.

The heat and humidity of summer added to the physical stress of living in the field, which was further exacerbated by our inability to employ creature comforts we would enjoy in the rifle companies, such as sleeping bags and shelter from the rain. At any time, if the patrol were compromised, we would be required to have our kit packed away in a matter of seconds and put a massive rate of fire on the enemy while withdrawing from them as fast as we could. Therefore, any equipment that slowed this process could be catastrophic. We were always waiting for the inevitable training staff who would continually attempt to find us to assess our break contact drills (firing and moving until you lose contact with the enemy).

Sleep deprivation is part of the job for a recon patrol, and experiencing the 3 RAR recon course prepared me well for commando selection. If our risk of compromise was high, we would always have one person awake and on watch; for a four-person patrol, this did not leave much room for a whole night's sleep. During the last few days of the course, the staff would ask for the grid reference to our hide, then charge at us with blank rounds, forcing us to break contact, which we did for almost 48 hours straight.

The anxiety of waiting to be 'bumped' put us in a heightened state of alertness that caused even more fatigue. The sense I experienced on the course of never being able to relax was like the feeling I would have on patrol in Afghanistan, where we would endure long periods of boredom and monotony, interspersed with high degrees of stress and physical output. There is a saying in the army: 'Train hard—fight easy', and the training I completed on the recon course was an excellent foundation for my special operations career.

Of all my experiences in the military, the most stress-inducing was being lost alone at night on a navigation assessment. For soldiers to operate in the field, they must learn to use a compass and a topographical map to ensure they always know where they are without relying only on technology such as the Global Positioning System (GPS). Even when GPS is available, it's essential to always have a backup system. Not knowing your exact geographical position can be a matter of literal life or death.

Soldiers are generally expected to have a basic understanding of land navigation: it's taught at Kapooka for enlisted soldiers and at the Royal Military College at Duntroon for officers. Combat corps such as infantry and the armoured unit are required to develop further competency as part of their role. Specialised infantry soldiers such as recon/snipers and SF must, however, have exceptional skills in individual land navigation by day and night. The theory of navigation itself is simple, but there is a significant divergence between understanding and applying the theory. The only way to get better at navigation is to get 'time on feet', navigating in the bush.

Navigation assessments—'nav ex'—involve a soldier walking with a map, compass, weapon and all their equipment across varying types of terrain, looking for prepared checkpoints that validate the soldier finding them; these can be a numerical figure or code on a piece of paper or marker panel that is communicated via radio to the command post.

Once the command post is satisfied you are there, they give you another grid reference to plot and move towards, and this continues for the entire activity window. Some tests have a minimum number of checkpoints to meet, and some are based on the median number of checkpoints the soldier's cohort achieve.

On the first night of my 'nav ex' on the recon course, I quickly smashed out a few checkpoints, giving myself a false sense of confidence. I saw myself disregarding my paces and bearings, and instead attempting to match the map's features to what I could see around me.

Map-to-ground navigation largely depends on the type of terrain one faces and the navigator's skill; neither factored into my decision-making. Around 1 p.m. on the first day, I jogged up a slight hill, full of confidence and very happy with my progress thus far. I glanced at my map to reconfirm what was over the mountain, which was supposed to be a slope rolling down to a creek line junction where the checkpoint was.

When I reached the top of the hill, however, I saw only a few kilometres of cliffs, gradually leading to a prominent feature in the distance. I stood there stunned, looking down at my map and the terrain. Nothing that I saw with my eyes looked remotely like anything on my map. Confused, I turned around to look at the ground I had covered since the last checkpoint I had reached, which was now 4 kilometres to my south.

Confused and panicked, I turned around and ran back the way I had come, still unsure exactly where I'd gone wrong. I got about

100 metres or so, stopped, realised I had no idea why I was running that way, and screamed, 'Cuuuunt!'

My experience in the infantry and special operations, as a trainee and then an instructor, has taught me that land navigation is a mental battle as much as a navigational one, where some of the best lessons are learned from previous failures.

There is a feeling of complete helplessness when you are alone, lost, with time ticking away. The military, predominantly a team environment, does not allow many opportunities to work in complete isolation. But solo navigation activities enable the individual to experience and control stress and anxiety, think logically and find solutions.

Many candidates have failed the navigation phase of selection purely due to their inability to control their emotions and stay focused on the task at hand. The significance of this is self-evident— SF operators are required to withstand stress and anxiety and remain mission-focused.

I took a few deep breaths, moved to the top of the hill and began a resection, using multiple features in the distance to triangulate my current position. The triangle of error I calculated placed me roughly 800 metres to the west, or where I thought I was when I realised my mistake. Not counting paces and bearings, I had slowly drifted away from my approach to the west, which on the map I could see looked almost the same as where I thought I was going, map-to-ground.

I cursed myself for this mistake, which would now cost me valuable time to backtrack, as the grid to my next checkpoint was directly through thick scrub. I double-checked my calculations, took a large swig of water from my CamelBak, and sprinted down the hill. I managed to pass that nav ex, but I had learned a valuable lesson that day, from a mistake I told myself I would never repeat.

*

The fourteen-day field phase at the end of the recon course concluded with a three-hour PT session, with each NCO in the recon/sniper platoon handing out their punishment, before a barbecue and beers on the beach to mark the end. I had been promoted to lance corporal the year before, and as the only NCO on the course, I was almost sure of a position in the platoon. My competition, a highly competent soldier and good mate, had broken his ankle on the course, taking him out of the race. Had it not been for that, I am not sure I would have got into the platoon.

The recon course was followed by the RAPSL Course, held at an airfield in the town of Ayre, in Queensland, and it was something I had been looking forward to for a long time. By day and night, we completed just under 30 jumps from 4000–6000 feet in clean fatigue or combat equipment. Unlike civilian square sport canopies, military chutes were much more robust to account for the higher altitudes and extra weight they would be required to hold up. After a few days of ground training, we would jump all day and, towards the end of the course, into the night, which I always found thrilling. The inside of the aircraft would have a slight red glow for visibility, and when the plane ramp came down, we just saw a large black hold, thousands of feet in the air.

As well as being a lot of fun, military jumping can also be very stressful.

Special operations freefallers and RAPSL jumpers today use modern equipment that has developed significantly in the past ten years or so, including navigation tools to track their location and movement under the canopy. At 3 RAR in the early 2000s, however, we had our helmet, an altimeter, a ditter (an altitude warning device), a compass and green Cyalume sticks to identify our location in the sky.

There are times when you are jumping with nothing but your helmet and uniform on a brilliant morning, and at those times, flying around the sky at 8000 feet certainly is fun—many times I had to remind myself I was getting paid for this and thought how unbelievably lucky I was. On the other hand, there are times when you wonder why you do this job and if it's worth it. I experienced one such moment when we did a 10,000-foot RAPSL insertion into the Hunter Valley with recon/snipers.

We were up at 2 a.m. to pack all our gear into trucks for the drive out to RAAF Base Richmond, where we would begin the long, slow process of sorting ourselves into jump teams and getting our names and numbers of parachutes recorded. In rifle companies it can take hours to get hundreds of paratroopers ready and onto aircraft, but recon/snipers would typically insert days before the companies. We'd had a late night beforehand, planning and preparing, and I was already feeling fatigued by the time we finally got our parachutes and were ready for the jump on two hours' sleep.

Just as we were dressing for our parachute parade, we were told that the winds were too high and the jump had been delayed, a typical occurrence in parachuting. I looked at my pack, which must have weighed more than 50 kilograms, and was quietly relieved that I would no longer have to carry it around.

When the exercise did take place, two recon patrols and sniper pairs would insert into the exercise area via parachute, then patrol 11 kilometres to locate and identify an enemy camp, before walking back to the static-line drop zone to pathfind for the rifle companies back to the enemy camp so they could conduct a deliberate attack. It would be tough, backbreaking work, but it was precisely the role we had been trained for. A few hours later, we were told to pause for the day and that we'd try again tomorrow, and then were directed to find somewhere to sleep.

The next day, after shivering through a cold June afternoon, we finally got some meals brought out before commencing para-parade and repeating the process. Once we were checked, we threw our packs onto our shoulders and walked the few hundred metres to the awaiting C-130 aircraft; anyone who ever did this 'death march' to the aircraft at Richmond knows it was not easy, but nobody ever dared to admit that.

After a short flight, we stood up in the plane. We attached our static lines to the internal cable, our backs in agony under the strain of our packs, webbing, weapons and parachutes clipped onto our parachute harnesses with all the weight hanging off our shoulders. After what seemed like an eternity, we got the one-minute call, then the green light, and we jumped into the pitch-black night above the Hunter Valley.

As I exited, I tripped on the ramp and went face first, making my opening much more complicated than I had anticipated; after the mandatory awareness counts to wait for the parachute to open, I saw my entire suspension lines in a twist. The drill to overcome this was to kick yourself free of the twists, which was difficult when you had combat equipment hanging off your front. I strained and struggled to kick the twists free as best I could while trying to ascertain my position in the six-person stack; we needed to link up under the canopy before heading towards the target.

Glancing at the altimeter on my wrist, I saw I was at 6000 feet, having already lost 2000 feet due to twists, which motivated me to kick harder, and the twists eventually did straighten out. Finally, I grasped my toggles and assessed the wind direction while frantically looking all around for a sign of another patrol member. This dilemma is easily solved for today's jumpers through NVG, digital tracking tools and radios.

All I could see, though, was clouds and sky and not a single Cyalume stick; I rechecked my alti, then turned downwind to get a better view of the sky behind me, but still nothing. Realising I might have to find an alternate drop zone, as I couldn't make out the luminous markers on our designated drop zone, I glanced at my altimeter again, which read 4000 feet. I turned into the wind to try to identify a clear area to land, cursing myself the entire time for the fuck-up this exercise was becoming.

As I turned, I saw a row of five Cyalume sticks floating away from me in the distance, in perfect formation. There was nothing between me and the rest of the team but the thick vegetation towards which I was rapidly descending, leaving me no option but to find an alternative landing area. Yet even then my alti still read 3000 feet, and all I could hear was the ribbing and slaying I would get for being the only dude in the jump who landed off target when we got back. I yelled, 'Fuck it!' and turned towards the patrol. A few moments later, I looked at my alti, which now read less than 2000 feet, looked at the rapidly approaching bush below me, and knew straight away I had severely fucked up—again. I was now in complete terror, having turned into the wind to slow my landing down, but I was getting zero penetration as the wind was more substantial than the forward speed of the parachute. Then, glancing behind me, I saw I was heading towards a large dam.

A few dangers in military parachuting strike fear in the heart of any paratrooper: trees, water and wire. Somehow, I flew towards two of these on my first night jump with recon/snipers. Water parachute jumps have flotation devices, but not the land-jump setups to which I was attached, leaving me at risk of drowning. I was now faced with a critical decision—turn into the wind and have a slow landing, which could be above trees or into a dam, or turn and go with the wind in the hope of clearing the trees and barrier but guaranteeing myself a hard landing.

I decided on the not-drowning-by-myself-at-night option. As I approached 80 feet, I lowered my combat equipment, freeing it from the front of my legs so it wouldn't impede my landing, and then my parachute started picking up speed; the closer I got to the ground, the faster I seemed to be going. I was sure I would break a leg at a minimum, but at least I had cleared the large dam by about 40 metres and was heading towards a clearing—that meant no trees. Just at the last 20 feet or so, as the ground came rushing towards me, I felt as if my body was being ripped in two. I frantically glanced below me to try to see what was pulling my legs and saw my combat equipment stuck in a barbed wire fence, the lowering line straining against the top of the wall as the force of the travelling parachute battled the fence posts. I couldn't believe it. I had hit the paratrooper trifecta: water, trees *and* wire.

Of course, it had to be me. I pulled the jettison device on my harness to cut my pack away, causing my body to surge with the parachute. I eventually stopped after landing hard and being dragged a good 30 metres or so. I lay there staring at the stars, slowly moving each limb to ensure it still worked, wishing I was anywhere else but in this paddock, and thinking that there had to be an easier way to make a living.

Despite a few nasty jumps, the RAPSL further cemented my love for parachuting. When I was sixteen, I completed the civilian accelerated freefall course at Skydive Sydney in Picton, south-west of Sydney. The father of Pete, one of my best mates from growing up in the Hills, was a founding member of Skydive Sydney but had tragically passed away from cancer a few years before. Pete was completing the course to pay homage to him, and I of course was happy to join. I had left school and was working as a painter for $200 a week, so it took me a while to save enough money for the course. Although I had not done freefall before, I had done my two static-line jumps in cadets the same year, which gave me more confidence.

The initial stages of the freefall course were conducted over a weekend. Some theory and written tests were followed by a half-day of dry drills covering awareness counts, opening procedures and malfunction drills. The course is completed in about nine jumps or 'stages', each requiring the student to display a particular key element of freefall. The instructor involvement decreases after the first few jumps, for a first 'solo' exit around stage four. So, at sixteen, with an instructor holding onto me on either side, I jumped from the ramp of a Skyvan aircraft at 14,000 feet on a brilliant spring morning.

The pure exhilaration, adrenaline and thrill of falling through the sky at 230 kilometres an hour is something to which words can never do justice. I was instantly hooked, and I still skydive to this day.

CHAPTER 8

OPERATION ASTUTE

It was a pay Thursday in late May 2006, and after we hit the gym, a few platoon lads and I headed into the Rocks for a few beers. We had heard rumours of another possible deployment to Timor, and as the army's current online Battalion Group, we knew if the balloon went up, 3 RAR would definitely get a go. We also knew the 4 RAR (Cdo) lads across the road were on the move, though nobody knew when and what they would do.

On 24 May 2006, the acting prime minister, Peter Costello, announced that Australia would send an advance party to negotiate a deployment of ADF at the request of the East Timorese government to quell unrest and return stability. Within days, forward elements of a multi-national force, under the operational name 'Astute', touched down in Dili.

Around 1 a.m. that Thursday morning, I was sitting shitfaced on a pub dancefloor, lying through my teeth to a cute young back-packer who never really got a chance to form an opinion of me. This was because her less attractive friend, who was getting no attention from the other lads, did her best to continually interrupt me, rolling her eyes and challenging everything I said. On my way to the toilet, I pulled out my phone to see thirteen missed calls from Platoon Commander Vando and ran straight out of the pub to call him back.

'Ryder, where the fuck are you guys?' he asked. 'Get back to work ASAP. We're on!'

I ran back inside to round up the lads, kissed the cute back-packer on the cheek to say bye, then gave her annoying bodyguard the finger on the way out, much to the disgust of both of them.

We arrived back at Kapyong Lines early in the morning. The battalion was already humming; all the company office lights were on, and soldiers were running around in a frenzy with papers and bags, every second person stopping to give me their opinion on what was happening.

The next few days were a bit of a blur. First we drove to RAAF Base Richmond to catch a C-130 flight to Townsville, where we would spend a few days before having a night in Darwin, then flying into Dili the following day. After we found some space in Townsville's Lavarack Barracks at 2 RAR, we were told to link up with their recon/snipers to get last-minute training in image capture and transfer kits, as we would be deploying with them as soon as we were wheels down in Dili. After endless briefs and intelligence updates, we pushed into the RAAF base in Darwin to get our ammu-nition and high explosives before our flight in to Komoro Airstrip in Dili, which 4 RAR (Cdo) had just secured.

I was the patrol 2ic, so I was responsible for all patrol administra-tion, including ensuring the team had conducted all its mandatory checks of weapons and equipment. Once we got our ammunition, we started filling magazines and stowing away our grenades, 40mm grenade launcher rounds and Claymore antipersonnel mines. Claymores are electronically initiated explosive devices, so their electrical circuit needs base-testing to ensure they will fire when needed. In training, as with all explosives and live firing in the ADF, there are strict rules and protocols about where and how this base-testing should occur.

Our first task once we landed in Dili would be to get our hands on a crew of M113 APCs that would be inserting us 20 kilometres or so east of the capital to conduct surveillance on a major supply route. I therefore needed to ensure that, as soon as we arrived, we had everything on us that we needed for the mission. I chased around the signallers to ensure we had the correct frequencies and codes for our two types of radios, accurate maps and, of course, batteries and food.

An hour or so later, the company executive officer (XO) came running over in a panic to tell the few hundred of us preparing our equipment that buses were on the way. Timings had slid left—we were leaving in 40 minutes. I looked at my team's kit, strewn all over the tarmac in the blistering sun, and wondered how on earth we would get it all good to go in time. I stopped the patrol, called them in and gave them priorities to work on if we ran out of time. Firstly, ammo and base-testing Claymores, followed by radio checks and water—everything else would have to wait.

I grabbed all the patrol's Claymores and looked for a quiet area away from everyone where I could lay out the devices and check the black and tan electrical cables for continuity. The heat on the tarmac was unbearable in the midday sun, so I took off my shirt, which was dripping in sweat. I placed all six mines, evenly spaced apart, about 30 metres from the main body of troops.

I had begun unrolling the spools when a dozen or so buses appeared and parked right next to all the mines. An RAAF WO I didn't recognise slowly walked off the bus, staring at me with his mouth open and taking in the sight of a dude with no shirt on setting up a bunch of mines by himself on an airfield in broad daylight.

There is a general misconception that every soldier in the army regularly plays with guns and explosives and develops marksmanship and confidence through the process. In fact, the vast majority of roles in the army only require soldiers to shoot twice a year, which can be done on a massive weapons-simulation computer system. Anything more than this is not required as there is an almost zero per cent likelihood that that person will ever have to employ or fire a weapons system in real time. Seniority of rank, therefore, does not equate with more experience with weapons and explosives. A private in a recon platoon would be vastly more experienced and competent than a WO who was a pay clerk.

So when this RAAF WO saw a young lad by himself setting up a bunch of Claymores on a tarmac not far from hundreds of other troops and other ammunition, he did what I expected him to do and erupted into a rage, which was concealed from the rest of the team by the buses. The WO was so angry that he couldn't find the right words. After getting me to stand to attention, he stammered and stuttered for a while, before firing questions at me.

'What rank are you?' he yelled. 'What unit? You can't set up explosives here! Where the fuck is your shirt?' That he called them 'explosives' and not 'Claymores' told me everything I needed to know about this fuck. Armed with this intelligence, I decided to see how far I could push him without risking my deployment.

'Apologies, sir. Could you please tell me what I'm doing wrong?' I asked, knowing the answer but hedging my bets that the WO didn't.

'You can't set up here; it's against policy,' he replied.

'Which policy, sir?' I responded with a cheeky, smartarse grin. 'I don't think I'm familiar with them. If you could kindly provide me references, I would be happy to take this as a learning opportunity.'

The WO's rage was boiling. He leaned a few inches from my face. 'I know what you're doing. I'm going to charge you and throw you in the cells,' he barked.

I stood there and locked eyes with him.

'Shut the fuck up,' was his next order, even though I hadn't said anything.

As I stood there, I could feel a laugh brewing in my gut. Every second, it grew in intensity, eventually reaching my face. I tried in vain not to laugh, pushing my lips together, but it was hopeless. I gave up and laughed with such force that I had to bend over and rest my hands on my thighs. I don't remember what he said next, but he went storming off towards the main body, frantically trying to find someone to help him deal with this shirtless soldier whose abhorrent behaviour had to be dealt with. I never did see that WO again, and I often wonder how far he got with his plan to incarcerate me.

After an unceremonious landing at Komoro Airstrip, we grabbed our packs and found a shaded area to rest up in while waiting for our first job. We knew that in a few weeks our platoon would combine with 1 RAR and 2 RAR to form a combined reconnaissance and sniper platoon that would service the Battle Group that 3 RAR was part of. For the moment, however, we would be operating as a stand-alone patrol, which we were chuffed about.

It was a swelteringly hot afternoon in Dili, the air thick with smoke from scattered fires burning all over the city. Most of our task group were scattered around the airport terminal, finding whatever shade and seats they could. Everyone was living out of their packs, as the logistics supply chain was yet to be implemented. A few hours later, the platoon commander returned with details of a road move for us recon/snipers and one of the platoons from Bravo Company 3 RAR that had flown in with us.

We were to load up in trucks and replace 4 RAR (Cdo), which had just cleared and secured the heliport a few kilometres from Komoro that would be Battalion Headquarters. After a lot of confusion and yelling, we loaded into the trucks. When we arrived at the heliport, our recon patrol and the snipers were tasked with finding a position for overwatch while Bravo Company secured the perimeter.

As we unloaded our packs, I saw a mate from Alpha Company 3 RAR who had done the SF entry test with me in 2004. I walked over to him while he sat against a wall with his SR-25 marksman rifle, black runners and baseball cap, and shook his hand. His platoon had seconded a bunch of white fleets (civilian vehicles), four-wheel drives, and 2nd Squadron, SASR (2 SAS Sqn) was tasked and re-tasked all over the capital. I listened enviously to the commando's stories of the last few days.

A few minutes later, all their earpieces crackled into life, leaving the commandos sprinting for their vehicles, and then they were off out the gate in convoy, beeping their horn at anyone who dared get in their way. At that moment, I knew I really wanted to be with SF, but I couldn't focus on that too much—we in recon/snipers had busy days ahead.

We moved into a two-storey building on the eastern side of the heliport that had a tower with two more levels. We had an observation post (OP) on the roof with the snipers, so we had claimed the upper level as our bed-down and planning area.

We received our orders and began planning. As my patrol's 2ic, I would help the patrol commander, Dan, with planning. We pored over maps at varying scales of the area we were inserting into, to form an appreciation of the terrain, and agreed on a ridgeline adjacent to the main supply route where we would be tasked with observing and reporting back to Regimental Headquarters. We then coordinated with the APC crew, to make sure they were happy to insert us there. The M113 APC has been in use since the late 1950s. Although it is a capable and robust vehicle, there are other platforms of choice for inserting a clandestine recon patrol. It was the only available asset, however, as the SF contingent were using all the Black Hawk helicopters.

We refilled our packs with rations and water, double-checked that the batteries on all our comms and image capture and transfer kits were charged, and then started the ritual of camouflage.

A lot of work and planning goes into an operation, and applying camouflage to your face is the final step before grabbing your kit and heading out into whatever is out there. This final step marked the psychological transition from rest to preparing for battle, a pivotal moment for warriors throughout history. We jumped off the ramps of the APCs around 11 p.m. and commenced our infiltration to the OP, which was around 1 kilometre to our north. We walked this final distance because of the noise inserting any closer would create.

Our task was to observe and report on a main supply route (MSR) into the capital so that the commander could get an appreciation of the patterns of local life and enhance their situational awareness of the area.

The ground was sparser than the maps had indicated, and as we got closer to the OP site, we knew we would have to move to the alternative OP we had chosen, as the risk of compromise would be too high once the sun came up. We eventually found a suitable hide site around 400 metres from our planned OP location, which still gave us an excellent view of the main supply route.

We then began our occupation routine. For a small recon element, survivability depends on the ability to remain concealed, with courses of action determined by specific standard operating procedures designed to maximise the chances of getting away if a compromise does occur. We very slowly took positions in a tight perimeter in the middle of a thicket of spiky bushes below the crest of the ridgeline to minimise our silhouettes during the day. We commenced setting up our Claymores as perimeter security. As I gave Beau, our scout, the field signal to set up one of the Claymores, I smiled, recalling the incident with the RAAF WO in Darwin.

As this was still the first few days of the entire operation, we had yet to learn exactly what the threat picture was, so we maintained constant watch on the OP site, looking at the road and the ridge-line to our north. The Claymores were placed all around the OP to delay any threats that would follow us and, more importantly, clear a way off the ridgeline, as behind us lay 40 metres of sheer cliff falling into the ocean, leaving only two tracks off the feature into our pre-designated rendezvous locations. After we set the Claymores, I started to draft up a radio report with our OP grid and an initial account, then settled into the monotony of sitting around for the remainder of the night.

Everything in an OP is done slowly and methodically, under the assumption that we may be required to break contact and withdraw from a numerically superior force at any moment. One person at a time ate; one person at a time would have their pack open; and two people in the four-person patrol would always be awake.

I tapped Beau on the shoulder around 2 a.m. on the second night. After my two-hour turn on watch, I informed him that I had just changed the batteries on the thermal imaging (TI) device, and handed him the OP log with its attached micro-torch to record all our observations.

I slowly fell asleep, listening to the waves crashing below us, but was startled awake by someone violently tapping my leg. I sat up and lowered my NVG to see Beau giving me the thumbs-down signal—the signal for the enemy or a potential threat. I took off my pack to get closer to him.

'What did you see?' I asked.

'Mate, I just saw a ute pull up and four people carrying weapons disappear in the tree line below us,' he replied.

I wasn't 100 per cent sure that his eyes weren't playing tricks on him, mainly because TI is known for its inability to provide clear pictures, but I wasn't taking any chances. I tapped the rest of the patrol on their legs. 'Stand to! Stand to!' I whispered, causing a flurry of movement while the guys put on their NVGs and covered their sectors.

The patrol commander slid over to us to confirm what was happening, and Beau explained again what he had seen.

'Scott, did you see anything?' Dan asked.

'No, mate, I was asleep,' I replied.

'Beau, how sure are you?'

'They had weapons and were moving in this direction.'

Dan continued to quiz Beau.

'Mate, I'm telling you what I saw,' he responded, his voice getting slightly more strained.

Dan called me over to quickly go through our options.

I agreed that what Beau said wasn't enough to call in a compromise, but that if four men really were approaching our OP, it would almost certainly be a compromise and see us having to extract regardless. I suggested we at least send a situation report back to HQ to keep them informed while we waited to see how this played out. This was back in the days before we had drones at our beck and call that could quickly fly over and verify what we couldn't see. On this trip, we had to do it the old-school way, with our eyes.

As I grabbed the radio to call in the report, we heard twigs breaking below us from the direction Beau had seen the four men approaching. We sat there, frozen, with our mouths open, straining to hear anything that would indicate the location or intent of the threat. I rested my right index finger on the square safety latch of my Steyr rifle, double-checking that the press switch for my night-laser device was still there, as I would need it as an aiming mark to engage accurately.

With my left hand, I slowly released the safety bail on my Claymore. The Claymore was pointed directly at the area the noise came from, and I intended to fire it the moment contact was initiated. Then we waited. Ten minutes later, still nothing. Twenty minutes later, still nothing.

Eventually, I realised that whoever Beau had seen wasn't coming up our way. Suddenly tired as the adrenaline wore off, we stood down and got ready for a few hours' more sleep. Even though we hadn't been compromised or brought into contact, it felt good to know we were well prepared. We could rely on our equipment, attitude and drills all coming together, and I was proud of how the team had performed. I was disappointed, though, that we hadn't fired a shot.

On our return to the heliport, we discovered that our bed-down in the tower was now occupied by brigade storemen, who had not even done us the courtesy of packing up the food and rations that we had brought into the country but opted not to take to the OP due to weight. A few days earlier, when we had replaced 4 RAR (Cdo), the only people in the area were SF and infantry. Now, the rear echelon was slowly arriving, and with it came dozens of officers and WOs, each with their agenda, whose tasks and roles—in their eyes—trumped everyone else's.

Dan tried in vain to secure our old spot, as recon/snipers were still manning the OP on the tower, but a storeman told him to piss off. Dan flew into a rage and threatened to bash him and throw him off the balcony, which of course was not well received. This was the first time in my career that I witnessed at first-hand the poor treatment of specific roles, mainly infantry, by non-combat corps leaders.

Beyond our official ranks, there seemed to be an unspoken pseudo-hierarchy in environments where large bodies of troops came together. Somehow, although infantry faced the greatest risk and had a physically arduous job, they were considered the lowest in the pecking order, always relegated to the worst living areas and the last to enjoy anything that could improve a soldier's quality of life. Moreover, a 'grunt' could never get away with even the tiniest deviation from regulations. We were always expected to maintain the highest standards of dress, bearing and behaviour, but we never got first pickings on anything.

Back in Dili, we spent a few days at the heliport while the rest of the army seemed to slowly fill every square inch of the rapidly growing base. Signs suddenly appeared about what state your weapon had to be in or where you could or couldn't drive, walk, eat or smoke.

As the weeks went by, the frequency of negligent discharges (NDs) of firearms increased, as different areas of the base required weapons to be in varying states of readiness. With many support staff not used to carrying and working with firearms every day, this meant more accidents.

After our unsuccessful bid to reclaim our living quarters, we were told to head to HMAS *Tobruk*, which had arrived in Dili Harbour, where we could shower and change clothes. While we sat in the back of the Uni-mog truck, a group of white four-wheel drives screamed past in a tight convoy in front of us, and as I peered through the front of the truck I caught a glimpse of a mate of mine in 4 RAR (Cdo), as he held on for dear life. Every interaction I had with SOCOMD, they were doing something I wanted to be doing.

While I was about to have a shower on a navy ship, the commandos were in four-wheel drives chasing down bad guys—I knew where I would rather be.

We were standing on the deck of the *Tobruk*, waiting in line with around 60 soldiers when a navy NCO came out and told us he only had the capacity for twenty or so people to shower. This caused a bunch of soldiers to start pleading their case as to why they should get picked. I thought I mustn't have heard right when one said he hadn't showered in two days and needed to get in today.

I realised at this point that our patrol had gone almost eleven whole days without a shower. Our cams were white with sweat stains, our collars were covered in cam cream from our necks, and we must have stunk to high heaven. We stood there patiently while more pogues—non-combat corps—jostled for a shower. Eventually, realising this was a waste of time, I signalled for the patrol to follow me, and we put our packs on to head out into the fresh air.

One of the navy personnel, who must have caught sight (or smell) of our patrol, walked over and asked us where we were from and the last time we had showered. I informed him it was more than ten days ago in Townsville, and that we were recon/snipers, 3 RAR. He ushered us to the showers past everyone else on the deck, who suddenly fell silent.

When we returned to the heliport, 1 RAR, 2 RAR and 3 RAR recon/snipers were combined into a Task Group Intelligence, Surveillance and Reconnaissance (ISR) asset under the command of 3 RAR and given accommodation in tents. Military-issued cot stretchers under mosquito dome tents would be our home for the next six months, a bunch of old fans the only means of comfort. We got to know the other members of the platoon, and we quickly bonded over count-less games of poker, Risk, and Presidents and Assholes.

Dan had been sent home for personal reasons, so I was leader of the patrol, with another guy from our patrol, Sam, acting as my 2ic until a new patrol commander could be sent over in a few weeks. The Australian Federal Police (AFP) had recently formed the Operational Response Group, which had been deployed to the Solomon Islands and now Timor, and elements of the task group, including recon/snipers, would be working with them in specific areas of responsibility around Dili and its surrounds.

We spent much time patrolling and driving in our locations, taking on more of a policing role than a military one. Most of our work was trying to identify arsonists and violent offenders who posed a risk to the population and to the rapidly growing number of displaced locals living in the internally displaced persons camp just outside Komoro Airstrip.

Each weekly intelligence report would have a new directive, policy and acronym, which was typically useless. The best acronym that some genius conjured up was 'gang-aged youths', or GAYs, which we were to use over the radio when reporting on gang activity. Some readers may think this was by design, perhaps for morale. I can assure you, though, that some officer would have come up with it in total seriousness and, despite everyone around him knowing it was a terrible idea, no one in command meetings would have said anything, allowing it to be sent out.

We operated in small teams with the AFP, patrolled the streets and spoke to locals to gauge militia activity. While there was a lot of activity in the city at first, within the first week or two of the operation everything simmered down quickly.

Towards the end of the trip, we spent a few days at the base at Bobonaro, in the west of Timor, where I had spent time during my 2002 deployment. On that trip, I'd become friendly with one of the town kids who would try to sell us CDs, magazines and biscuits.

He was eleven or twelve years old, and I had got to know him quite well over many hours in the top piquet tower overlooking the base.

In 2006, we were walking down to the local markets when I heard a man with a deep voice calling out my name: 'Mr Scott! Mr Scott, it's me.' As he approached, I recognised him straight away. Now in his teens, he was about 6 feet tall, which is quite rare for a Timorese person. We enjoyed catching up and getting some photos together. I was surprised he remembered me, as many other Australians would have been rotating through the base in the four years since I'd been there.

CHAPTER 9

THE BODYGUARDS

After we had been in East Timor for about three months, my patrol was tasked to head to Gleno, 30 kilometres south-west of Dili, where Bravo Company was stationed. Our task was to provide security to an influential political ally of the new government for the next six weeks, living in his front yard, while Bravo Company provided our logistics sustainment and an immediate quick reaction force should we need it.

So we packed our gear and headed off to meet Major Tara, who would be our sole task for the next few months, and arrived at his house with our local interpreter, provided to us by Bravo Company Headquarters (CHQ). The modest, single-storey, four-bedroom home, painted bright green, was by Timorese standards a pretty good house, and sat in a relatively quiet side street near the centre of town.

A small-framed man who looked to be in his early sixties walked out to greet us with a few military officers, his wife and kids in tow. He introduced himself and we exchanged formalities. We discussed where we would be sleeping to avoid getting in his way, but to ensure we provided security during the night. My orders on this task were light, and I was not offered much background, but I knew this was more about the optics of a personal security team for intelligence/ strategic reasons than any actual threat to Major Tara or his family.

Infantry soldiers are not trained in the close personal protection (CPP) work. For lower-ranked senior military officers, it's usually conducted by military police, and for senior officers and government officials, including the current president of Timor, Xanana Gusmao, it's usually conducted by SASR and 4 RAR (Cdo).

I had heard the term 'imposter syndrome' before but had never experienced it myself until now. The whole night before, I lay awake trying to work out how I would provide Major Tara protection with no formal training in CPP while maintaining the illusion of credibility in front of not only him but also Bravo Company, to whom we were attached for the duration of the task.

The acting 2ic, Sam, and I had discussed at length the critical issues with completing this task, and we both agreed we needed to develop a base plan on the first day we met Major Tara. There was a delicate balance between gaining insight into Major Tara's habits, routines and movements before developing a plan, and having something tangible to brief him on if he asked about our 'vast' experience in providing CPP.

Contrary to popular opinion, nothing about SF is particularly 'special'. The funding and resources certainly are vital factors, but once I got into SOCOMD, I realised that the thing that made SF stand out was that they continually honed their skills based primarily on mastering the basics. Which is what I began to do in this case. Without CPP training, I had to look at the situation in terms of the training I did have. And so I viewed Major Tara as a vital asset. I then incorporated basic infantry minor tactics, techniques and procedures to give the patrol confidence in the task ahead.

I got the patrol together and began rehearsals on how we would protect Major Tara. It made sense that we always had one person providing CPP as the bodyguard, so we developed a roster for that role. Then we practised simple infantry formations such as box and diamond on foot, with Major Tara and the bodyguard in the centre.

I assessed that the formation's distance should depend on the threat and environment, so we practised a 'box in' or 'box out' call to reflect this. In an infantry obstacle crossing, you always send a scouting element over the obstacle at the outset, so we concluded that in both foot and vehicle moves, we would always send a recon element first to scout the conditions.

In this manner, we hashed out a bunch of possible scenarios. We developed standard operating procedures for everything from moving between locations to breaking contact, which involved the bodyguard carrying Major Tara while the patrol broke contact. I recall thinking at the time how frustrating it was that we were the ones who'd been landed with this job, given the number of SF blokes in Dili, and how having even one of them here would have been immensely helpful.

The year before that Timor trip in 2006, a group of NCOs, including me, were tasked to develop an introductory urban operations course, which we essentially made up. Then, too, I had been frustrated and didn't understand why some of the commandos across the road could not devise and run the course for us—it was their speciality, not ours. Getting their advice and guidance would have meant we would be teaching contemporary and tested methods, not relying on guesswork and improvisation.

Years later, when I was a student on the armed response protection team course, the qualifying course for commandos to be employed in personal security detachment (PSD) operations overseas, I was looking forward to learning all the special trade secrets to PSD work.

As it turns out, though, the basis of nearly all of the physical drills on foot and some of the vehicle drills that we learned weren't too dissimilar from what we had done in Timor, which we had of course based on basic infantry minor tactics.

This gave me a valuable lesson before my SF career had even begun: nothing that happens in SOCOMD permits the erosion and abdication of core infantry skills, something that some SF blokes seem to forget. During my time as an instructor at the ADF School of Special Operations (ADFSSO) years later, I would constantly reinforce this to the trainee team commanders and trainees.

As it turns out, our preparation was not wasted, as the first thing Major Tara wanted to see was how we would protect him in certain situations. Using one of his aides, we demonstrated our formations on foot and in vehicles, and actions on contact, including a 'man down' drill, which was a withdrawal with Major Tara as a casualty.

We finished our little demonstration and stood there dripping with sweat, waiting. I held my breath as he turned to his interpreter, trying to gauge his response through tone and pitch, but he gave nothing away. 'Major Tara said he is very grateful to have such a highly trained CPP team with him and wishes to invite you inside his home for dinner tonight,' the interpreter translated.

I was relieved. As I debriefed the patrol afterwards, I praised them for their effort and hard work. I also informed them, however, that this was early days, and the monotony and lack of sleep while guarding Major Tara's home would get very old very soon, and we would have to remain vigilant. Before dinner, I drove to Bravo CHQ to back-brief the OC and get his blessing. I told him our sustainment plan for rations and water, with which he seemed pleased. When I returned to the patrol, we set up our 14 by 14-foot (4 by 4-metre) tent in Major Tara's front yard; this would be home for the next six weeks.

As predicted, the monotony of the task soon set in, and regular piquets and sitting around in cars while Major Tara went about his business in and around Gleno and ate and slept got old very quickly. We were thankful, then, to be re-tasked for a few days while Major Tara travelled north to visit family. He apparently didn't require a security element for this, which further fuelled my speculation as to the real motives behind our CPP task. Regardless, I enjoyed my autonomy with the task and liked working with the rest of the patrol.

We farewelled Major Tara and met the Bravo Company OC for our next task. The OC, a former British Army officer, had a strange habit of wearing his issued parachute smock daily, despite the heat and humidity, earning him the nickname 'Smocky'. Australian paratroopers, unlike those in the British Army, don't wear their parachute wings on their camouflage uniforms, only on a smock—the smock is a sort of lightweight jacket, whose only real purpose is to show off our wings when it's reasonable to do so. The 42-degree heat we were in was perceived as unreasonable to everyone but Smocky.

At the meeting, we sat through the most eccentric, broad, unrealistic set of orders I had ever received, all centred around coffee trucks. Smocky was convinced that the anti-government militia was smuggling weapons in the back of coffee trucks, with key coffee traffickers allegedly based in Gleno—as it turns out, on the same street as Major Tara. Even the analyst providing us with the intelligence picture seemed sceptical as he offered some minimal information, which essentially summarised that there was coffee, trucks and maybe weapons in the area.

Still unconvinced this wasn't a practical joke, I quizzed the intelligence officer how the coffee/weapons hypothesis was reached, glancing at Smocky, who indicated that 'many coffee trucks have been seen on my street'. My disbelief grew even more as I was given my mission statement, which included 'taking imagery of any people involved in the coffee/weapons trade in a clandestine manner'. I was informed the suspects were based at a 'safe house'. When I checked the grid reference for the safe house, I saw that it was the house across the road from Major Tara, on the street where we had already been living for the past month.

I spent a few hours drafting a set of orders for the patrol, who were just as bewildered as I was about how exactly we were supposed to take photos of people living in the house across the road from us without being seen.

As I sat down for my meal of mie goreng noodles, wondering how on earth I could perform this task, one of the locals with whom we had become familiar stopped by on his bike, asking us if we wanted to join him in watching the soccer World Cup, as Australia was playing that night. Not wanting to offend him, I said we would get back to him—having four armed Australian soldiers watching soccer among dozens of drunk Timorese spelled disaster, despite how personally appealing it sounded to me. Then, suddenly, a cheeky smile spread across my face.

'Ryder, whatever idea just came into your head, it's a terrible idea,' Beau said, grinning.

I got the boys together to reveal my grand plan. 'Okay, so tonight we'll all watch soccer with old mate,' I explained. 'But we tell him we have to keep an eye on Major Tara's house, so we'll need to watch the game at the house across the road.' This, of course, was the 'safe house' Smocky had told us about. 'Then, after the game,' I continued, 'we get a big group photo. I'll edit it and crop each of the faces out, then write up a detailed patrol report on them. Any detail we don't know, we'll just make some shit up,' I finished proudly. The boys stared at me. Some started to nod slowly, despite the plan's fundamental disregard for the motivation behind the task. And then, acknowledging the ridiculousness of said task, everyone agreed. We devised some critical actions in the unlikely event they would be needed.

Shaun Taylor—who would fill in as the team 2ic after I took over the patrol and would also complete selection for commandos not long after me—found the local who'd invited us to watch the game, as well as the owner of the safe house, and confirmed the plan would work. A few other locals pulled out machetes before the game, then sat back, waiting for kick-off. As game time approached, the number of house guests started steadily growing. Initially it was the dozen or so we expected, then twenty, then 30, then 40. By the time the game started, we had a hundred or so drunk Timorese sitting in what I thought was a hall but was actually an empty lounge room, with one main door as the entry and exit.

A small part of me was severely regretting my decision now, and it only got worse when the locals ushered us towards the front row of seats, giving us cold beers as we sat. The lads looked at me, unsure if they should be drinking, waiting for my lead. I saw my career flash before my eyes and imagined the front page of the *Daily Telegraph*: 'Australian soldiers bashed after weapons stolen in alcohol-fuelled World Cup party'. But that was future Scott's problem—right now, I decided to crack a cold one and watch the World Cup while we ran a one-person watch at the main entrance to the hall in case every-thing went pear-shaped.

After a few too many beers, the game ended and, as planned, I grabbed the patrol's D90 Nikon camera out of my bag. Cheering, I told everyone to get a photo with the patrol to celebrate Australia's win. I took some group shots before we shook hands with the locals and headed back to our tent.

I spent most of the following day drafting the patrol report and cropping photos, then headed in to submit the USB to Smocky's clerk for his review, which by all accounts was received very well, with numerous mentions in orders of our patrol's stellar performance during a sensitive ISR task. The patrol and I took enormous pleasure from this, given our unorthodox methods and blatant disregard for the job. It never blew up in our faces.

After six weeks with Major Tara, we said our farewells by exchanging gifts, hugs and many photos, and headed back to reunite with the rest of the platoon in Dili and be given our next task. Major Tara was almost tearful as he waved his final goodbye, as were some of his aides. We had built a significant rapport and got to know him well during our time there, and I often wonder what ended up happening to him and his family.

My career in the army has allowed me to travel worldwide to train and fight with a variety of international armies and other organisations. Australian soldiers have always been welcomed with open arms and well liked by whomever we work with; we are known for being respectful of other cultures and capabilities, and I always took pride in ensuring I played a small part in maintaining this reputation.

If the seed was planted in me to attempt selection for commandos before the 2006 Timor trip, then our joint task with Alpha Company 4 RAR (Cdo) was the nail in the coffin for my regular army career.

I was given orders for a joint operation with a platoon of commandos from Alpha Company. It focused on the capture of Oan Kiak, a guerrilla leader with the L7 movement, which opposed the current government. Kiak was wanted for the murder of an unarmed truck driver, but was also gaining a significant following from elements of the local population. Intelligence had indicated that Kiak was hiding among the locals in a coastal town just outside Dili, where he was alleged to be conducting regular meetings with other guerrilla leaders.

My patrol would be working with 4 RAR (Cdo) by conducting 24/7 clandestine surveillance of the coffee shop where local sources claimed Kiak held his meetings. The commandos, meanwhile, would stage nearby at a soccer field, ready to drive up and detain Kiak once spotted. On arrival at the soccer field, I met up with the platoon commander and team leaders to discuss our plan, then found a suitable OP on a nearby hill from which I would be able to identify Kiak's face through our optics.

We would work in pairs, inserting into the OP at night for 24 hours before being replaced by the other team the next night. To ensure we had a clear line of communication with the commando platoon, one of their signallers, who had specialist radio equipment we did not, was attached to us. I was one of the pair who inserted the first night, keen to get a good look at the OP. The walk to the site was up a steep 100-metre ridgeline; as always, it was much more complicated than it looked to climb. But the place was suitable enough, and after building a hide with some nearby foliage, we settled in for the night.

Thirty minutes later, a torrential downpour began, which didn't let up for the whole night. A horrendous onshore wind battered our position, making sleep impossible. Day 1 of the OP, and I was already over it. The next night, after we were replaced, I walked into the soccer stadium like a miserable drowned rat and trudged over to where we were sleeping on our thick foam mats on the concrete under the grandstand. When I looked over to the commandos' spot, I was shocked. The teams had lined their cars up facing the exit, with all their gear neatly laid out on the seats, and a one-person piquet on the radios.

They had acquired half a dozen 14-foot (4-metre) tents, rarer than rocking-horse shit for 3 RAR, and were living on stretchers under mozzie domes, three or four to a tent. Off to the side, two boys with their shirts off and wearing cut-off shorts were cooking breakfast on a barbecue.

One of their tents had been turned into a kitchen, for which a few would drive into town to acquire fresh food; the back of one of their four-wheel drives even had a large fridge for their drinks and meat. I could not believe it. While we slept on foam and ate ration packs, these boys had a bunch of civilian cars, tents, cold drinks and fresh food, and spent the day with their shirts off, listening to music, kicking a footy and doing fitness circuits.

We never did see Oan Kiak, at the café or anywhere else, and within weeks he would hand himself in to security forces. But I did get my first taste of the mature, adult environment of SF and the contrast in funding and resources between regular army and SOCOMD. The SF guys had all the best guns, gear and radios, along with freedom and trust from their commanders—something that we never did. I sat there eating my dehydrated tuna mornay, filled with envy as I watched the commandos. At that exact moment, I knew my heart was no longer in 3 RAR.

And while I was contemplating a future in SF, operators from Delta Company 4 RAR (Cdo) were being deployed to Afghanistan on Rotation III of the SOTG. There they would see some of the fiercest fighting of Australia's involvement in the Global War on Terror to date, cementing the reputation of Australian commandos in the Afghanistan theatre. Delta Company 4 RAR (Cdo), SASR and the US 10th Mountain Division conducted Operation Perth, which lasted nine days, to clear the Chora Valley, a known Taliban stronghold. SASR provided overwatch and battlefield commentary, while the commandos and 10th Mountain cleared from north to south, initially based out of the governor's compound. This compound was later named FOB Locke after Sergeant Matthew Locke from SASR, who was killed the following year.

Working with Alpha Company 4 RAR (Cdo) through the Timor deployment, I would hear snippets of information about what was going on in Afghanistan from both SASR and 4 RAR (Cdo), which only fuelled my desire to get 'across the road' to become a commando and finally have my turn at actual, real combat.

On our return to Dili a week or so later, I filled out and submitted my application form for SF, my sights firmly set on becoming a commando.

CHAPTER 10

CANDIDATE 19

To the outsider, selection is discussed and viewed as the main hurdle to being accepted into an SF unit. There have been countless books on building the resilience to pass selection, with tips and tricks for succeeding on the course. The entry test and physical elements of the selection are designed to meet policy and safety frameworks for further SF training. For example, the 3.2-kilometre run is designed to test a soldier's ability meet the minimum level on the military's work/rest tables (which outline safe levels of physical exertion in certain climates) for arduous defence training or a 'tough' training policy. The selection program is mainly physical, with some essential military written and practical tests to determine basic, all-corps soldiering skills.

But the SF community itself regards the 'reo'—the commando reinforcement and training cycle—as the main qualification and the real test.

The reo involves more than twelve months of back-to-back courses to qualify soldiers to a level where they can be employed in the commando teams. Some reo courses are more physically gruelling than anything on selection; the physical element is just the nature of the business. The one thing that cannot be assessed in selection is cognitive capacity, specifically, how a person reacts under various forms of stress. Once the reo starts, trainees are expected to assimilate and absorb vast amounts of information, which increases in complexity as each course progresses.

There is a perception about getting into SF that it's purely a fitness competition. If that were the case, it would be no different from CrossFit or any other sport. In reality, selection and reo are intended to identify soldiers with the necessary physical *and* mental attributes, the ones who want to be in SF for the right reasons.

As it turned out, I wasn't the only one wanting to apply for commandos or SASR—every second person I was in Timor with claimed they were putting their 'apps' in for SF. It seemed like just telling people you were doing it was somehow status-elevating—I know more than a few soldiers who made that claim for years, never going so far as to actually apply.

Having applied after our return from Dili, I had my sight set on the commando selection in February 2007. The last time I'd come home from Timor, back in 2002, I had spent months drinking and partying; this time, I had a focus, so partying would have to wait until after selection. From the very start, I doubted my abilities, looking at all the other lads who had their apps in, knowing that I would compete with them for a spot in 4 RAR (Cdo). But this just further fuelled my desire to get stuck into training.

I, along with the other SF applicants who'd been in Timor, got hold of a copy of the SASR's thirteen-week training program, which we had to shorten due to our arrival back to Australia having been delayed by a few weeks. We forensically analysed how we could adapt the program to redress our weaknesses. For me, the 3.2-kilometre run in webbing with a rifle was a challenge, and I needed help to comfortably beat my current speed of fifteen minutes 30 seconds, just under the sixteen minutes allowed. But this same run had been the fitness test for 3 RAR, so I had experience, which was an advantage.

My size meant that I knew I had to work twice as hard as the other lads at activities such as torsion bar circuits (a series of exercises with a 15-kilogram metal pole, used as a torture device in selection) and pack marching. So I decided that these must form the largest part of my training program.

After a few days of visiting friends and family at home, I began my seven-week leave period—and my training. I started to build up my pack fitness through twice-weekly stomps, which I would increase in weight and distance up to 35 kilograms and 20 kilometres.

I broke this regime up with weight sessions, swimming, running and circuits from the thirteen-week program. Friends and family around the Hills would regularly drive past on my runs and stomps, beep their horns and yell obscenities or encouragement.

About a week before Christmas, I was doing a 15-kilometre stomp around Kellyville on a stinking-hot 40-plus-degree day when I ran out of steam and had to sit on the side of the road in the shade. I had heavy cramps in my legs—despite knowing I was overtraining, I had still pressed on, causing me to burn out completely. Some friends of mine drove past and pulled over, asking me what the fuck I was doing. 'Training for commandos,' I told them.

A couple of them helped me into the car while another went to pick up my pack. 'Fucking hell, how heavy is this thing?' he asked. Two of them picked it up and threw it in the boot. 'Mate, how is your back not fucked?' they asked. Good question. Again, future Scott's problem.

In the last stage of training, when it was time to return to work, I worked up to 30-kilometre walks with two of the boys I had decided to train with. We trained as a group, getting up early to complete our longer stomps. The other guys were still faster than me, but my training over Christmas leave had paid off.

In January 2007, we drove up to Singleton Military Area to complete our SF entry test, which was required to get a place on the selection course in a few weeks. It was a humid and hot summer's day in the Hunter Valley, which only served to drain our energy before the first test began.

We did the pack march at night, and I felt comfortable and confident when we stepped off. To my surprise, around the 10-kilometre mark, dozens of candidates pulled off or went down with exhaustion, no doubt due to due to poor preparation. A dozen or so others even decided to pull off voluntarily due to blisters.

I had spent months training and worrying about whether I had done enough to prepare. Selection had consumed me, from the first moment my eyes opened to the last thought before bed. I could not fathom how somebody would attempt this with such poor preparation. My surprise at the other candidates' lack of staying power deepened when we did the 3.2-kilometre run, where a portion of them struggled so much in the first few kilometres that they came in at around eighteen minutes, two minutes after the cut-off time!

My whole career, I was never the best runner, the best at pack marches or the strongest during strength sessions, but knowing this, I had worked hard to ensure I was adequately prepared. My SF entry test busted the first of many myths I had heard about SF and selection. For years, I had read statistics about selection courses all over the world where '140 started and only 40 finished', and I would often wonder if I had a chance of being one of the few who finished. I now realise that a decent chunk of those applicants didn't fail because they weren't good enough, but purely because they hadn't even tried to prepare or research.

Plenty has already been written about SF selection courses, so I will only go into some details in this book. Our course in 2007 was five weeks and was called the commando selection and training course, as it combined selection and the introductory team tactics course. Later, these courses would be separated into selection and the commando team tactics course, following the SASR model of separating selection and the patrol course.

Of course, it was physically demanding, and no matter how fit you were, you were pushed to your limit. Aside from the physical element, however, was the constant stress. Every second of every day for 35 days, your every move was scrutinised and criticised; the lack of sleep compounded the stress, making it almost impossible to retain information and instructions for tasks, which led to further punishments.

We were given tasks that seemed absurd, and even when we completed them to the detail instructed, we were told we needed to improve. Fairness was not a thing on selection, which caused many candidates to get frustrated to the point of quitting immediately. We each carried a card in our pocket known as a discharge on request, which we could present to directing staff (DS) when we'd had enough.

Officers and enlisted men were treated equally on the course, our individual identities taken away and replaced with candidate numbers by which we were addressed for the duration. Our aim was to remain as far from the DS's attention as possible—repeated mentions of your candidate number not only indicated that you had fucked up, but that you were on the radar of the other DS members. This was problematic for a few reasons.

Just like trainees, not all DS are created equal, and having your number called out all the time—even if it wasn't to reprimand you—might lead to some junior DS assuming you were a problem to report on. That would provide inaccurate data for the senior instructors, known as the board of studies, who would periodically remove certain candidates during the course.

It was only years later, when I was a DS on selection myself, and had worked under commando officers for the best part of seventeen years, that I really thought about the fact that officers lose their rank on selection and, just like the diggers, become a number. Officer trainees are expected to complete nearly all the courses on the CRTC, apart from specialised skills that they would never employ, such as explosive breaching.

There is a separate module for them layered on top of the selection course, known as the 'Officer' or 'O' mod, which is run by qualified commando officers and focuses on their communication and planning skills. This is an essential skillset for SF officers to build upon during the CRTC, as there aren't too many opportunities to train in important military planning.

When I was a DS on selection, I would identify the officers and send the youngest-looking DS, usually a recent commando graduate, to overtly target an officer and speak down to him so I could gauge the officer candidate's reaction. 'Candidate 07, is there a reason you're standing there not moving while people in your team are still working?' the young operator would ask an officer candidate. 'Candidate 07, why is another candidate helping you? Are you not capable of carrying out tasks by yourself? What type of fucking officer are you?'

The idea was to see if there was a point where the officer candidate could no longer deal with the perceived disrespect from a subordinate and finally lash out or 'break', which I would report on immediately. We needed officers who would have the presence to lead while still acknowledging and respecting the vast amount of combat experience that existed in the teams with which they were charged.

Will Hetherington was a captain in 6 RAR and spent six years in 2 Cdo Regt, completing selection and reo in 2018. He explained to me the unique position officers are in during the process, being required to demonstrate their ability to command while also acknowledging their place as a trainee. 'You need to exercise humility,' he said:

> Officers need to know when to demonstrate officer attributes such as communication while still accepting that when you walk into a room, you are not the smartest or most experienced; some officers cannot find the right balance.
>
> There is an expectation that you come into the process having already mastered critical trade skills such as planning, so officer instructors can build on this knowledge and tailor it to special operations planning concepts.

Will actually attributed his success in the regiment to his respect for his subordinates: 'I had much respect for every operator in my platoon, particularly the NCOs—they had vastly more real-time combat experience than me, so I had to balance my ability to make decisions with the experience in the room.'

In a regular army unit, a trainee completes basic training, then a specialist course known as initial employment training before posting to their unit; the receiving unit has no buy-in or investment into the people they receive. Regular ADF units post their workforces to different locations around the country as they progress through their careers, making it almost impossible to maintain an element of quality control or culture.

SASR and the commando regiments, on the other hand, along with state police tactical groups, are the only organisations that peer-select their workforce, which creates a distinctive culture and typical personality types in those units.

As the trainees progress through the CRTC or equivalent training modules, they are constantly assessed by dozens of senior operators as potential new additions to their team. Once qualified, the trainees are spread evenly among the companies, filling gaps in critical unit capabilities.

When I was going through the selection process, other candidates would be removed for relatively minor infractions that could have been quickly remedied with further training from a competent team leader or instructor. This was a waste of time and money. These days, removal by a candidate's DS requires significant reporting and evidence. Some DS baulked at this curtailment of their autonomy, but I always saw it as a good thing, as it forced DS to get their paperwork right. This was someone's career we were talking about.

Selection is a transformational process. Willingly putting yourself through weeks of abuse, gruelling physical work, mental fatigue and lack of sleep comes down to one key thing: how badly you want it. People want to be in SF for many reasons, some of which don't hold when they've reached their limit. The course quickly finds those who truly want to be there and either removes the other candidates or provides a mechanism for them to remove themselves when they decide the effort isn't worth it.

Part of our selection was Sherwood Pass. This was a three-day solo navigation assessment where candidates were required to reach a minimum number of checkpoints, day and night, to be deemed competent. Thankfully, my previous experience in navigation activities had prepared me well for this part of the course. One silly mistake nearly cost me the entire assessment, though. I had already covered about 24 kilometres on the second day when I was given a checkpoint directly on the other side of a large hill, so I decided to go straight over it instead of taking the safe option and contouring around it.

When I was about halfway up the feature, I slipped on a steep dirt mound at the base of a rockface and fell a few metres onto my back. Thankfully I landed on my pack, so I didn't injure myself, but I shattered my pack frame. I was able to get on the radio, inform the DS and get a replacement, but making my way down from the high ground to a road cost me valuable time, and I reached fewer check-points than I would have liked. I was given the pack frame by a DS called Kane, and I still have it on my pack to this day.

The navigation phase was made difficult by the walks at the end of each day. As the training area we were working in was a little small, the last task given to each candidate would be a 10–15-kilometre walk from one end of training area to the next. In addition, some checkpoints were back at the command post tent where the DS was located, on top of a steep hill, to make us walk more. I enjoyed the nav phase despite the distances, because I was left alone and didn't have to worry about dozens of DS watching my every move.

Whatever your motivation for joining SF, it is certainly tested during the phases of the courses where you are deprived of food and sleep for up to 74 hours. On the east coast, for commando selection, this is known as 'demarcation'; on the west coast, for the SASR selec-tion, it is known as 'lucky dip'. Regardless of its name, the idea is the same. Candidates who are already weary from selection must forgo sleep and food and continue operating without respite on six-hour activities.

In my selection, demarc was where the mind games were stepped up, causing a few candidates to withdraw. Every time someone pulled out, it gave me strength, making me feel like I was one step closer to finishing.

After days of no food and sleep, we were malnourished, exhausted and barely able to keep our eyes open, yet the torture didn't stop. On the last day, we rotated through a scenario set in Afghanistan, attending a meeting with a tribal elder who would offer us food. Unsure of what to say, we nodded at the pretend elder in agreement, and a large pot of boiled offal, sheep's tongues and eyeballs was offered up. Despite not having eaten for days, the sight and smell were enough to make us gag, but any attempts to refuse the food would send the villager into a rage.

Towards the end of demarc, knowing the finish line was in sight, we were given a location on a map and told this was where we were to meet trucks that would drive us back to warm food and a shower. Once we got close, however, the truck drove off into the distance. We walked for another few kilometres before we were finally allowed on the truck. A few hundred metres down the road, the truck 'broke down', and we had to walk back to the start to get on the next truck, a DS screaming at us all the while to make the timings to meet the trucks. This continued well into the night and seemed like it would never end.

Finally, after the longest five weeks of my life, we finished selection and were driven back to the SF precinct at Lone Pine Barracks in Singleton to wash and de-service our equipment from the course. We hadn't slept or eaten for the last 74 hours, our backs were covered with chafe marks, we were full of tick bites, and some guys' feet were wholly cooked to the point where they had to get around on crutches. I had prepared my feet well in my lead-up to selection with methylated spirits, so I was still walking, but the chafing on my back and hips had opened into festering sores that were starting to get to me.

Everyone had their own reasons for attempting selection. Andrew Riley, who completed selection in 2009 and spent eleven years as an operator with 2 Cdo Regt, mainly in Alpha Company, had a brother in the military and had always been interested in following in his footsteps.

'I never felt like I was good enough,' Andrew explained to me. 'I was intimidated by the RAR guys [fellow candidates from the Royal Australian Regiment; selection is tri-service and open to all roles in the ADF], but once I got on the course, I realised that they weren't excelling as much as I thought, which gave me confidence in my ability.'

Andrew also mentioned the change he noticed in himself during the final stages of the course. Through the shared hardship, his own identity became less important, and was replaced with the group identity so critical to working in SF teams. This mentality is also a key attribute instructors look for in candidates. Andrew explained:

Looking back, I can see I was selfish when I joined the military, and you never really think about others. However, when I saw how much the other guys were putting in, I didn't want to be known as the 'jack guy', which made me work harder for the team, despite my wishes or needs. The most challenging part of the selection course is the constant grind of being under assessment and the lack of feedback. The whole time, you have instructors with their notebooks taking notes, which adds to the self-doubt. You must take it daily to get through.

I often asked myself precisely what motivated me to become a commando. Firstly, I believe it was my desire to be in the best unit; I hated looking over the road at the boys at 4 RAR (Cdo) and wishing I was doing what they were doing with their guns, cars and the latest equipment. The thought of being a small cohort of hand-picked soldiers to do a job that few in the country could be capable of specifically appealed to me.

Whatever had brought us there, though, those of us who had completed the selection course had pushed our bodies and minds to the limit. Now we stood outside some old demountable buildings, nervously waiting to hear our fate.

Once we heard our name, we would walk into an office of the DS, where we would be told we had either passed or failed and, if we had failed, whether we would be allowed to attempt the course again. I watched one of the candidates, a fit, bright lad from a Townsville infantry battalion, walk out of the demountable, turn away from the waiting area, find a spot in the shade and then sit down to weep. He had been told he had failed and was unsuitable for re-attempting selection.

My name was called, and I walked into a small office where a WO and a captain sat behind a desk. They directed me to sit down, which I did. They kept it short, telling me I had succeeded and that I would receive my course report later that day.

I thanked the staff, left the room and turned away from the other lads who were still waiting to be told their news. I was elated and couldn't keep the smile off my face. I found a quiet spot to sit down and stared into the distance, happy, proud and excited to begin my SF journey.

My sister and me in Thamel, Kathmandu, Nepal, 1991, where I was born and lived until we moved to Australia a few years later.

A photo from my first deployment with 3 RAR in 2002. On a 'blue hat' peacekeeping patrol with the United Nations near Dili, Timor Leste.
Photo: Private Jamie Clark.

Private Jamie Clark. Jamie would lose his life on a deployment with 3 RAR in the Solomon Islands. *Photo: Virtual War Memorial.*

Searching a suspect after an arson attack on a government building during Operation Astute in Timor Leste in 2006, as part of the 3 RAR recon/snipers platoon. *Photo: Rob Tanner.*

My recon team during the Special Operations Task Group (SOTG) Rotation VII to Afghanistan in 2008. From left to right: Ben Chuck, Garry Robinson, Tim Hale, me, Davis Pain and Lance Elder. *Photo: Private T.*

Back at our vehicles after a Direct Action raid and another 24 hours of no sleep. This was the first opposed raid of the 2008 rotation that saw the target killed—and the first time I would see an enemy killed in action up close. *Photo: Ben Chuck.*

Private Ben Chuck on Rotation VII, 2008. Ben would complete three SOTG rotations to Afghanistan before losing his life in the chopper crash.

Downtime on a sixteen-day vehicle operation in Afghanistan in 2008.
Left to right: Dean Burgess, Ben Chuck, Ryan Walker, me, Tim Hale and
Daniel. *Photo: Private R.*

Contact in Mirabad Valley, 2008. Ben Chuck midway through a gunfight where we
were receiving accurate enemy machine gun fire from multiple Taliban positions.
I (background, left) am preparing an 84 rocket while Garry (background, right)
observes and reports on enemy movements. *Photo: Ben Chuck.*

Our team during an RAAF combat search and rescue exercise, recovering downed pilots, in Townsville in 2009. *Photo: Josh Alvarez.*

Some of the company vehicles during a short break at an Afghan National Army base near Helmand province, 2008.

Our recon team minutes before being attacked by enemy fighters in the valley below us. My ATV would be shot in this contact, requiring me to be towed off the hill. 2008. *Photo: Tim Hale.*

A typical scene on long vehicle operations. We would try and sleep in the morning before the midday heat made it almost impossible. Tim Hale (left), me (right) and Ben Chuck (walking). Summer fighting season, 2008. *Photo: Davis Pain.*

The range at Tarin Kowt—not much more than a Hesco wall where we would test fire and zero out weapon systems.

With my Barrett after a gunfight in Doab, northern Kandahar in 2013. Captured Taliban fighters are being escorted away in the background. *Photo: Ben Chuck.*

A typical 'green belt' in Southern Afghanistan. The high terrain provided great vantage points into the valleys— both for us and for the enemy. *Photo: ADF.*

The second wave of Task Force 66 operators landing in Gizab in 2010 during the local uprising against the Taliban. *Photo: Trooper M.*

Anthony Dimov (left), Ben Chuck (centre) and me (far right) engaging enemy fighters in northern Kandahar with our .50-calibre Barrett rifles. An assaulter kneels behind us, observing with binoculars. *Photo: Davis Pain.*

A commando team being extracted by a UH-60 Black Hawk from the 101st Airborne, Task Force No Mercy, who would provide rotary wing platforms for our rotation in 2010. *Photo: ADF.*

Our sniper team and attachments during an operation in northern Kandahar, 2010 (left to right: Anthony Dimov, Davis Pain, Garry Robinson, a signals operator, me, a US SF attachment and Ben Chuck). *Photo: Corporal P.*

'My last recollections before impact are looking out the door and seeing the ground rush by.' This photo shows the tail of the crashed Task Force No Mercy UH-60 Black Hawk. By sunrise, all the wounded, including me, had been evacuated back to Kandahar. 21 June 2010. *Photo: Corporal D.*

A macro view of the crash site showing the wide spread of debris. The main fuselage was still on fire when this shot was taken. *Photo: Corporal D.*

My .50-calibre Barrett sniper rifle, recovered from the crash site. The rifle was between my knees when we hit the ground. *Photo: ADF.*

The bodies of Private Tim Aplin, Private Ben Chuck and Private Scott Palmer during their ramp ceremony at Tarin Kowt, being escorted to the plane by members of Alpha Company. *Photo: ADF.*

'Gordon Chuck told me, "We knew Ben as a boy and a young man—but not as a commando. We got to see where Ben ate, worked, slept, and got a glimpse into his army life, and we're grateful that we were given the chance." Laying a poppy next to Ben Chuck's name during the closing of the war ceremony, in front of the families of the fallen. Tarin Kowt, 2013. *Photo: Gordon Chuck.*

Taking a rest next to my ATV on Rotation XX to Afghanistan in 2013. Unlike in earlier rotations where we would have entire teams on ATVs, later rotations often saw us inserting via helicopters.
Photo: Private B.

FE-B and our partner force walking from Camp Russell to the flightline for a helicopter assault. Camp Russell's famous boxing kangaroo sign can be seen in the background.
Photo: ADF.

The beautiful and unforgiving terrain of southern Afghanistan. As SF snipers, climbing the terrain to higher ground with all our equipment at night could be torturous.
Photo: ADF.

Posing with two members of the Afghan partner forces during an operation in Patan, Uruzgan province, in 2013. *Photo: Private B.*

My team of Australian and US Special Operations Forces advisors at the range in Baghdad in 2017 (left to right: US SF soldier, Geoff William, another US SF soldier, me and Kyle Christopher.

Posing for a pic with the then Australian prime minister, Scott Morrison, on our return to the UAE after a successful visit to troops in Iraq. I was his bodyguard for the visit. *Photo: Private J.*

This picture was taken at the end of the advanced close-quarter battle (basic and supervisor) course I ran for the navy's clearance divers during my time at the Defence Force School of Operations. Me (centre) and my 2ic Nick (far right) are in high-vis shirts. *Photo: Sergeant T.*

My last live-fire assault as a commando, in 2022. As instructors at the training wing at the School of Special Operations, we conducted a live-fire hostage recovery exercise, with candidates on the selection course acting as hostages. After being recovered, they would find out they had completed SF selection.
Photo: Corporal T.

A private viewing of the engine cowling that was used to evacuate me from the crash site. The cowling stayed on the walls of the hospital at Kandahar airfield before being given to the Australian War Memorial in Canberra. I would only see the cowling for the first time after I left the regiment in 2023.
Photo: Sarah Ryder.

CHAPTER 11

THE REO

In 2007, our CRTC courses were split between SFTF at Lone Pine Barracks in Singleton, and Holsworthy Barracks in western Sydney, where 4 RAR (Cdo) was located.

Our physical limits were tested, and we were expected to continually display the required 'commando attributes'. Trainees on the reo had to perform back-to-back courses for twelve months, learning corps commando skills needed for employment in the commando companies of either 1 Cdo Regt (Reserve) or 2 Cdo Regt (the later manifestation of 4 RAR (Cdo)), SOCOMD's permanent, full-time element.

Each course on the reo comprises two separate streams: one is an introductory course to qualify the commando trainees in a specific skill set; the second is a supervisor course in that same skill to allow senior operators to complete their supervisor training. The trainee supervisors in the supervisor course deliver day-to-day instruction and mentoring to the basic trainees in the introductory course. The trainee supervisors are themselves overseen by qualified supervisors.

The SFTF instructors—the senior instructor and course manager, typically a sergeant and a corporal—form the course management framework. This unique framework ensures quality control and safety, as well as oversight and investment from across the regiment. It both trains prospective commandos and qualifies operators who can manage safe training back in their home subunits. For example, after a senior operator attends the commando breaching and demolitions course as a trainee supervisor, they will then teach the course content to the basic trainees on reo.

In this way they provide a workforce for the ADF School of Special Operations (ADFSSO) staff from the training wing, who could not reasonably run and teach every course themselves, given the size and length of the reo.

Most of the supervisors on my reo were from Delta Company, and had recently returned from leave after Rotation III of the SOTG. They had fresh combat experience, which us trainees listened to eagerly. This was new to me, as most of the courses in 3 RAR were delivered by soldiers who had spent time in Timor but had yet to experience actual gunfights. The SFTF courses included weapons, qualifying us to use the full spectrum of SF weapons that commando companies employ. We also learned SF roping: how to fast-rope, rappel, climb ladders into helicopters and scale cliff faces in complete equipment. As well as this, we learned how to build and fire various explosives and breaching charges, how to use specific radios, and how to apply first aid with a focus on combat trauma.

In 2007, as I said, selection and the commando team tactics course were combined, which saw us move straight into the rest of the reo. Since then, the commando team tactics course has developed into arguably one of the world's best war-fighting courses, and is often cited as the most challenging course on reo due to the enormous learning curve it provides for the trainees.

Trainees' ability to absorb a vast amount of information is a crucial assessment criterion throughout the CRTC, and it's known as 'trainability'. Trainees are expected to keep up with the pace of the course, and though there is always room for retraining or reassessment, if the training of the majority is hindered by the extra effort or instruction required by one person, then typically that person is removed.

Adding to the difficulty of the course is the constant strain of managing real-life training with live rounds and not compromising safety. Trainees are allowed very few safety breaches on the reo. The senior instructor, supported by the officers, makes the final decision, and they are empowered to exercise their discretion in removing any trainee guilty of a breach. SF training inherently involves more risks than training in conventional defence units, even at the basic level. Safety is therefore always paramount, particularly with fatigued and stressed candidates. The margin for error is too small.

Trainees who are highly capable and intelligent and who have the right aptitude, but are yet to be trained in crucial infantry skills, absorb the knowledge they need and move on. Infantry trainees like me, on the other hand, usually must unlearn bad habits and learn new skills, which places more pressure on them.

Non-infantry guys are told that taking a fire position in the open increases their chances of being shot, which makes sense, and they always look for a large tree or rock or depression in the ground to shoot from. But some infantrymen, who have years of training in section attacks, always look to ensure they are evenly spaced and in a nice straight line with soldiers on either side of them, which can leave them and those around them vulnerable to injury during live-fire attacks.

*

Three required courses are seen as significant hurdles on the reo, and if you complete them, you are almost guaranteed success and a beret at the end. The first of these courses is commando team tactics, the introductory rural warfighting course. The second is ACQB, recently renamed the precision strike direct action and recovery continuum, which teaches operators how to fight in built-up areas, rooms and structures, and also qualifies them to hold a position on 2 Cdo Regt TAG-E. The final hurdle is the commando amphibious operators course, which trains commandos to operate in the maritime environment.

For my reo in 2007, the ACQB course was split in two. The introductory course, basic close-quarter battle (CQB), taught all operators the fundamentals of room combat. The full ACQB course was, however, reserved for those who were going to join the TAG-E, which back then was held by Charlie Company, but after 2009 rotated through the companies.

By the end of the first week of the basic CQB course, I think I had already fired more live rounds from our 9mm submachine guns, Hecker & Koch MP5, and USP 9mm pistols than I had in my entire military career thus far. If you think you are okay at combat shooting, CQB quickly lets you know you still have much to learn. Those first few weeks were all about non-stop shooting, spending six hours a day on the range, honing critical martial skills with our primary and secondary weapons, before moving into two-man room combat. The course took a graduated approach, consolidating one skill before building and moving on to the next.

Despite the long hours and the strain on our backs from shooting and assaulting in body armour, I thoroughly enjoyed the course—this was a skill I desperately wanted to master. A key aim of my becoming a commando was to work in the TAG. The idea of being the forces of last resort for severe domestic terrorism incidents in Australia was something that I was personally invested in, and the elite status of the TAG around the globe was something I badly wanted to be part of.

Our commando amphibious operators course was in the middle of June 2007, it was held on HMAS *Cerberus* outside Melbourne, Victoria, and it was the worst five weeks of my reo. I still shudder when I recall it. We spent every day wet, cold, tired and miserable out on the water in Zodiac inflatable boats, learning how to drive, repair and operate in the maritime environment. It's fatiguing enough in itself, without being a reo trainee.

The amphib courses back then were almost another selection course as opposed to the teaching course they should have been. Constantly being punished for not doing something well enough while being wet and cold takes a physical and emotional toll to a degree I had never expected.

One night, after de-servicing the craft, which took until 1 a.m. as we had only come off the water around 11 p.m., we finally hung our gear out in the drying room, which never seemed to fulfil its purpose. We got our heads down for a few hours' sleep—reveilles on the course were always 5 a.m. But at around 3 a.m., the instructors began shouting from below our accommodation block to get up and get dressed in our amphib kit, in our cams, not in dry suits. It was around minus 1 degree, and I dreaded what was coming.

The DS lined us up and told us they weren't happy with the overall standard of the course's trainees, so we would conduct retraining until they were satisfied that we were completing tasks fast enough and to the instructors' satisfaction—a fancy way of saying we were being punished. We were to perform an activity on rotation in three stands.

The first was capsize drills, where we worked on correcting a flipped craft. The second was high-speed transits, which served no purpose but to make us colder with the wind chill after we were wet. The third was swimming with a pair of fins attached to our boots, in pairs, back to the start. In addition, we were informed that this would only stop once at least two trainees self-removed from the course.

The water was bitterly cold, and after an hour, it's fair to say a few of us were close to hypothermia. One trainee succumbed to it and was withdrawn by the medics. When I got to the finning stand, I started cramping up in my right leg, which made the 500-metre swim even more complex, and I started swallowing water.

After the second round, I thought, 'Surely this must be over. There's no way this can keep going.' But the DS told us to continue until they had achieved their goal of two trainees self-removing, which they did around the three-hour mark. Eventually, we returned to the base to clean the craft, which brought us to just before first light and the next day's start.

The course was challenging enough, but having never driven a boat or had any watercraft experience certainly didn't help. The first time I coxswained a craft was on the amphib course. One morning—again, a bitterly cold Melbourne winter's morning—we were working on reversing the craft around a pylon with the twin outboard motors, and as coxswain, I was the driver. Of course, I hit the pylon repeatedly, which the instructor attempted to remedy through threats and warnings of 'getting wet'.

On my second attempt, I again hit the pylon, so as punishment I had to 'get up to my neck' in the cold water before re-attempting the task. If I had difficulty without being wet, being nearly hypothermic didn't help, and to nobody's surprise, I kept hitting the pylons. That morning was the start of my steady decline in the course.

The constant focus on me made me ever more nervous, which meant I made even more mistakes. Every instructor would watch me like a hawk, and I began to get disheartened and stop trying. A week before the end of the course, we were doing transits at night, and I was on my retest as a coxswain. One of my outboard motors malfunctioned, and after fault-correcting, I needed to change a fuel bulb, which required a flathead screwdriver. The craft was full of fuel, making me feel sick, and the sea state had been gradually declining through the night, adding to the seasickness and nausea. Two of the trainees had already thrown up over the side.

While the DS yelled at me to hurry up and fix the outboard motor to catch up with the rest of the flotilla, my hands were barely working due to the cold, and as I tried to unscrew the bulb, I dropped the screwdriver into the water. The craft fell silent, and the instructor stared at me with disdain. I knew my fate was sealed.

Looking back, I can see that my cockiness and comfort in my performance on the reo thus far led to my downfall. I knew the DS didn't target me as they did the other trainees, so I got lazy and stopped putting in as much as I should have. At the same time, I have always had difficulty operating in the cold, which seemed to affect me much more than the other lads. This time it compounded my poor performance, eventually leading to several senior instructor warnings, and my subsequent failure of the course.

I was gutted but partly relieved to end the course and return to Sydney. Once I got back, however, I was sent back to 3 RAR, where I would have to wait another three months before picking up where I left off on the next reo, as two reo cycles were being run that year. Within a week of returning to 3 RAR, I was again in the recon/sniper platoon, and we were jumping into Exercise Talisman Sabre, a sizeable annual defence exercise in North Queensland.

As I sat in an OP for three days, I had much time to reflect. I kicked myself for my shit performance, and forensically analysed all the adverse reporting I had received on the course that led to my removal from the cycle. I was thankful, however, that I had been given a second chance, and I swore to myself that I would not fuck it up.

I joined the reo again in late 2007, and the first course was the ACQB. That year, the decision had been made to qualify the whole regiment in ACQB, in preparation for the twelve-month rotations on the TAG-E that would begin in 2009. Having completed the basic CQB course, I had no issues and passed with flying colours.

I thoroughly enjoyed ACQB and felt like I was finally doing the things I joined the army to do. We learned how to assault buildings, buses, trains and planes, and we spent hundreds of hours shooting and attacking, practising how we would recover hostages from multiple scenarios, day and night.

Following ACQB, I was back on the amphib course. This time, despite the focus on me, I knew what to expect and had prepared myself well. I passed. In December 2007, I lined up in front of the regiment with the other successful trainees at Tobruk Lines at Holsworthy, where we were presented with our famed Sherwood green beret. My girlfriend, Sarah, who I had been dating for a few months, was there. To this day, it is one of the proudest moments of my life.

Sarah was working as a manager in retail fashion outlet, and I had met her through a mutual friend. To impress her, I would come into the shop, splash some cash around and buy a whole bunch of ugly clothes. Turns out she thought I was a dick for doing so. Regardless, my plan worked. We began dating, and a few months later she moved into my apartment.

The bond between trainees is especially powerful in SASR and commando selection. The constant pressure and shared hardship over many months create a strong esprit de corps. Relationships formed on reo last a lifetime. Inside the reo itself, hierarchies form, based mainly on competence; this culture mimics the regiment, where an operator's reputation is everything.

When an operator sees another operator with his beret in his pocket, without knowing anything else about the man, he knows that he has been through the same experiences as him. He knows that the other operator can be trusted and, without knowing his name, knows he will have his back if needed. This level of automatic trust doesn't exist in the rest of society and is a crucial reason for the loss of identity commandos suffer when they leave the regiment.

While I was busy on my reo, the commandos suffered their first killed in action (KIA). In November 2007, Rotation IV with Bravo Company was conducting a night raid on a Taliban leader's bed-down location in the north-eastern Mirabad Valley. In a company-sized raid on a complex structure of numerous compounds, Quebec platoon cleared the main structure. The company silently approached its entry points; there was traffic from signals intelligence, not even dogs being alerted to the assaulters' presence.

Private Luke Worsley's team breached the door, and as he made entry, a Taliban machine gunner who was crouched in the corner shot him in the head. For the first time in the history of commandos, Bravo Company heard something no operator ever wanted to hear: 'All callsigns, Quebec platoon has a KIA.' Every operator stood silent, shocked, trying to find out exactly who had been killed, before continuing to push on with securing the compound. The focus of the mission now changed to getting the body of the first commando killed in Afghanistan back to Camp Russell.

Fellow Bravo Company operator Lance Corporal Cameron Baird continued the assault, killing the enemy in the compound, and the fight was over moments after it had begun. Cameron Baird would later be awarded the Medal for Gallantry (MG) for his actions that day; he would take on legendary status in the regiment for years to come.

Eventually, the company found out that Luke was the KIA. Helicopters would not risk landing in a contested area for a dead body, so Bravo Company were instructed to walk his body back to the vehicle drop-off (VDO).

Nobody enjoys holding onto a stretcher weighing more than 100 kilograms for kilometres. Normally, operators are happy when someone offers to change them out of carrying the stretcher. It was a different story, however, on the night Luke was killed. 'You had to force people off the stretcher physically,' recalled Dave Parker, one of the operators walking Luke. Operators who were there on the night described it as one of their most arduous walks—hills that seemed to go on forever, and jagged rocks littering their path in poor visibility. Eventually, the company got Luke back to the VDO.

CHAPTER 12

THE VIKINGS

In February 2008, after a much-needed Christmas break, I started my first year in the regiment with Alpha Company, which was due to replace Delta Company on SOTG Rotation VII in Afghanistan in a few months. Each company in the unit was identified with a logo, and ours was Vikings. I was to work in the company's recon team, and my role was number one scout.

However, the build-up to our deployment was interrupted on 27 April by the news of the death of Lance Corporal Jason Marks from Delta Company in the Uruzgan province. An operator who was present on the day told me later that intelligence had been getting more indications after a direct action (DA) on a dry hole[13] earlier that morning. The company sat in the *dasht* (desert) waiting for the intelligence picture to develop, which when it did indicated the Taliban were laying improvised explosive devices (IEDs) on the path the company had taken. Orders were issued to find and kill the enemy laying the IEDs, which would see coalition elements spread through the valley. The main effort involved an IRR-led route clearance (removing the IEDs) back towards the town of Chineh Kalay.

Dismounted to support IRR, the operator I spoke to was told through intelligence that the enemy were talking about him specifically, as they had him lined up as he walked around a set of compounds. The enemy was ready to 'start the work'. It was later determined that there were multiple enemies inside the very compound he was walking around, lying in wait to spring the ambush.

As Delta Company approached Chineh Kalay in a large vehicle convoy, a complex ambush was sprung from the ridgelines around them. In the opening seconds of the ambush, rocket-propelled grenades (RPGs) and automatic fire pounded the convoy. The company moved into a defensive posture, still trying to ascertain exactly where they were being attacked from.

Jason Marks's special reconnaissance vehicle (SRV) was hit multiple times, disabling it, and a bullet hit an ammunition liner near his head, the fragments cutting his face. Private Rudi, the team driver, returned fire with 66 rockets. As Jason moved around the vehicle, he was shot in the back and killed instantly. Moments later, Jason's gunner was also shot in the arm, throwing him back into the vehicle.

Another operator, still serving in the regiment, ran to assist Jason from a nearby car and was shot four times. The company was then engaged from multiple directions, receiving accurate and sustained fire from RPGs and PK machine guns (PKMs). To the rear of the convoy, the joint terminal attack air controller (JTAC) was also shot. In the opening ten minutes of the ambush, Delta Company had one KIA and three wounded in action (WIA). When the calls came over the radio, everyone recognised the dire situation.

A few minutes later, as the mortar team were setting up their baseplates to the rear, one of the mortarmen was also shot. It seemed like every bit of high ground around them had an enemy pouring fire into the convoy. Dozens of vehicles were shot at as the company returned fire with everything they had in a bid to repel the ambush.

'I was on my reo a few months prior and had been sent to Delta a few weeks after they arrived. When we heard Jason was killed and we had multiple WIA, it hit home that this was no longer training; it was the real deal,' recalled one operator.

Delta Company remained in contact for the next few hours, eventually holding off the attack long enough to get Jason and the four wounded into Bushmasters so that they could get out of the contact site for proper medical treatment and evacuation. They were under fire the entire time, with bullets ricocheting off the vehicle as the boys did their best to suppress enemy positions and support the evacuation of the wounded. 'The adrenaline was insane; my mouth was dry the entire time. We never expected to get hit so hard that day. It was horrendous. I had dirt and dust in my mouth from bullets that landed close to my face,' explained another operator, who was on foot during the gun battle.

After evacuating the wounded and Jason, the company drove back to Tarin Kowt (KT), fatigued from the battle and still coming to terms with the day's events.

The role of my recon team was to act as pathfinder, and conduct surveillance and reconnaissance in support of the company. While the two assault platoons and headquarters got around in a mix of SRVs and Protected Mobility Vehicles (PMVs, aka Bushmasters), the recon and sniper teams were mounted on all-terrain vehicles (ATVs)—what civilians know as quadbikes. Getting my four roller bags of equipment from the main quartermaster's store, I was like a kid at Christmas, and spent the next few days sorting through it all, or 'tinkering with kit', as it was known. Operators spend an inordinate amount of time ensuring their gear is exactly as it should be, and it seems to take years to perfect, if ever. It was trial and error, and over my career in SOCOMD, I would continually change every pouch, strap and clip, always working to find a balance between comfort and practicality—and, of course, looks. As they say, 'The first rule of SF is to look good; the second, refer to rule one.' I would wake up every day excited to go to work and could not wait to put myself to the test for our upcoming deployment.

Our team commander, Garry Robinson, was an ex-3 RAR sergeant who had completed selection in 2004 and lost his rank (as all NCOs do after selection), but due to his competence was promoted within twelve months. A quietly spoken leader who had grown up in the western suburbs of Sydney, Garry was a supremely fit operator and, as well as the commandos, was also in the Australian short-course triathlon team. I would dread our weekly runs, where we all struggled to keep up with him—impossible to do, as hard as we tried. Garry was well respected, he chose his words carefully and he never seemed to get stressed or angry—leadership qualities I try to emulate to this day.

The culture in our regiment around how new guys were treated was utterly different from what I had experienced in 3 RAR. In 3 RAR, it took years to be viewed as someone worth listening to. My experience as a 'lid' in 3 RAR had me approach my first year in 4 RAR (Cdo) with some trepidation, as I expected much of the same. But I was pleasantly surprised. There was no name-calling for new guys or expectation that they would get all the shit jobs. It seemed to be the opposite. The experienced guys were not only expected but willing to take on the lion's share of the more demanding jobs.

For example, in 3 RAR, the new guys were typically given the team machine gun, which weighed significantly more than rifles, and was more cumbersome to move around. The idea was that the experienced guys should carry less. In Garry's team, however, one of the senior operators had the machine gun. The idea was that the team's organic firepower came from the machine gun and so the more experienced operator should carry it.

And despite being new, I was given a surprising amount of autonomy. For instance, Garry called me one morning and tasked me with inventorying and reordering the team's image capture and transfer kits. Many parts were missing, Garry said, and he asked me to 'spend the next few days sorting it, mate. Have it done by Friday, please.' I spent the day finding all the bits of the kit, then called him around 5 p.m. to ask if I could knock off for the day.

'Mate, you don't need permission to go home, you have your task,' he said. 'I'll see you on Friday.'

As a private in 4 RAR (Cdo), I seemed to have more trust than I did when I was a section commander in 3 RAR. This would take some getting used to.

A commando team is a five-person team comprising a team leader (TL), 2ic, breacher, a medic (who is a commando trained in advanced first aid), a signaller and a scout, which was my role. Our team 2ic was Lance Elder, a former 2 RAR infantryman who had been in the regiment for a few years and was also a man of few words. Lance's nickname was 'Wireless'.

Benjamin Chuck, or 'Chucky', another quietly spoken operator, this time from Far North Queensland's Atherton Tablelands, was known as 'the most beautiful man in 4 RAR (Cdo)'. My girlfriend, Sarah, and her mates would all giggle like schoolgirls when they saw him and drool over him. Chucky was chiselled like a Greek god and highly fit, never missing an opportunity to take his shirt off for a quick circuit, which provoked many eyerolls from us.

Chucky also had an excellent temper, although he often lost his shit on our long night-time ATV rides in Afghanistan. Riding over rugged terrain in the dark with NVG was at times extremely frustrating. Hitting a rock or hole would violently turn your handlebars, which would then smash your hands onto the front of your plate carrier against the M4 carbine magazines. Over time, this would become very painful and cause your hands to swell.

Many nights we would hear Chucky's bike increase in torque as he attempted to negotiate a piece of terrain leading to a large bank, and the diff of his bike smashed against a rock, leading to screams of 'Cuuuunt!', much to our amusement.

Tim Hale was an ex-3 RAR who had completed the recon course at 3 RAR and would work with me intimately over the next few years as my number two scout. Tim was another quiet lad who was never phased by anything, and he, along with Chucky and Wireless, was a veteran of Alpha Company's previous SOTG in 2007, leaving me as the new guy who had not yet seen actual combat, something I constantly reminded myself.

I would eagerly listen to their stories of contacts and DA assaults and could not wait until I had some stories of my own. Like Garry, Tim had a laissez-faire attitude to everything; his heart rate never seemed to change. Whether he was having a coffee in a café or engaged in a gunfight, his temperament remained the same.

Despite our different personalities, the whole team got along well. We would train together, drink together and do other things as a team, too. Garry took us white-water rafting before our second trip, along with lots of other social stuff, which only served to improve and build our team cohesion. This was something I replicated when I was a team leader years later.

The fifth team member, Davis Pain, who was our signaller, had completed reo with me in 2007. He was an infantry soldier from 2 RAR in Townsville, after his infantry initial employment training in 2001. Davis had completed his commando training a bit later in life and was a little older than the rest of us, turning 29 on the reo, so his nickname was 'Old Balls'. Davis was a likeable operator who was also good for a laugh, and we never got tired of making 'old man' jokes at his expense. He could also give as good he got and was always plotting some prank in our downtime.

We spent a few weeks training at Holsworthy before driving to Cultana Training Area in South Australia to complete our mission rehearsal exercise (MRE) before our deployment. The MRE was a task group–wide validation activity that needed to be signed off as 'ready' before we could deploy. Run by Special Operations Headquarters (SOHQ), it included 4 RAR (Cdo), SASR, IRR and all other enablers, such as the Primary Health Care Team (PHCT), which comprised doctors and medics. We would be accommodated at the Baxter Detention Centre outside Port Augusta, which had only just stopped holding refugees. Cultana would be the destination for SOTG MRE until the ADF withdrew from Afghanistan in 2013, and it was ideal for working on the sorts of vehicle operations that formed most mission profiles.

As a company, we spent days firing all our weapons systems on and off vehicles, driving our ATVs, pathfinding for the company and rehearsing our DA profiles. This is where I got my first taste of how complex pathfinding on bikes is; I almost fell asleep one night on my bike while we slowly followed IRR conducting a route clearance with their Minelab metal detectors.

Long nights continually turning your head with a helmet and NVGs would constantly leave your neck and shoulders stiff. Role players would fill the role of enemy, and we would use paint bullets to engage threats during DA training. This realistic and relevant training highlighted the complexities involved in identifying and engaging threats in confined spaces at night.

Even though we worked in the same compound as SASR, the toxic culture that existed between us meant we had almost no inter-action, and this would continue well after the final rotation of the SOTG in 2013. Despite belonging to the same task group, we had zero interoperability with 'the cats', as we called them, either in training or on deployments. Our lack of interaction with them was based on their transparent disdain for commandos, or 'dos', as they disparagingly called us.

I'd mistakenly presumed that both force elements (FE)[14] would support each other in similar operations, but that didn't occur until well into the later SOTG rotations. I failed to understand it then, and still don't fully understand it now. Regardless, I was the new guy and had bigger fish to fry on my first trip than SOCOMD rivalry.

After months of lead-up, we said goodbye to family and partners. We flew to Afghanistan via Kuwait, our final logistical preparation area before flying into TK. Later, Al Minhad air base outside Dubai in the United Arab Emirates was established as Australia's logistical node, but in 2007, the ADF was still leveraging support from the US forces staged in Kuwait.

The base in Kuwait was huge, and it was the first time I witnessed the scale of the US war machine and interacted with US soldiers. The base had a Pizza Hut, a Dunkin' Donuts and a KFC, which always seemed to have a line outside regardless of the time of day. One evening I chatted with a young US Army truck driver who was going home after a twelve-month deployment to Iraq. He excitedly told me about everything he would do with the money he had saved on his trip, and showed me pictures of his family and the car he planned to buy.

Curious, I asked him how much he had saved after a twelve-month deployment; I guessed it would be substantial. He proudly informed me that he had held onto $20,000, which confused me. A twelve-month deployment would allow an Australian to save substantially more than that, even with the exchange rate. This was when I discovered that the US military only gets around $3 a day extra as their war allowance, which they call a 'per diem'. I was shocked. The savings the truck driver had managed to put together were just from his usual salary, and didn't include any extra funding for deployment.

Finally, we kitted up in our body armour, helmets and guns and boarded a C-130 Hercules bound for TK. I spent the entire flight looking out the window at the vast arid landscape and mountainous regions. I was surprised at the juxtaposition of miles of flat desert and the extensive green areas and mountain ranges that seemed to stick out randomly.

The green patches, known as the green belt, were vegetated areas around water systems, typically centred around inhabited areas and providing fertile ground for crops and animals, which all Afghans had. I stared at the terrain and wondered how many battles had been fought over the centuries across that very landscape. I couldn't wait to get my turn.

The C-130 started its steep incline into TK and, after a short taxi, we were walking off the ramp. The first thing I noticed was how beautiful the landscape was. Vast mountains as far as the eye could see, broken up by the massive base at TK.

TK was a multinational base that included Australians, Dutch, British and local Afghan forces. The central part of the base was to the south of the main airstrip, and was always a hive of activity. The Australian SOTG had its own compound, Camp Russell, named after Sergeant Andrew Russell from SASR, the first Australian KIA in Afghanistan. It housed SASR, commandos, mechanics, cooks, transport and admin staff.

For this rotation, Rotation VII of the SOTG, we were accommodated in wooden huts called bee huts, and each team had a room along a narrow corridor. Of course, SASR had partitioned off their end, but the remainder of our task group lived communally, sharing toilets, showers, a mess hall and a gym. Later in this rotation, we would be the first FE to move into the new building being built on the other side of the camp. It was still one room per team on bunk beds, but they had hardened concrete structures with a toilet and shower block at each end.

We spent long days in the vehicle sheds, checking and packing our bikes, which would be our main form of transport for the next five months. They were Polaris farm bikes that came in either a four-wheel or six-wheel version, chosen according to the operator's preference, but also depending on the weight of equipment. Although the mechanics would work miracles keeping these bikes going rotation after rotation, when we first came across them they all looked worn and tired. The idea of using ATVs was to provide the FE with an element of manoeuvrability that could not be matched by the SRVs or PMVs that were used by the remainder of the FE.

We also spent countless hours at the range, testing all our weapons systems before our first job came up in a week or so. We all endured days of mandatory briefings, intelligence updates and lectures on camp rules. At the same time, the team leaders (TLs) pored over maps and began preparations to deliver orders for our operations.

CHAPTER 13

OPERATION MCDOUGALL

In the first few years of Australia's involvement in Afghanistan, Prime Minister John Howard explained that the role of SF was to 'enhance provincial security by disrupting Taliban command and control supply routes and directly support the Australian reconstruction task forces'.[15] Essentially, the role of TF66 was to find and get in a fight with the Taliban, allowing the reconstruction effort to continue unhindered. If this sounds broad, it was. The overall strategy in Afghanistan, or what 'success' looked like, was never really mentioned. In all fairness, we didn't care; we knew our job was to get in gunfights with the bad guys—precisely what we had joined the commandos to do.

The improvised explosive device (IED) threat in 2008 was most definitely a consideration, but it was not yet at the stage it would be in later years. But that time, there were so many IEDs that it was almost impossible to justify having any vehicle other than a PMV outside the wire. These were purpose-built vehicles that had an angled chassis, which meant that when they struck an IED, the wave would be more evenly dispersed away from the centre of the blast, minimising the effect of the explosion on the occupants.

A flat chassis, on the other hand, bore the full brunt of the blast, placing the occupants at a much greater risk. As each rotation of the SOTG progressed, the IED threat increased, forcing subsequent rotations mainly into PMVs or ultimately rotary wing (RW, i.e. helicopter) insertion.

Having two teams on ATVs (recon and snipers) gave the OC the ability to move more freely in the battlespace, and provided him with more situational awareness from his men, in the absence of other assets such as information provided by ISR drones. These assets were predominantly owned by the US. There was a small detachment of Australian drone operators based in TK who operated one ISR platform, but it was nowhere near the standard of the US drones, although even these were still in their infancy during the early years of the Afghanistan campaign. Over time, however, there was a dramatic increase in the use of drones, by both the West and later ISIS in Iraq. Having small, agile teams also meant we could find routes or 'pathfinders' for the larger vehicles, particularly at night— which we called 'period of darkness', another piece of unnecessary jargon that the military loved to use.

We each had a MAG58 Fabrique Nationale 7.62mm light machine gun fixed onto our bike frame, with a metallic cage for the gun's ammunition liners. (Team bikes either had MAG58 light machine guns or 84mm short-range anti-armour weapons.) We also carried our sleeping gear—a swag with a pillow and a lightweight sleeping bag—on our bikes.

The bike side bins are where we would keep all the smaller items we needed daily, such as batteries, cooking equipment, snacks and water. The assault teams primarily used the SRVs, having two per team, and although they had vastly more room than our vehicles, they had to share the space with two other men, which after weeks got a bit old.

Although we got less rest on the ATVs, we had complete autonomy over where we went, when we stopped and which routes we took, which I much preferred. I could stop and piss when I wanted and didn't have to consider other operators, which made life a little easier, even if we had to work twice as hard on the bikes.

After long days of preparing, we finally received our orders for our first mission: a vehicle-mounted DA in a suspected IED facilitator's compound, followed by four nights of DAs around the Baluchi Valley, north of the main base at TK. Although this was only a few kilometres' drive as the crow flies, the IED threat and the need to stay off the main roads turned an easy drive into a day-long affair.

Our first operation was named McDougall, after Australia's Sergeant Stanley McDougall, who was awarded a Victoria Cross (VC) in France during the First World War. It was the first hit-out for Force Element Bravo (FE-B; the commando arm of the SOTG), and we were all busting to get out of the gate. As the number one scout of the recon team, it would be my responsibility to always be in the lead and provide routes for the remainder of the company, or to call the IRR engineers forward to clear any areas. I called IRR in if I deemed an area a probable IED location, such as a creek crossing or an area where the terrain might naturally channel us into taking a particular route. At any time, I could get on the radio to ask for a PMV to take the lead if I thought the road might not be worth clearing but also not worth the risk of getting blown up on my bike.

As we drove out of the base and turned left onto the main road in TK, it was such as surreal feeling. After a long year on reo, followed by months of training and talking about Afghanistan, I was finally here and riding an ATV through an actual warzone. That first drive out of TK, I had such a feeling of contentment, such certainty that there was nowhere I should be on the planet right now other than leading a convoy of nearly 50 vehicles through the desert to capture or kill bad guys.

All the countless hours of pack marches, runs and sleepless nights filled with self-doubt were suddenly worth it. As we got through the central part of town and over the main bridge, Garry, my team commander, directed me to the right of a set of compounds and into the desert, away from the main roads. Thus began our long day of driving to our VDO.

Tim and I, as number one and number two scouts, would support each other in contact or split when we came to a crossing that the SRVs wouldn't be able to make. If something looked suspicious or we weren't sure it was passable by other vehicles, I would call him forward and we would devise a plan. If it wasn't crossable, we would inform Garry, then Tim and I would go in opposite directions to identify a more suitable crossing.

Although it may not sound like difficult work, having to continually be alert day and night, looking for the best tracks, watching out for IEDs and people moving in compounds, and tracking your GPS map gets very fatiguing. And the cost of getting it wrong could be not only my own safety or life, but that of the remainder of the company. So I took my role very seriously.

We arrived at the VDO around 6 p.m. on that first night and, after ensuring the perimeter was tied in—a circular defensive perimeter with operators on security watch—we rested a few hours before we stepped off for the DA, which was currently set for 11 p.m. I used the time to stretch my back from a long day of driving and stare at my map and the route we would take to the target compound, trying to imagine myself walking the route and taking in critical features I would see along the way. Even though Garry, as the TL, was responsible for navigating, getting a better understanding of the route meant I would have to turn to Tim or Garry for directions less frequently. As the scout, my job was staying alert to what was ahead of me, which I couldn't do if I was constantly looking at my map or GPS.

Finally, the time came. After a confirmatory set of orders, I stepped off on my first operational commando night-time raid.

As the recon team, we were to lead the FE to a specific point short of the target compound. There, everyone would split off into their areas, as per orders, then lead the assault teams who were breaching and making entry to the compound. We would act as the ladder team, to get over the wall and provide supporting fire or commentary for the assault.

We travelled through the night, crossing a series of aqueducts, and moved into the thicker area of the green belt, which was littered with compounds, but we had to find another way of getting to the target building as the terrain was too steep for our planned approach. I had my M4 5.56mm modular rifle (the standard personal weapon for SOCOMD) on my shoulder. My finger was on my infrared switch, as I was constantly scanning dark areas of foliage and the open doorways in the walls of compounds.

As the scout, I did not have the luxury of having anyone in front of me, so I was required to remain extra vigilant. After about two hours of slow, methodical patrolling in the green belt, my back was already starting to ache under the load of my plate carrier and grab bag. I was completely drenched in sweat, so I knelt behind a wall to take my helmet off and wipe the sweat from my eyes in order to see better through the monocles of my NVG. At that moment, the JTAC jumped on the company channel: 'All callsigns, from ISR, three tangos moving from the east with weapons.'

I got my helmet and NVGs on and had moved to a better position of cover from the east when I heard gunshots ring out behind me; we typically constantly patrolled in single file to minimise the risk from IEDs, so I knew the engagement must be about 50 metres to the rear of where I was, at the forward lines of our own troops.

A couple of dozen shots from a suppressed weapon was followed by two large thuds, which I recognised as a friendly 40mm high-explosive weapon. I then saw an assault team moving, which I identified as Lance Corporal Mason Edwards's when he reported on the radio: 'Two enemy KIA.' I am still trying to work out what I had expected, but the first contact for the company was over in a few minutes, and most of us needed to be told what was happening.

The ISR platform,[16] which was following us, identified three enemies and used its infrared lights to 'sparkle' or illuminate the target, prompting Mason's team to break from the conga line[17] we were in and conduct a quick attack on the enemy position, only 40 metres or so from their own position, with 40mm weapons and small arms.

The Afghan National Army (ANA), which had checkpoints spread through the province, were less trained than the other forces and at times their incompetence posed just as great a threat as the Taliban. On our foot infiltration towards the target compound, we were engaged by the ANA checkpoint, some of their rounds almost finding their mark, multiple operators ducking for cover as rounds came within inches of them.

After a short stop, we continued with the infiltration, eventually coming to a set of compounds on the far side of a wide aqueduct close to the force separation point, where all the teams would split into their predesignated positions. I welcomed the break, as the adjust-able ladder on my back was digging into my ribs and I needed a few minutes to take it off and prepare it for the wall team, by extending it to the correct height.

Once all the teams were in position, we got the word to move into the final positions we would take before breaching and entering the target compound. The JTAC, G-train, gave us constant feeds from the ISR, indicating four to five suspects in the compound. This was consistent with the intelligence in our orders, which stated that the commander had a security detachment of three or four fighters. Chucky helped me carry the ladder, while Garry went ahead and indicated where he wanted the ladder on the wall. We had rehearsed and trained for this hundreds of times.

The compound was a large, enclosed double-storey structure centred around a large courtyard with chicken pens, a metal gate on one side, and an aqueduct running adjacent to the entrance on the other side. This is where our ladder was to be placed, from which we would provide support to the teams assaulting. We moved painstakingly around the compound, always cautious of IEDs but more focused on the walls and doorways we were walking past. As we drove past the lead assault team, I could see their TL, Mark Cook, covering the door as his breacher placed an explosive charge on it, and I remember thinking how this just felt like training, except it wasn't, and we had no idea what was on the other side of the gate.

Chucky and I slowly raised the ladder and once it was set, I gingerly made my way up, careful to make as little noise as possible, so I could get a quick look over the wall. I needed to check that I could see the assault teams from the ladder, and to make sure I could climb up onto the roof if needed. At the top of the ladder, though, I got a good view of the roof and saw it was half a metre wide and covered with broken glass, making our position useless.

I turned around and gave Garry the no-go signal, and he directed me to come down; we would have to look for an alternative ladder point. My earpiece crackled to life as I approached the bottom of the ladder. 'Compromise, compromise, compromise,' came the call from one of the assault teams on the western edge of the compound. Despite being compromised, however, we would have to wait for the platoon commander, Sam to give the H-hour. As ground forces commander, it was his call. 'All callsigns, go, go, go!' came the command.

A second later, I heard Mark's team's explosive charge go off, which was the first live charge I had seen outside of training, and I was surprised at the sound and power of the explosion. 'Fuck the ladder off, make entry, make the entry,' Garry directed Chucky and me. I dropped the ladder and rushed around the corner to the metal gate, where the team had still not made entry due to the dust from the charge, making it impossible to see through our NVG.

I raised my gun with laser over the shoulders of one of the assault team and saw four or five lasers poised inside the compound, ready to engage any threats as soon as the dust had settled. My heart was racing, and I could feel myself breathing heavily when someone made the call to go. The first man through the door went to the right to clear the way along the perimeter wall, leaving Mark to go left, with me as the third man just to his right. Mark's other team members filled the remaining gaps to ensure all areas of the compound had a gun up, in case a threat appeared.

From my left, I heard Mark engage, rapidly firing five to six rounds while I continued to train my weapon and laser on a doorway that still hadn't been cleared. I was waiting at the door for another operator to back me up and had turned on the infrared torch on my gun to get a better view into the small room, when I heard female screaming coming from the direction Mark had been firing towards. Once the small room was cleared, I continued to clear areas of the compound until the call came that it was clear. Garry called our team to the entry point to reposition into a defensive posture around the target, in case of any follow-on attack. It was all over in under a minute.

I climbed onto the roof of the compound and got a better look into the areas where most of the engagements had occurred. A frail old man with a long white beard who had sustained a gunshot wound was lying on his back and being treated by the platoon medic, Smiley. The older man wasn't making a sound; he just lay there staring at the sky, refusing to make eye contact with anyone. To his rear was a young girl, about twelve years old, who had also been shot. She was screaming hysterically, while CFAs and other medics cut off her top to identify if she had other wounds hidden under her clothing. (Each team had a CFA and each platoon also had one medic trained to the paramedic level.)

The older man and young girl had sustained their wounds from the entry point fired by Mark, who had seen the old man reach for a weapon next to him in the dust of the compound. Mark engaged the man, and a round over-penetrated his body and hit the young girl sitting behind him.

Standing on the compound roof at 3 a.m., in the middle of Afghanistan after a night raid deep in Taliban territory, I paused to reflect on how surreal this was. Of all the things I could be doing in my life, here I was. But I was brought out of my reflective mood by the screaming of the girl who had been shot. I could hear platoon HQ coordinating an AME[18] to get the two injured civilians out for treatment, but we ended up carrying them out with us.

Our first DA on what was supposed to be a Taliban commander, and we had zero Taliban and an old man and a young girl as casualties, leaving me to wonder just how solid the intelligence was that had led us to this compound. I leaned against a roof wall, faced the green belt and realised how tired I suddenly felt.

I'd had zero sleep before we stepped off and had spent the whole day in the summer heat pathfinding to our VDO. Even the night before, my excitement and apprehension had made it challenging to sleep. I looked at my watch and was surprised to see it read almost 4 a.m. Waiting for the AME had chewed up our time, which meant that if we didn't leave very soon, we would be walking through the green belt in daylight after a night raid, which was less than ideal. I looked forward to returning to the VDO for food and sleep before it got too hot.

When we finally stepped off around 5 a.m., we could already see the local population up and about to start their day in the green belt. As the sun rose, the entire village started to slowly come to life, and things looked very different from the way they'd looked through the green tubes in my NVG. Well after first light, company headquarters intelligence was reporting enemy indicators in the area.

The path back to the VDO was a few hundred metres to the north of the way we had come in, and from my map recon, I remembered a large, dry creek bed would be coming up in the next kilometre or so. As I approached it, the sun now fully up, I stopped to find the best way across. It was a significant creek bed, about 40 metres or so across, and deep enough that we had to walk with care.

Marcus Wagstaff, then a private in one of the assault teams and now a serving member of the commando regiment, was there that morning too. He recalled a boy of around nine or ten walking up and down the line of operators asking everyone who the 'Tajiman' was, a local term for an interpreter. The Taliban were known to target the interpreters, or 'terps', as this detracted from our ability to communicate with the locals. After Marcus had crossed the creek bed, he took position on the far side and recalls looking into the creek as the two casualties were being carried across. 'Holy shit,' he said, 'I'm glad we didn't get hit with an IED. I looked down and saw at least fifteen operators carrying or walking nearby. It would have been disastrous.'

Once I too had crossed the creek and was on the other side, Garry informed me on the radio that the OC wanted us to travel further to the north, and he directed me to come back to the other side of the creek. The OC wanted to get as far away from another ANA checkpoint as possible to avoid another blue-on-blue engagement (friendly fire), so he instructed the company to cross further up the creek line. As our team was now split, one of the assault teams would take the lead. I was sweating profusely, on my last litre of water, and frustrated at the seemingly unnecessary change to the crossing point, especially as now we would have to spend longer in the green belt. But as soon as we could get clear of the creek bed, we would be back in the desert and could pick up the pace to get back to the cars, take our rigs off, get some water and stretch our backs.

As directed, I crossed back over the dry creek bed. At the same time, the company signaller began updating more frequently on enemy radio traffic, which seemed to be talking specifically about our movement around the creek bed.

By the time I got to the crossing point, one of the assault teams had already taken the lead, so I followed the last man of that team as we began our walk across and up the far side of the creek. Just as I reached the top of the creek bed, though, an almighty explosion went off behind me, and I threw myself to the ground in a ditch. I glanced behind me and saw bits of Auscam material amidst the black smoke and dust.

It is hard to explain or quantify to someone who has never been in a warzone what an explosion in that sort of proximity does to a person. One minute you are thinking about water and noodles, the next your cortisol shoots through the roof as your brain tries to work out what just happened. I looked around me, and everyone had taken cover, unsure of precisely what had occurred, but knowing that a decent IED had just been triggered. We hoped that it was a remotely triggered, radio-controlled IED that had missed its mark, as opposed to a pressure-plate triggered IED, which would mean there was an enemy watching us and potentially getting ready for a follow-up attack. But the bits of Australian uniform that lay around the creek bed led me to lose hope.

Over the radio, the lead platoon commander gave his report to the OC. 'Lead elements have struck an IED, two x friendly Cat A[19] casualties.' The OC acknowledged and then directed the company: 'All callsigns, intelligence indicating ambush, lead elements secure the casualties. Prepare for contact.' I looked around and saw Garry running around making sure our team was okay. He then positioned us higher up on the far side of the creek bed to secure the location.

My mind was racing, trying to think which group was behind me and wondering who the two friendly KIA had been. As I moved to a better position, I could see the medics working on two torn-apart bodies, and one leg sitting 5 metres away from one of the bodies, but I didn't have time to look at the faces. Intelligence was indicating contact was imminent, and I needed to get to a position that covered a series of compounds in front of me.

We waited in position for an attack that never came, and after ten minutes or so were given orders to prepare to move out. A radio call finally came in that the two KIA were not our own operators but an Afghan and a US interpreter. The Taliban had been following our movements, and we just happened to cross the part of the dry creek bed where they had laid a radio-controlled IED, which they triggered as we crossed.

It just so happened that it only hit the two terps. Either the Taliban had targeted the terps, who were dressed the same as us, in Auscam, but without weapons, or it had just been pure luck that no Aussies had been killed. I think I speak for everyone who was there that day when I say that as sad as it was that we had lost two people, I was thankful they were not our boys. I remember thinking, if this is what the first operations are like, what do the next five months have in store for us?

I had known that the deployment would be hard work, but until that exfiltration off target, I don't think I appreciated just how tough it was going to be. And as I was still not fully acclimatised to the heat or to carrying such heavy loads for long periods, that walk out after the IED strike was still, to this day, one of the toughest physical challenges I have been through.

The build-up, excitement and adrenaline of the past few weeks all seemed to hit me at once. Low on water, severely dehydrated and with the ladder's weight on my back in the mid-morning heat, every step was an effort. I recall thinking: 'This is why there is a selection course.' All those days of no sleep and strenuous physical activity had provided each operator with a high-water mark on his physical capabilities. I had been through three days of no food and no sleep before, when I was on selection, so I knew I could get through this. My other thought was that if this were back in 3 RAR, we would have a lot of guys 'go down' with exhaustion and dehydration, but not a single operator in the FE did so.

CHAPTER 14

HELMAND

Rotation VII would see the first Australians go into Helmand province, as part of a coalition-wide infrastructure project to install a turbine engine at Kajaki Dam. For our part, FE-B was tasked with drawing the enemy away into a fight so that others could focus on the transit and installation of the turbine. Our mission, basically, was to drive around and get into fights. It was the job we wanted.

Helmand province, even back in 2008, was known as the 'real badlands' and was home to the British troops and US Marines well into the final years of the war. Up to this point, though, no Australians had been operating in the area, and we were excited to be the first. Later SOTG rotations, predominantly with Charlie Company, brought some of the fiercest fighting Australians would see in the Afghan campaign, and would claim the lives of numerous 2 Cdo Regt and Special Operations Engineer Regiment (SOER) operators (formerly IRR).

The insurgents of Helmand province were part of the Alizai tribe; they were ferocious fighters whose main motive was to protect the heroin poppy trade that funded the resistance. Since the days of the Soviet invasion, the Alizai had mobilised to repel any incursion that risked their rapidly growing primary industry.[20]

It was a long, slow, hot drive. The heat of my ATV engine, which seemed to get hotter on the right side, sometimes had me side-straddling. I had recently read a book on the two-year occupation of Afghanistan by Alexander the Great and his army, which detailed their struggles until they reached the Helmand River and Lashkar Ghar, the capital of Helmand province.

Not much had changed since 330 BC, when Alexander's army had walked on the ground we were now driving over. I imagined them sitting in the desert, probably complaining about the same things as we were more than 2000 years later.

To get to Helmand, the teams who were usually in Bushmasters opted for US Humvees so that they could negotiate the infamous Chambarak Pass, while us recon and sniper teams remained on ATVs. The pass is notoriously steep and leads straight into the village of Khenjakak in northern Helmand, where we expected to encounter the most resistance. We weren't wrong. As soon as we got close to the pass, intelligence indicated the Taliban were reporting on our movements through the spotter network, which we had expected, but we were still surprised by the frequency and accuracy of the enemy reporting, which seemed more detailed and thorough than that of the enemy fighters in Uruzgan province.

Before we got to the pass, we were to meet up with a Green Berets platoon, which would join us for northern Helmand's clearance. This was my first interaction with the Green Berets, the US Army's special forces. I had the grid reference for the meet-up location and was ahead of the main convoy by a few hundred metres. As I got closer, I informed the platoon chook (radio operator) that I was 500 metres out, then slowly drove around a slight hill to the Green Berets' location.

It was a hot day, and all I had on was a T-shirt, baseball cap and body armour. When I turned the corner, I saw the US platoon in a defensive position and waved. The closest vehicle occupants sat there looking stunned, all inside the Humvees with the doors shut. I rode up to the first car, and one of the occupants slowly opened the door with his mouth open.

'G'day, fellas,' I said with a smile.

The two guys inside both just looked at each other. I was still determining what exactly I had done wrong.

'You guys are on fuckin' ATVs?' the passenger asked. 'You guys fuckin' crazy?'

'Yeah, mate, I like the breeze,' I replied.

We all broke out in laughter and began our introductions. The Americans thought we were nuts for riding bikes into Helmand. Looking back, they were probably right.

We crept along Chambarak Pass, IRR sweeping the road the entire way with their Minelabs. We knew the pass would be heavy with IEDs, as it was the only eastern approach into Khenjakak and northern Helmand. I was on my bike on the other side of the pass to the assault team, and was watching one of their team's SRVs come off the hill when the car exploded, sending debris and car parts into the air. One of our SRVs had hit an IED.

I sat there stunned as the car and the boys in it disappeared in a thick cloud of smoke and dust. I strained to see movement, anything indicating that they were okay. The other cars in the valley raced over to help them, as we started to see movement and counted off the bodies. We could see all three blokes moving—they were alive. IRR swept the area for further devices and, once they gave the green light, we moved down to look at the damage to the SRV. It was destroyed. The chassis was twisted, and part of the car was unrecognisable from the blast. How anyone survived is beyond me, but the boys only suffered a few broken bones. Still, it was a fitting welcome to Helmand province, and only a taste of what was to come.

Once we had stripped all the equipment from the damaged SRV, coalition fast jets dropped a bomb onto the vehicle to destroy its remains, and we moved away from the pass towards Khenjakak. To our west were the villages of Labe Joy and Sultan Rabat, which intelligence indicated were the most likely areas the Taliban were located.

Us recon and sniper teams were being used to overwatch and secure the north and east of the company VDO, which was placed a few kilometres out of Khenjakak for the first two days of the operation. On approach, we received fire from 107mm rockets, but we had no idea where they were shooting from. Most of the 107s went high off our flank, but one flew right through the middle of the patrol and exploded behind us. We remained in overwatch for the first day, watching with envy as the assault teams took part in a running battle in the valley below.

Each incursion we made closer to Khenjakak was met with more rockets and heavy automatic fire. On the second day, we were moved to the southern edge of the VDO while headquarters planned our eventual assault into Khenjakak itself, and I was looking forward to finally getting a piece of the action.

Oscar platoon, one of the two assault platoons in Alpha Company, received such fierce resistance on one of their incursions towards the Khenjakak that they were almost surrounded, requiring November platoon to support their withdrawal.

They had received sporadic fire on previous advances towards northern Khenjakak, so they decided to advance further to the west to gauge enemy activity. They were already down one SRV, and as they pulled up on a slight hill, the sky around them erupted. Private T, one of the drivers, got out of his SRV to check the ground to his front for IEDs when the enemy unleashed ferocious fire at him. Private T zigzagged back to the car as rounds landed all around him from a nearby village. Marcus Wagstaff, who was in the same platoon, fired his .50-cal machine gun into the village, hoping to suppress the enemy machine gunner. 'I just don't know how [T] didn't get hit; there was so much fire,' Marcus recalled.

Marcus and his team were tasked to push further towards the village, but were engaged by a Dushka machine gun,[21] forcing them to return to the VDO until a plan was formulated to return to the green belt the next day. The next morning, Oscar platoon pushed back close to the green belt and began a running gunfight for the next two hours, where every team was in contact, firing into the green belt at an enemy nobody could see, so well were they dug into the village.

Oscar platoon was wholly pinned down and started receiving RPG and mortar fire, and an overwhelming amount of small-arms fire. The teams got on the radio and requested November platoon to support them. The platoon's SRVs were not armoured, and the last thing they wanted was a vehicle to be disabled and trapped in the kill zone of multiple enemy positions all around them.

November platoon established a base of fire and a path for Oscar platoon, to allow them to withdraw, and then both platoons moved back to the VDO. Multiple vehicles had been hit; some operators found bullet holes in their packs and sleeves and in the mounted weapons on their vehicles. 'To this day, after four SOTGs, that was the most intense contact I have ever had,' Marcus said later. 'After that TIC [troops in contact], I slept for eighteen hours, I was so exhausted.'

That evening, the company was resupplied via a parachute from an Australian C-130 Hercules, one of the few times I would see them used in the Afghanistan theatre for this purpose. The Herc came in low and fast, dropping half a dozen loads of ammo, food and water. We had become so accustomed to US, British and Dutch aircraft supporting us that seeing Aussie aircraft in Helmand was a welcome change.

On the third night of the operation we sat around our vehicles as relentless bombing from US aircraft shook the ground we were on throughout the dark hours. Again, I was in awe of the scale and power of the bombs, and the devastation they would wreak on the Khenjakak and surrounding villages. Each 2000-pound bomb sent a kilometres-wide shockwave to our VDO, and I often tried to imagine the carnage they were causing the enemy. I was glad the bomber aircraft were on our side. Before the last light, we spotted some movement on the edge of the village while I was on watch, and took the opportunity to call in a mortar mission.

I had spent countless hours in 3 RAR working a mortar tube and training to call in fire, so I was thrilled to get the opportunity to do it operationally. I identified a large dome-shaped building where I had seen enemy movement, and called in a mission to the mortar team set to our rear. The third adjusting round landed a few metres in front of the compound, and I called for 'fire for effect'. Moments later, half a dozen 81mm high-explosive rounds destroyed the structure and surrounding walls, rendering the building useless as a fighting position and, I hoped, killing the enemy inside.

For us in recon and snipers, however, boredom, not the Taliban, was the main enemy. Joining the assault platoons on our bikes for the incursions towards the enemy villages was seen as too risky, so we chased shade, ate and talked shit to pass the time. One afternoon, after we got bored with our 300th game of cards, Chucky challenged the team to the complex game of rock throwing, which, as you guessed, involved throwing rocks at a water bottle. From smaller rocks we went to enormous rocks and then started throwing them at each other. The TLs were busy planning in the command vehicles, so we were left to our own devices.

This was followed by cricket, with rocks. To be safe, some of us wore our helmets. 'Boys, what the fuck?' Garry asked no one in particular as he came back from planning, taking in the sight of us in shorts with our helmets on, dozens of water bottles, makeshift cricket stumps and our area littered with hundreds of rocks. 'Cut it out. Bring it in for orders,' he said, with the look of a disappointed father on his face.

Garry started his orders with a smirk, which we knew was a good thing, as it usually meant we had an excellent task coming up. Our task was to conduct a company-level advance into the edge of Khenjakak—the last few days had given us a better idea of the enemy locations, and the risk of taking in bikes was now accept-able—from where we had been getting shot at for the past few days. We would be supported by Dutch Apache attack aircraft, British fast jets, and multiple ISR platforms. I couldn't believe it. We were driving head-on into an area we knew would be heavily contested. We packed up our gear and began the assault a few hours later.

It was 2 September 2008. The company shook out into an extended line, with the CHQ in the rear with the mortar teams. Before we stepped off for the assault, Harrier aircraft repeatedly flew over us towards the town as a show of force, designed to deter any potential insurgents by letting them know what could be unleashed if we wished. As soon as we stepped off, signals intelligence went ballistic as the insurgents reported on the company charging towards them.

About 2 kilometres or so away from the edge of the enemy-held village, I looked over my right shoulder, and saw something that will stay with me forever. Close to 50 of our vehicles were charging in extended lines, trailing dust clouds, as Apache gunships flew low over us. It was a modern version of the Charge of the Light Brigade at Beersheba, and it was an incredible sight. There was nowhere else I wanted to be.

As we got closer to Khenjakak I suddenly felt vulnerable on my ATV. My experience in the Mirabad Valley in Uruzgan province had taught me just how little cover the bike provided. The build-up— the running gunfights, the bombing and the intelligence—in the last few days had suggested the possibility of a more formidable, more prepared enemy than we'd encountered there, despite the relentless bombing and mortars from our side over the past few days.

I looked at my GPS, which said we were less than a kilometre from the place where we were to break into the town, an open area that ran parallel to a dry creek system. At that moment we got a call on our radios: 'All callsigns, stop, stop, stop!' We weren't to know this then, but to our north in Ana Kalay Valley, near the village of Khas Uruzgan, Force Element Alpha (FE-A; the SASR arm of the SOTG), which was working with the US and the Afghans, had just been ambushed and had suffered nine casualties out of the twelve Australians in the patrol. Trooper Mark Donaldson would be awarded the first Victoria Cross for Australia in this battle. FE-A repelled a relentless attack for three hours, during which the enemy convoy covered a distance of just under 4 kilometres. The ambush was well planned, and the enemy attacked with automatic fire and RPGs; it was a miracle no Aussies were killed.

During the ambush at Ana Kalay, an IRR explosive-detection dog, Sarbi, and her handler, David, were injured by shrapnel from an RPG that exploded close to them, and Sarbi fled. Sarbi, a Labrador/ Newfoundland cross, had worked with FE-A and FE-B on this rotation, and many had grown fond of her. Her story would become famous worldwide. She was eventually found and given numerous awards, including the Purple Cross from RSPCA Australia. She was the second animal to be awarded this medal for wartime service, after one of Simpson's donkeys, Murphy. The Australian War Memorial website recounts Sarbi's story:

> Knowing that Sarbi had gone missing when temperatures were about to plummet had made leaving difficult . . . They left some of David's sweaty clothes out around the perimeter fence to help her pick up his scent. An Australian military official reported that Sarbi had returned to the base, but Afghan guards had shooed her away. At one point, an Australian intelligence officer was monitoring telephone conversations when they heard the Taliban talking about a dog, trying to decide what to do with it. During one phone call, it was apparent that the dog was causing trouble and getting into the chickens . . . Intelligence reports later confirmed that Sarbi was with local Taliban commander and village elder Mullah Hamdullah. Coalition forces tried to arrange a trade, offering to release the mullah's father from prison if Sarbi was returned, but the deal was rejected. Special Forces wanted to go and get Sarbi, but the risks were too high. Eventually, the mullah agreed to sell Sarbi to the coalition forces. In October 2009, almost thirteen months after Sarbi went missing, David was working at the School of Military Engineering in Sydney when he received a call from Corporal Murray Young. 'Mate, we think we've got Sarbi.'[22]

Back at TK, headquarters decided we should stop our assault until we had rotary-wing AME assets, in case we suffered a casualty. Nearly all AME assets in the southern operating areas had been directed to evacuate SASR and US casualties from Ana Kalay.

We then stood static, guns trained on the village, and we could see movement as the enemy prepared for what they thought was the inevitable attack.

Some .50-cals did engage when movement was spotted in the compounds on the edge of the village, but begrudgingly, we turned around and drove back towards the pass. To add insult to injury, as we drove away the Taliban declared victory. 'They own the desert, but we own the green; *Allahu akbar.*'[23] It was a frustrating day, which I named 'the greatest assault that never happened'.

On the drive back to TK from Helmand, the infrared headlight on my bike stopped working. I needed it to avoid potholes and depressions in the ground; without it, my depth perception of the terrain at the front of the bike was poor. Each time my front wheels came into contact with a hot rock, my handlebars would judder to one side, crushing my hands against the magazine pouches on the front of my plate carrier vest.

After hours of this, I had enough and got on the radio to ask Tim if he could take the lead. I was tired and covered in sweat and dust, and my hands were starting to swell. I needed a break from the strain of leading the company back to TK. Tim pulled up beside me, asked if I was all right, and then drove ahead to find a path.

I took out a water bottle and was having a sip when an almighty flash in front of me, in the direction Tim had taken, shook me to the core. The explosion echoed in the valley around us, and my heart sank, knowing Tim had just driven over an IED. I dropped my water bottle and ripped my throttle as hard as possible to get to him, while hearing the cars reporting over the radio that recon had just triggered an IED.

Despite the flash and explosion, something was different about this IED, something which I had still not registered in my panic. It wasn't that loud. Still, IEDs come in varying sizes and scales, and it wouldn't take a big one to kill or severely injure a dude on a quadbike.

As I drove towards Tim, I prayed that he was okay, cursing myself for asking him to take the lead. If Tim was dead, it was my fault, and a wave of guilt came over me as I frantically searched for his body, mentally rehearsing how I would treat him and apply a tourniquet to his legs, which would surely have been amputated in the blast.

I kept a wide berth as I neared Tim's location, hoping to drive around any secondary devices, when I saw Tim's bike. As I got closer, I let out a gasp. I was relieved to see that Tim's legs and body were intact, but he was slouched forward on the handlebars of his bike. I pulled up next to him, my heart rate through the roof, terrified that we had just lost him.

'Fuck mate, that was close,' Tim said as his head came up and he had a drink of water. He hadn't been slouching down because he was hurt; he was merely getting water from his pack.

Relieved, we both started laughing and tried to determine what had happened with the charge. IRR conducted a clearance and dug it up, finding only a bunch of detonators. The main charge had failed to initiate, as it had been in the ground for a while and the electric cables looked corroded due to water ingress. Tim rode on unfazed. I swore I would never ask him to take the lead again.

CHAPTER 15

MIRABAD VALLEY

After months of extended vehicle operations with constant dry holes, a term we used to describe abandoned or empty compounds, I was beginning to think we might be the first commandos not to get into a gunfight; it was all I thought about. The team grew tired of my continual whingeing about the lack of action. I couldn't believe, after all the build-up, the rotation had been such a non-event for me, particularly given that we had missed most of the action in Helmand province in the past weeks. But a series of operations into Mirabad Valley would give me everything I hoped for.

Operation Peeler was the clearance of the Mirabad Valley, a place where previous SOTG rotations had seen significant combat. The Musazi district of the valley was home to a well-known IED facilitator, Abdul Hai, given the codename Objective Rapier, who would remain on Australia's most-wanted list for many rotations.[24] (Objectives were given English names to identify them, to avoid confusion between similar and/or common traditional names.) And more generally, Operation Peeler aimed to disrupt the Taliban network in the region, inhibiting their ability to command, communicate and conduct attacks on coalition and ANA forces. As well as going around being shot at, we would be conducting a series of DA assaults in the valley. Surely we would see some action, I thought to myself.

The vehicle insertion into the valley's edge was horrendous, with two team members having rollovers on their ATVs—a common occurrence when driving at night. Late on the first evening, I found myself on a knife-edge ridgeline. I got on the radio and told Tim to take the vehicles following me on a different path while I worked out how to get myself off the 12-metre cliff. I had two left tyres on the track, giving me inches before a 12-metre drop off the mountain. My front right tyre was halfway up a large boulder, with only my rear right tyre providing traction.

People always ask me if I was ever scared in Afghanistan. In combat, some fear is a normal response. But the most scared I have ever been was riding around on a quadbike at night as the number one scout. One wrong move, and I was guaranteed to get seriously injured—and this was one of those times. Everything I tried, I felt like I would roll the bike over the edge. The rest of the team was ahead of me as Tim had found a more suitable path for the convoy, and I was all on my own, feeling completely helpless.

I had to try something. I kicked the bike into reverse, leaned back on its rear-right corner, and inched my way back, keeping my eyes on both sides to ensure I didn't roll off the edge. Eventually, I was back on flat ground and sat on the bike shaking. I got off and walked to the drop-off, which looked much higher from below. Another night, another close call on an ATV—not my last for this deployment.

Our recon team and the sniper team would retain our ATVs to support the dismounted clearance of the valley by the assault teams, as the bikes, with their MAG58s and rockets, would give added fire-power and manoeuvrability to the company commander during the clearance.

We arrived at the vehicle harbour early the following day, and after a few hours' rest, our team crept up the edge of the desert, looking down into the valley from the western side. We scanned the area, but nothing seemed out of place, so we stayed in position while the assault platoons made their way on foot, some fifteen minutes behind us.

We had a long day ahead, so Garry advised us to get some food down, as we had all opted for a sleep instead of eating when we'd arrived at the harbour. Eating was also a lot easier to do before it got too hot. I was cooking some noodles on my Jetboil when I heard Garry's report on the radio: 'Be aware I see around 200 women and children heading north up the valley.' I looked in the direction Garry was facing and saw, less than 400 metres below us, a steady stream of women and kids hurrying away in a single file.

'Where are all the men?' I asked Garry.

'Waiting for us,' he responded, with a look of concern I had not seen on his face before.

My heart skipped a beat—we were on.

Garry wanted us to spread out along the high ground, and directed me to move 60 metres or so further to the south to get a better view of the southern side of a series of compounds in the valley. I jumped on my bike, then looked down at my noodles, which had just finished cooking. I assessed that the ground was flat and so I could ride with one hand and hold my noodles in the other, finishing them once I got to my overwatch position. A stupid decision.

I was distracted by the constant chatter reporting on Taliban when my front left tyre hit a rock. Unable to control the handlebars, I was flipped over to the right, down a 15-metre rolling hill. Stunned, I let go of my noodles and handlebars and covered my face to try to protect it as I rolled dozens of times down the hill. Once I stopped, I saw my airborne bike coming straight for me.

Unable to move due to the pain in my legs, I just covered my head and hoped for the best. Somehow, the bike bounced off the ground right next to me, then entirely over me, missing me by inches, before rolling further down the hill and stopping, spreading my guns and equipment down the bike path. My earpiece crackled into life. 'All callsigns, one of the Romeo [recon team] bikes are down: bike rollover,' said one of the assaulters as he rushed over to help me. That instant, gunfire erupted.

Davis and Lance had crested the high ground near where I had rolled my bike and started receiving machine gun fire from at least two positions in the compounds in front of them in the valley. Davis responded with his machine gun and fired a 66mm rocket launcher, forgetting to put his hearing protection on; he still suffers from severe tinnitus due to the damage his ears sustained that morning. Lance and Davis continued firing 66mm rockets, and one of Davis's went straight through a compound's front door. 'Contact,' I heard Davis scream on the radio as the assaulters ducked for cover and the rest of our recon team began firing into the valley.

This was Davis's first contact, and he recalls hearing the bullets crack over his head, thinking, 'This is what it sounds like.' The intensity of the fire grew, causing Davis and Lance to break contact back towards the crest of a minor hill, where the remainder of the team would meet up with them. Davis recalled his thoughts during the gunfight: 'You don't think about it. Like you always read about, the training takes over and you act. I fumbled around with the 66—the adrenaline made my hands shake.'

I couldn't believe it. Finally, we were getting into a gunfight, and I was lying there with what felt like broken legs. 'Cuuuunt!' I shouted. As soon as the contact started, everyone's focus shifted from the rolled bike to the enemy, leaving me to myself. As I stood up I had trouble putting weight on my legs, and wondered how on earth I would get all my weapons and equipment and roll my bike upright. Just then, Chucky came screaming down the hill on his bike while enemy fire cracked above our heads. 'Scott, get on the back, fuck your gear, just grab some ammo,' he yelled over gunfire.

I grabbed some liners of 7.62mm link for the machine guns and jumped on Chucky's bike. We rode up the hill to where the rest of the team was now laid out in extended lines behind their bikes. The team's position was about 500 metres from the edge of the nearest set of compounds, and I yelled out to them to get a target indication of where we were being shot at from. The sniper team had also joined us, and Dan, who carried the .50-calibre sniper rifle, was lying prone next to his bike, engaging targets, when a burst of enemy machine gun fire stitched up the ground next to him.

I took cover behind Chucky's bike and he started engaging the compounds and surrounding green belt with his MAG58, where he perceived the Taliban to be engaging us. Incoming rounds were kicking up dust around us, and our bullets and rocket fire were also kicking up dust around the compounds in front of us. The incoming fire was consistent and accurate as the Taliban machine gunners adjusted their shots.

Despite not having my bike and guns, I was thrilled to finally be in a decent gunfight, nearly eight years after joining the army. I had to control my anxiety, take deep breaths and remain aware of my surroundings. I could not have been happier.

Our machine gun fire was having little impact on minimising the incoming fire, so I ran over to Chucky—who had the SR25 Marksman rifle with enhanced optics—to see if he had any visibility on which compounds we were being engaged from. I also realised that Chucky was wearing a blue singlet under his body armour, which I found amusing.

Chucky told me he thought the fire was coming from a compound directly in front of us, so I returned to his bike to get his binoculars for a better look. Just as Chucky had indicated, I saw two fighters ducking around a large wall in front of us, and I could also see our teams' rounds kicking off the wall, having little impact as the Taliban were behind hard cover. Straight away, I considered using an 84mm short-range anti-armour weapons round with a near-surface burst or proximity fuse. I hoped to see the projectile detonate in the air and shower the enemy with shrapnel from the rocket, as it was designed to do.

I waited for a lull in fire, then grabbed Chucky's 84mm launcher and loaded a rocket into the tube. Now, I wish I could say I had the clarity of mind to get the laser range finder and the exact distance to the compound, then set the fuse as I was taught. But a burst of enemy machine gun fire spiked my adrenaline, so I just guessed the distance, prepared the launcher, and ran out into the open to ensure the weapon's back blast did not injure any of the team.

My heart was racing, and I was out of breath after a small sprint. I aimed the sights at the compound wall, calling 'ears' for anyone who didn't have hearing protection on, and fired. By pure chance, the airburst round detonated directly over the compound wall, kicking up a large plume of dust and instantly stopping any fire from the compound. We did not complete a battle damage assessment on that compound, but it is fair to say the round was 'effective'—it was pure luck where the rocket exploded. I'm not sure who was more surprised by the accuracy of the rocket, the rest of the team or me. Of course, I didn't tell them that it was a complete fluke, happy for them to falsely praise my marksmanship with the 84.

The fire eased up over the next ten minutes, completely stopping after the platoon JTAC started calling in 500-pound bombs from the US fighter jets that were now stationed above us in support.

The bombs ripped through the green belt of the valley, destroying compounds, trees and walls, leaving me wondering if any civilians in the area were being injured. The shockwave rushed towards us, visible in the open desert. The noise alone was enough to scare the pants off you, let alone the chance of having one land on top of you. We had been fired upon and were left with no other choice than to bomb, but the scale of the destruction it caused was intense.

During the contact, I recall thinking how similar the sound of being shot at was to the sound of being in the butts of a rifle range: it was like a whip being cracked over your head.

As the senior instructor of the SF weapons course at ADFSSO in my last few years in the army, I drew on this experience by creating an exercise where trainees had to stand in the butts of the rifle range without their hearing protection while I had firers cycle through different weapon systems, in a bid to expose the trainees to the sounds of incoming fire.

I would start with single shots above their heads, fired from within a few metres, then off the flank so they could hear the difference. I also cycled through subsonic and supersonic rounds[25] for the trainees to help them distinguish the two.

This also exposed them to the difficulties of communicating in heavy contact. I got all the officer trainees at one end of the butts, with the remainder at the other end. On command, I would ask one of the officer trainees to give a simple command to the rest of the course, less than 50 metres away: '100 metres, slight right, two enemies with machine guns in the open.'

At the same time, I had four operators 100 metres away fire automatic burst over the trainees' heads, replicating heavy enemy fire. After the allocated ten seconds, I would ask the group receiving the command what the officer had detailed. In almost every serial, the officers could not pass on the simple target indication, reinforcing the need to 'fight' to communicate during enemy contact, keeping your head on a swivel and always passing messages on to operators around you. In some cases, ten seconds of experience is more valuable than weeks of instruction.

After watching dozens of bombs being dropped on the compounds, I returned to the spot where my bike had rolled, and found that aside from a few bends in my weapon rack,[26] it was working fine. But the morning was not over for us. We received orders that we would be moving into a large compound further to the north in the green belt, to provide more intimate support to the assault teams who had begun their clearance there. Our day was just beginning. My baptism of fire would continue well into the afternoon.

Garry directed Tim and me to clear a large compound that had a good view of the built-up area that Oscar platoon would soon be clearing, and we drove the few hundred metres to the edge of the green belt to find a path to the compound. As we had been in contact already that day, the laying of hasty IEDs by the Taliban was a real threat, so we picked rocky areas that would be harder to lay IEDs in, which made for slower riding.

We parked our bikes outside the compound and carefully cleared the interior. The main structure was a single-storey, multi-room building with a flat roof that took little time to clear. A contact rang out below us in the green belt, so we ran back to our ATVs to drive into the compound we had just cleared on foot, where we could use our MAG58s and rockets to support the team in contact. We took up position along the waist-high wall and informed Garry that the compound was clear and that we were in position, facing east into the valley. We requested an update on all our friendly teams' locations in the green belt.

The IRR engineers started scanning the compound with their Minelabs, and one of them yelled out, 'Everyone freeze! IEDs.'

I glanced over at Tim, knowing exactly what he was thinking: 'Fuck, that was close.' The engineer stood only a metre from the path I had taken to lead Tim into the compound. Other IRR operators then came to assist with the clearance and found not one but three 25-kilogram IEDs made with home-made explosives with pressure plate initiators. It was pure chance that we had not stood on or ridden over them. One step in a different direction, and we would have been pink mist. Regardless, we had a job to do, and didn't have time to ponder what may have been.

We weren't the only ones to have a close call with IEDs that day. A team from Oscar platoon to our south attempted to take up a position on some high ground when they were engaged with RPG and machine gun fire from multiple enemy locations. The first two team members ran to cover and jumped into a ditch, which ended up being an empty grave—they were standing in the local cemetery.

The TL got on his radio and began calling in mortars onto the enemy position, while the team 2ic found a plastic cable hanging off a small branch near him. He carefully followed the cable, which led right to the grave he and the team commander were in—he found three mortar rounds as the main charge of an IED under their feet.

Every assault team seemed to be in contact—we had stirred up the hornet's nest in the valley that morning. The signals intelligence reporting was coming in every few minutes, yet either the enemy were unwilling to target our compound, or they were too consumed by the assaulters fighting multiple positions in the valley. Either way, our compound had not engaged, leaving us out of the fight. Still, we diligently tracked all friendly teams' movements on our maps.

Combat is a stressful and exhilarating experience, yet the anxiety for me came not from the fear of getting shot, but more from the fear of making a mistake. Mainly, I was scared of being responsible for friendly fire. Countless times in my career, in both training and operations, I have had to exercise extreme caution and judgement before pulling the trigger to make sure I don't hit someone on my side. Movies have you believe it is relatively simple—bad guys on one side, you on the other. But real-time operations are dynamic, and the enemy can dictate your movements, regardless of how robust your planning has been.

Aside from the infrared strobes on operators' helmets, which are visible at night through NVG, it can be tough to distinguish friend from foe. Regardless of rank, every operator needs to track the movements and locations of all teams, as the cost of not doing so could prove catastrophic. As the saying goes, 'No plan seems to survive first contact'; operators must think on their feet under stress—a critical assessment criterion during the commando selection and training process.

Night operations added more stress. It was not unusual to land on the wrong landing site, where teams would be running off in different directions. The gunfire, poor visibility and confusion on the landing direction would add to the chaos, making it challenging to identify Australian, US and ANA forces while receiving effective enemy fire.

Back in the compound Tim and I had cleared, Tim decided to throw an Australian flag over the wall so it was visible to the enemy, and the moment he did, an immense weight of fire was laid on the compound. Automatic fire tore up the walls around us and we did a good job keeping our heads down; the enemy numbers were growing as a team from Oscar platoon fought for their lives a few hundred metres away.

Mark, one of Oscar platoon's experienced TLs, proposed a plan to draw the enemy into battle with this team. The local Taliban would only occasionally take on forces the size of a company group, so Mark's plan was to push his team further up the green belt, where they'd be dislocated from the rest of the Australians in the valley, and therefore seem like a weaker target. Adding to this, he took a pirate flag and speakers bellowing Western pop music—everything the Taliban hated.

As Mark's team moved along an aqueduct, they were ambushed from less than 40 metres away with automatic fire and RPGs. In response, they threw themselves on the ground and returned fire, throwing grenades, and firing dozens of 40mm. Having issues with a new ammunition type, Private Viv Hunt, the marksman in Mark's assault team, suffered repeated stoppages, having to field strip his weapon mid-contact. 'When you get hit from that close, with that much fire, you don't do what you think you would do—we just threw ourselves to the ground and tried to match the rate of enemy fire,' Mark said later.

Complicating matters, the Afghan provincial response unit (PRC) and Afghan tactical police unit were a hundred or so metres from the team's right flank, and in firing indiscriminately hit the area directly in front of Mark's team. Mark was concerned the fire would soon be directed at them and decided to withdraw. 'Moving forward was too risky, so I decided to break contact and go back towards the compound you guys [my team] were in; there was no use pushing forward.'

Mark's team, crawling on their stomachs, broke away from the ambush site after firing a 66mm rocket into a building they suspected the enemy was using to engage them.

Still unable to rectify his SR25 rifle, Viv found himself in the open, unable to return fire during the break. Scott, the team scout, repeatedly doubled back to cover Viv and ensure the team withdrew under fire, repeatedly exposing himself to fire as he did so. He would later be awarded the Star of Gallantry, one award down from the VC for Australia.

It had been an intense gunfight. When Mark's team came into our compound, you could see it on their faces. Again, it was a miracle none of them had been shot or killed. Upon reflection, Mark explained, what you think you'll do in an ambush and what you actually do can be different. 'We just reacted with as much fire as possible; there was no counter-ambush drill like we are taught—you just rely on instincts.'

Before Mark's team arrived in our compound, platoon HQ, tracking the movement of their assault teams and enemy chatter, had directed us to return fire further down into the green belt to facilitate their withdrawal, and had given us Mark's location. I grabbed my M4, took position behind a wall, and scanned the bush to my front to search for any signs of the enemy. Less than 70 metres away, I spotted a fighter in black robes duck behind a compound wall, then appear on the other side, firing automatic bursts at our compound.

I yelled a target indication and commenced engaging his position with rapid single shots from my M4. I recall thinking how surreal this was. Some bloke I had never met wanted me dead and was doing his best to send me to the grave. This was also the first time I'd seen a clear view of the enemy in full daylight, and I was surprised by how little he was carrying: dark, traditional robes and a weapon—that was it. I also realised I was more composed in this contact than I had been a few hours earlier, and my movements were less erratic.

To stabilise my shots as I continued to engage the compound where I had last seen the fighter, I rested my right elbow on the wall of our own compound. I had to change magazines on my rifle, so I took my elbow off the wall and conducted my magazine change behind cover—a split second later, two enemy bullets shattered the top of the wall exactly where my arm had been.

Once again, luck and timing were the only reason I didn't get my arm shot off. Despite our best efforts, the size of the enemy compound's wall was making our small-arms fire useless, so Garry devised a plan. On command, he would fire a few 84 rounds at it to destroy the enemy's cover while the rest of the team suppressed the position—Garry would have to stand over our own compound's wall to engage effectively, leaving him exposed.

I grabbed my machine gun off my bike and found a break in our compound wall to rest my bipod and, as planned, we fired into the compound while Garry fired the 84. As soon as I popped up to start firing, though, a burst of fire stitched the ground next to my head. The rounds were so close to my face they kicked dirt into my mouth. Two close calls in the space of three minutes, and it was only lunchtime.

The plan was effective, and we stopped receiving fire from the compound. Intelligence indicated the enemy was in panic, claiming two of them were dead, and their commander needed further direction on what to do next. It seemed there were more enemies around us than we had initially thought.

Despite being more composed than I'd been earlier, I was on a high from adrenaline. I desperately wanted to conduct a clearance of the compound to see the bodies, but doing so would serve no tactical advantage, so we stayed put. Despite the close calls, I don't think I have ever been as happy as I was that day. The first time you get into a good gunfight is something you never forget—although you will have more, the first one always stays with you. I finally felt like I was validated after all those years of training. It was a good feeling.

We were in radio communication with another assault team to our east, who indicated that the enemy had been seen moving in our direction. Mark's team had safely returned to our compound and would stay with us to rest up after their withdrawal. They were covered in mud and visibly fatigued from their fight, but were busy redistributing ammo and water, ready to go again.

We had stopped receiving fire from the series of compounds directly in front of us, and needed to be able to engage further out. After looking at the map to track the latest positions of the closest team, I suggested to Viv that we should take up a spot on the roof of the compound, as my machine gun and his marksman rifle could work together—we would be more effective up there than we would be on the ground, behind the compound wall.

We climbed onto the roof, and I immediately realised how exposed we were. Viv crawled over to me and, after realising the same, looked at me and said simply, 'Fuck bro.'

As we debated whether the other roof, which had a small lip around it, might offer us better protection, a massive volume of fire bore down on us. Automatic fire was going over our heads, and I could hear the teams in the compound attempting to return fire, but the volume of accurate fire we were receiving made it difficult.

Viv and I lay on the roof, unable to get up to return fire, staying as low as we possibly could. I was lying down with my face towards the fire, scared even to lift my head an inch, so accurate were the enemy bullets.

With each burst, the rounds got closer to my face, and it was apparent the enemy had locked onto Viv and me. The rounds then started to land directly next to us, skipping off the roof—the sound of rounds that close is something you never forget. The fire didn't stop. I closed my eyes. If it was going to happen, I didn't want to see it. I felt like an idiot. Why the fuck had we decided to get on this roof?

I then decided that closing my eyes wouldn't help, and as I opened them, a burst of fire stitched the enemy-facing side of the wall just below my position on the roof, inches from my face. An inch higher and it would have gone through my face.

Realising how dire our situation was, one of the team commanders directed everyone to suppress the green belt with fire so that Viv and myself could jump off, which we did in a hurry. Once back down behind the safety of the wall, I sat on my bike and lit a cigarette, realising for the first time how much my hands were shaking. I'd been sure I would die on that roof that morning.

CHAPTER 16

TETHERED GOATS

Mid-afternoon, we moved from the compound to the east of the valley, where we would rest up for the rest of the afternoon before pushing further up the valley on the last light. Garry moved us onto a slight hill 400 metres from the green belt, while the assault platoon's PMVs stayed on the top of the high ground to our rear, as the terrain was too steep for them to join us. The aim of having us on the slope was to deter any movement in the valley, as we did not want the Taliban to have a chance to escape before the clearance that night.

After the day we'd had, I was tired and dehydrated, and as the adrenaline wore off, I was starting to feel the pain in my legs from my rollover that morning. I'd underestimated how tired you get after a gunfight; as soon as the excitement wears off, you start to feel every bump, cut and bruise. Both recon and sniper teams were co-located in a half-circle facing the valley below, and we soon got into a routine of throwing oil on our guns and getting some food down while we kept one person on watch with binoculars behind one of the bikes. The assaulters were doing the same on the hill behind us.

Morale was strong within the team, as we had seen the most action of the trip so far, and although we were tired, our energy and mood were still high.

I took my turn on watch. The pattern of life in the village indicated that the fighters were still in the area—we could see no women or children in the compounds or men working the fields, a key indicator that our day was not done. Then I handed over to one of the snipers, giving him a rough outline of the movement I had observed during my watch, and settled down in the shade to try to get some sleep.

Dehydrated, I had just sat up to have a drink when an RPG suddenly exploded about 15 metres behind me, kicking up rocks and making me dive behind my bike for cover. The rocket had gone over our whole position. Despite the events of that morning, this was wholly unexpected and shocked us all from our siesta.

During the next ten minutes I was the most scared I have ever been in combat. Wholly exposed in the open on the bald hill, with no cover except our bikes, our position was hammered by the most accurate machine gun fire I have ever experienced.

It started as a bit of fun—another adrenaline spike and gunfight to tick off. I even heard someone shout out a 'Yeeha' after the RPG and initial burst of machine gun fire—to start with, most of the rounds went high. But this didn't last long. The boys who weren't already close to their bikes scrambled over to them as the only available cover. As the fire got closer, the Taliban machine gunner slowly got his eye in as he walked the rounds down to our position. One of the snipers, Chris, was to my rear, having found a depression in the ground, and was aiming to get his sniper rifle up, but every time he tried, the incoming fire saw him get down low in his hole.

Just as the fire started to slow down or stop for a short period, it would again kick off, allowing us no respite. As they were only a few hundred metres away, the cracks of the bullets as they broke the sound barrier were like mad bees frantically searching for something to sting. Even a terrible marksman would eventually get lucky.

Those of us with MAG58s on our bikes did our best to return fire, but we had no idea where we were being shot at from, so we sporadically fired into areas that we thought looked like likely positions. I screamed out to the sniper, who had been on watch, to see if he had any idea where we should fire, but every time I tried to talk to him, the sound of bullets cracking above and around our heads made communication impossible. Eventually, he was able to get his target indication out. 'The hill behind the tent,' he yelled as rounds kicked around him.

Three hundred metres away from us, on the other side of a dry creek bed, a Bedouin family had set up a tent; they had been there when we arrived. The family had a bunch of kids who had been running around playing, but they were now nowhere to be seen, presumably hiding once the gunfight erupted around them. That's what I hoped, anyway.

Our team's fire was now concentrated on the hill behind the family's camp, less than 50 metres from their tent. The fire was kicking up a lot of dust as the rounds impacted, which made it hard to identify the enemy position. I was concerned for the family and kept glancing at the tent to check for any movement. The Taliban fighters had deliberately placed themselves close to the tent, knowing we would be unable to call in any air support or use any of our heavy weapons, as doing so would put the civilians at too much risk. I was confident our team would be able to shoot without hitting the tent, but I had zero faith in the enemy, and nor did I think they would care if they did hit it.

I had just grabbed my binos to try to pinpoint where the enemy was when I spotted movement further up the hill, about 50 metres from where Paul, one of the snipers, had seen the enemy. Then I saw movement again a few seconds later, even closer to us. The enemy was attempting to flank us from the high ground; they mustn't yet have learned about the commando platoon tasked with supporting us on the other side. Regardless, a small creek line ran straight from the last-seen location to our location, which was out of view to them.

I yelled out a target indication and commenced pouring fire in and around the entrance to the creek line, hoping that the volume of fire would deter the enemy from attempting to flank us. Just as I had a stoppage on my gun, a burst of automatic fire cracked all around me. I got down behind my bike's tyres and tried to make myself as small as possible. I glanced over at Chucky, and his look said it all. The enemy bullets would soon find their mark if we didn't get out of here. There were no more smiles; I am sure my face had the same look as Chucky's.

In a slight pause in the incoming fire, I jumped up to rectify the stoppage on my MAG58 and realised I was on my last liner; I had fired 600 rounds of 7.62mm in this contact alone. We had an engineer with us, who hadn't got up from behind his bike the entire TIC, and I yelled at him to throw me some ammo. He reached up, grabbed a liner, and threw it in my direction—it landed between our two bikes.

Cursing, I jumped up to grab it, but as I did, a burst of enemy fire cracked around the tin, causing me to dive back behind my bike. I needed to get that last liner. I psyched myself up, gave myself a countdown, then leapt out and grabbed the liner before diving back behind my bike.

The enemy must have been watching me; as I jumped behind my bike, a burst of fire found its mark, going within an inch or two of my ATV and directly underneath it; my attempts to take cover behind the wheel had paid off. I then heard a loud 'ting' and knew my bike had been hit. By this stage, Garry had gotten onto the assault platoons, who were now heavily engaging the area with their 7.62mm guns on the Bushmasters as well as with team machine guns, which stopped the incoming fire in its tracks; the enemy, realising there was a whole platoon behind us, decided to withdraw back into the green belt.

When the fire stopped briefly, Garry directed us to grab our shit and 'get out of Dodge', and we were happy to oblige. But when I tried to start my bike, nothing happened. I didn't need to inspect it— I knew what was wrong with it. The team started to drive off, and I frantically jumped on the radio. 'My bike is fucked—I need a tow,' I yelled into the bone mic on my ear.

One of the assault platoons, who were on the same network, then increased their rate of fire towards the enemy as Lance drove over to me and began the towing drill, which we had been practising since the MRE back in Cultana. I jumped up and got a handle on my MAG58, ready to engage anyone who decided to target my very obviously broken-down bike. Within a minute or two, the towline was on, and I was being dragged up the slope to the assault platoons, out of view of the green belt. I glanced over at the Bedouin tent, hoping to see some movement, and I prayed the family were okay. I cursed the Taliban for putting innocent civilians at risk, but this would not be the only time I saw this occur.

As we were classified as TIC, supporting coalition assets were soon above us. The French Mirage jets had issues identifying our positions, however, and refused to drop bombs. The US jets were less hesitant and flew a few 'show of force' missions, flying low over the enemy and breaking the sound barrier. The Dutch Apaches were also willing to engage but would remain high, not wanting to get close to the action despite the continual commentary and reassurance we were receiving on friendly and enemy positions.

Oscar platoon, tasked with providing overwatch on the high ground, needed help getting some of their vehicles into position to support us. Marcus's SRV nearly rolled over while being shot at with RPGs as they made their way up the hill. As our team was engaged, they heard Garry's call on the radio, grabbed their MAG58s and other direct-fire heavy weapons, and ran to the top of the hill to support us. 'You guys were getting hammered. I have no idea why you were put on such an exposed hill; it's a miracle nobody was killed,' Marcus recalled.

Davis had been fast asleep when the contact started and, although startled by the initial RPG and incoming fire, thought he was dreaming. When he woke from his slumber, the gunfight was in full swing, and he jumped behind the gun on his bike, asking the team where the fire was coming from. Like me, Davis also fired most of his allocation of 7.62mm ammo from his MAG58; we were all shooting like mad, hoping to suppress the enemy, as we recognised how exposed we were.

But the confusion about where exactly the enemy was meant that a lot of our fire was ineffective. 'It's the most naked and exposed I have ever felt on that hill. Even at its worst, even when your bike was shot, I can't recall being scared. We had a great team, who communicated in contact well, and I had faith in everyone,' Davis explained.

Once we got back to the assault platoon, up in the safety of the high ground, I sat on my bike and lit a cigarette, my hands still shaking. I was amazed nobody had been shot—my bike was the only casualty. At one stage, I had been convinced I would get hit, and if it wasn't for the platoon being behind us, I think a few of us would have been.

I walked over to Chucky, who was sitting on his bike, deep in thought, with a water bottle in his hand, and when he looked at me, we both burst into laughter. Part relief, part adrenaline—I am not sure exactly what we were laughing at, but hearing us, Tim and Lance joined in, and we began swapping stories and slaying each other.

Sledging was a way to relieve tension, and it began minutes after we were convinced we would die.

'Fuck, at one stage I thought Scott was going to cry,' Chucky commented.

'Piss off, cunt, at least I fired rounds.'

'Hey everyone, if anyone needs ammo, Chucky still has six liners on his bike,' I replied while the rest of the team stood around in hysterics.

'What are you laughing at, Old Balls? You were in rapid eye movement through most of it, you old cunt.'

Nobody was safe once the sledging started. Humour was our antidote to stress; the more stressed we were, the more the jokes and pranks would increase.

After growing tired of sledging, I grabbed a torch and inspected my bike. As I suspected, there was a perfect 7.62mm hole in the engine cowling, inches from where my head had been taking cover behind the bike.

I had named my bike Dragula, after the Rob Zombie song featured in an old TAG-E video on YouTube that I had watched hundreds of times as a form of inspiration on flat days training for selection. As this was my third bike of the deployment, I'd grabbed a marker pen and wrote 'III' under 'Dragula'. While I wasn't paying attention, Luke, one of the assaulters, had come over and written a 'V' in front of the III, making it 'Dragula VIII'.

He then suggested he get a photo of me holding the cowling with the bullet hole, and I was happy to oblige, having still not looked at the cowling in my hand. I had been getting slayed for the past few months for the number of ATVs I had been through—even though that was expected for the number one scout, as I did most of the riding over poor terrain to prove routes. That didn't matter, though, as now there was evidence of me holding up a cowling with 'Dragula VIII', proof of my alleged acceptance that this was my *eighth* ATV of the trip. Well played, mate.

Not long after we re-joined the assault platoon, the other assault platoon moved closer to the green belt and was engaged immediately. Fast air was called in and British Harrier jets dropped 500-pound bombs in the valley, while the assault platoon guns on the Bushmasters fired into areas identified by the ISR platforms. The sight was spectacular, with tracer rounds flying, ricocheting off compounds while bombs destroyed entire structures. It reminded me of the footage from the first Gulf War, with tracer fire flying everywhere.

Not far from our position, 3 RAR, the regular army unit on the Mentoring Task Force rotation, was in a harbour on a task to provide the engineers with security during a reconnaissance of an area near the valley. The 3 RAR lads were growing frustrated at not being allowed to fight; the task group commander was an extremely risk-averse engineer unwilling to allow them to get into a TIC. Moments like this were the best recruiting you could do for SF. The infantry lads were babysitting engineers; they sat on their cars and watched the tracer rounds fly around the valley, in the full knowledge that Alpha Company had been in contact since first light.

One of the 3 RAR soldiers present that day put his SF application in the moment he got back from that patrol and is still a sergeant in 2 Cdo Regt at the time of writing. He recalls sitting on his Bushmaster, frustrated at the restrictions that were being placed on arguably some of the best infantry soldiers in the world. Years of training for a fight and not being allowed to partake in one, despite being so close, was the final straw for many infantry guys, me included, who bore witness to SF operations during the Timor and Afghanistan campaigns.

Later that night, we began our long, slow drive back to TK. Once the job was done, the drive back was the worst part, especially for

Tim and me at the front. It was always a constant balance between taking the lead and getting back as quickly as possible, overidentifying potential choke points that may contain IEDs and calling IRR forward.

If the engineers were called to the front, they would either take the lead in a PMV or physically clear the route. It was challenging, laborious work, involving manual clearance as IRR operators swept the ground with a Minelab. It could add hours to the drive home.

To make matters worse, a Bushmaster was now towing me, and the towline length had me in the middle of the dust behind the car. When I returned to TK, I was covered head to toe in Afghan sand. The sand had made its way into every pouch, magazine and water bottle, and it took me days to clean everything back to an acceptable standard. We had a few days off after our return from the operation, and settled into a steady routine of watching movies, training at the TK gym and relaxing.

CHAPTER 17

DA DAYS

Outside of disruption operations, DA raids on Taliban leaders and key IED facilitators took up our remaining time on the rotation. Earlier rotations had seen most of these conducted through VDO insertions, but as the IED threat increased, later rotations saw more helicopter-based DA insertions. On my last rotation in 2013, nearly all the mission insertions were by helicopters.

Intelligence gathered on the battlefield and through other means identified key Taliban members and placed them on a list known as the Joint Prioritised Elimination List, from which they would be removed once captured or killed.

The threat posed by the enemy leader would dictate the type of assault conducted. A 'soft knock' profile would be dictated if the intelligence was weak. This was more investigative than anything. We would cordon off the compound and call them out, hoping to uncover further intelligence to help the analysts build a better picture of the target or the area.

Enemy fighters higher on the Joint Priorities Elimination List, and about whom there was stronger intelligence, would trigger a more dynamic assault. This type of assault did not require a callout, and we would usually breach the doors to the compound with either explosive or manual tools. This was the DA that everyone wanted, and we got our fair share of them on this 2008 rotation. We conducted close to 22 DA raids, nearly all of them at the higher level.

To ensure our vast convoy of vehicles did not warn the target of our approach, we would usually site the VDO far away in the desert, and infiltrate on foot into the green belt to conduct the strike. These walks, although necessary, were challenging work, and after the stress of a long drive to the VDO, left little room for rest.

We would typically conduct three to four DAs per operation to maximise the time we were outside the wire, where the only chance we got to rest would be when the sun was up. The game of 'chasing shade' would then occur: the most reliable respite from the sun was offered by the shadows made by our vehicles, and we would continually have to drag our swags into those patches of shade as the sun moved through the day.

In summer, our water bottles got so hot that the only way we could cool them down to a temperature bearable enough to drink was to put a 600ml plastic bottle in a wet sock and hang it off our handlebars. The SRVs and Bushmasters had small fridges in them, so the recon and sniper teams were always at the mercy of the generosity of their occupants, hoping they would take pity on us and throw us cold water or Powerade on a hot day.

Eating during the day was also a challenge in the heat, and most of us would shed as much as 15 kilograms on this deployment. There was no time to eat at night, and it was normally too hot to eat cooked food during the day, so we became experts at stuffing muesli bars, chocolate and snacks in our dump pouches to scoff down during our short stops on the walk-ins. It was energy we desperately needed.

As all our DAs were planned for night-time, the days were spent in our VDO in the middle of the desert, where we would sit on camping chairs and play cards, read magazines, and pass the time shooting the shit. Despite the relentless heat, these became some of the most memorable moments for me. You get to really know the guys you work with when you spend every single waking minute with them, and deployments forge friendships that last a lifetime.

Night-time raids were the type of SF work that I had joined to do— a slow, silent approach to a village, then assaulting a compound in the dead of night, where we would often find the occupants in their sleep, completely unaware that we were there until we were screaming at them in Pashtun with infrared lasers pointing at their heads, invisible to the naked eye. We were the masters of the night, where our NVG and lasers gave us an almost unfair advantage. During the Afghanistan campaign, SOTG were the only Australians permitted to conduct night raids.

We had varying success with the DAs on this rotation, and captured two medium-value individuals in their sleep without firing a shot. But we also raided many compounds that had not been occupied for a long time. Assets such as high-fidelity ISR platforms were in high demand and were requested by every coalition SF unit, meaning we would only get them for high-priority missions or when going into contact.

When a coalition unit was in contact, radio communications would go back to the planning and command rooms, where they would mark a callsign as 'TIC'. This would see the unit in TIC prioritised for any assets that were available in the area.

A key frustration, however, was the prosecution of what were known as 'historical targets', or locations that had previously been raided. I am unsure of the utility of repeatedly risking lives to hit such targets, but they were staples in most SOTG rotations. Towards the end of our rotation, as one of the assault teams was about to breach a door in one such location, a man ran out of the compound and was nearly shot by the roof teams.

The man was yelling in Pashtun, and the interpreter later told us he was telling the teams not to damage the door as it was only new; the 'target' had opened it to make sure we didn't break it, so often had his compound been raided. We later discovered that Delta Company, which we replaced for this rotation, had raided it a few weeks earlier.

Aside from IEDs and the enemy, dogs also posed a threat, through potential bites and through the danger they might give our position away as we approached our target. Numerous times dogs would charge an assaulter as he entered, putting the fear of God into him. One DA, I was on the roof team of an unusually large compound when I saw a large black dog charge the first person who entered the compound, who was distracted by some occupants he was controlling. I yelled, 'Look out, dog!' but the assaulter didn't hear me.

Left with no choice, and with a split second to decide what to do, I flicked my safety catch up, aimed my laser at the dog's body and took up pressure on my trigger—when the dog was violently pulled back by a thick chain around its neck, causing it to stop short of the assault team. I had been a split second away from shooting it.

I always felt for the children who were in the compounds we raided. We only used explosive breaching if the threat level was justified, as it posed a risk to any occupants sleeping out under the stars, which they did on particularly hot nights. Having your home raided by strangers in NVG would be startling for any adult, let alone young kids, who reacted as kids anywhere would—by crying and screaming. It made me feel horrible every time it happened. That said, the Taliban were known to be ruthless, often arming their kids and using them as human shields, so we always had to be cautious.

On one DA, Chucky and I joined an assault team, and we entered a compound with numerous rooms where about thirteen children were sleeping on straw mats on the floor. We turned our torches on and scanned the room, looking for any weapons or threats. The shock of the assault sent one of the kids into an epileptic fit, and he was soon on the ground with his eyes rolled to the back of his head. The adults who lived in the compound, petrified of being shot, refused to help the kid, so I called the medic forward to treat him. The kid recovered, but it was a surreal experience and always stuck in my head.

On another DA, we conducted an explosive breach on a compound that looked more complex than the satellite imagery had shown—what was supposed to be a single compound with one large room turned out to be a covered area that joined multiple compounds, each with its narrow walkways, kitchens and sleeping areas next to the water system.

After the teams made entry, dozens of people seemed to be running around the compound, and all the soldiers were scream-ing at the occupants to get their hands up or sit down—in seconds, it became chaotic. Team integrity disappeared as operators moved to the highest-priority areas, leaving others to call for a buddy and continue the assault.

As I have mentioned, if I could identify one thing an SF operator needs in combat, it would be restraint. For a soldier, the decision to pull the trigger can have just as catastrophic a consequence as not pulling the trigger, and only training and experience provide the tools to make that decision. On that DA, I came close, but my training ensured I didn't shoot. As I moved down a small hallway, visibility was poor from the lack of ambient light and the dust that was getting kicked around the compound. As the direction of our assault had gone to shit, we just paired up and cleared everything we could. At the end of the hallway, I saw a figure with a weapon pointed at me. I placed my laser on him, flicked off my safety catch, and called out our codeword to identify friendlies. When I heard nothing back, I took up the first pressure of my trigger, ready to drop him. But I still did not have a clear positive identity as per my rules of engagement (ROE), so I moved closer, my barrel pointed at his head. In a few steps, the dust had cleared, and I could see it was another operator—his ears were ringing from the breach, and he hadn't heard my 'friendly' call. That's all it took. One bad decision under stress and the consequences could be catastrophic.

On these DAs, I was often surprised by the reactions of the non-combatant adult occupants of the compounds. The women would always turn away, refusing to make eye contact with us 'infidels', and the men had a type of steadfastness—they never seemed to show any emotion, which I always found off-putting; it also increased the tension, as it was easy to mistake ambivalence for ill intent. The men's hands would shake in fear, but their faces were hard to read. They aged quickly, a by-product of the harsh environment and lifestyle. Most compounds contained little more than cooking and sleeping quarters, with livestock and dogs scattered throughout.

Our own mood going in was always tense, as we never knew what awaited us in the compound. Regardless, most of the raids were unopposed, and we would clear and detain any suspects before they had time to react, which was, on paper, the desired outcome. Every operator hoped to win the golden ticket, though: an opposed DA where we could put our CQB skills to the test. Alpha Company did not have to wait long.

Objective Saffire was a medium-level commander in the northern parts of Uruzgan province and had been on the Joint Priorities Elimination List for some time. Previous raids had taken us into dry holes, which happened often. This time, the platoon-sized assault force would insert via Australian CH-47 Chinooks,[27] which were still operational at the time. Having Aussies fly us in rather than the Americans was a welcome change.

We were inserted early in the morning about 8 kilometres away from our target, well out of audible range, and commenced our long walk to the target village. We spent most nights staring through two green tubes, our NVG, which always gave me a headache after hours of use, but they were necessary to give us the advantage at night.

As we approached the green belt, I was surprised by the size and complexity of the cluster of compounds. High walls topped with a barbed wire fence, as well as a maze of walkways and aqueducts, made it difficult to get oriented. To make matters more difficult, the map we were using was outdated, and the satellite imagery didn't help due to tree cover on the main target compounds.

Our team was tasked with providing a cordon to the east for the first stage of the assault, then, on command, to clear a large compound that stood apart from the main cluster. The compound had a creek system to its east, with the remaining buildings running parallel to the north. The night was cold, and once we got to our cordon position, our clothes, drenched in sweat, had us shivering, praying to get moving again so we could generate some heat.

On receiving the order, the first assault team entered and engaged a guard positioned outside the main doors to the target building. We heard a succession of rapid suppressed shots, then our radios reported the occurrence: 'All callsigns, one enemy KIA, team in contact, wait out.' The engagement had alerted the village, and dogs started barking everywhere. The enemy began yelling into their radios, trying to find out what had happened.

As platoon HQ approached, 'G-train'—our nickname for the platoon JTAC—spotted a fighter running from a compound adjacent to the target building. The fighter was positively identified and G-train and Sam, the platoon commander, engaged him through vegetation. The enemy fighter, dressed from head to toe in white, narrowly avoided being shot, but would later be captured.

G-train and Sam advanced on the compound the enemy fighter had fled from, searching for an entry point. 'As I approached, about two feet from an external corner, a fighter ran around the corner and was so close that he almost ran his chest straight into my suppressor,' G-train recalled. 'At that range, his chest took up my full vision under NVG but I could see the middle of an AK variant across his chest. I immediately fired two rounds at point-blank range. The instant screaming was deafening. I didn't look down as he fell, knowing more fighters were potentially behind him. I instinctively went straight over the top of him as he fell screaming, got up and went around the corner, without realising what had occurred in the seconds prior. It just happened without thinking.'

Immediately after rounding the corner, G-train spotted an entry point with a curtain hanging over it. On his approach, another armed fighter pulled back the curtain to exit the compound. 'I fired another two rounds instantly and he either fell or withdrew, curtain dropping in front of him. I wasn't sure I had hit him,' said G-train. 'We quickly stacked either side of the entry. Sam prepared a fragmentation grenade and threw it into the room. After it exploded, I immediately made entry and on the way through, my NVG got caught on the curtain and flipped up onto the top of my helmet. Sam was straight in behind me, we're now inside a compound full of frag dust from the grenade, with potentially at least one active fighter inside. He has better eyes than me as I've just gone from night vision to zero vision.'

G-train moved to the corner of the room, unable to see. He didn't take his hands off his weapon; he was waiting for muzzle flashes to locate and re-engage the enemy. After clearing the room, they found the third fighter in the doorway, directly inside the curtain—he had been shot and killed on initial engagement. They called for another team to assist in the clearance, as they were facing a huge compound, with multiple rooms and doorways, one of which contained a dozen women and children. Another team came in to support them, and the compound was soon cleared and secured.

It was a fast, violent start to the assault. 'It was all reaction-ary; we went off instinct,' said G-train. 'It was a textbook DA raid. Helo'd into a neighbouring valley, a long foot insertion over high terrain, we didn't get compromised until we were on top of the target compound; a medium-value individual died on target. It's a credit to our training that it played out the way it did that night.' Hundreds of hours of training in room combat had paid dividends for the men of Alpha Company, as it would countless times for the rest of the men of 2 Cdo Regt in the Afghanistan war.

After all the compounds in the vicinity were cleared and secured, the dead enemies were searched and photographed. The enemy who had appeared in the doorway, below the curtain, was identified as Objective Saffire.

From my own team's location at the cordon, we eagerly scanned the bush near us to ensure we were not surprised by enemies who may have escaped from the compounds and decided to take revenge for their killed mates. The ISF platform operators then came on station and informed us there was a lot of movement in the compound directly to our north—the compound our team was to clear in the second stage of the assault. I could feel my heart beating faster, anticipating what was to come.

We shook out into an assault formation and moved slowly towards the compound, whose main entrance was directly in line with our approach. The ISF platform operators were still monitoring the compound and keeping us updated on the movement they could see. Tim and I arrived at the entrance first, and I slowly angled around the left side to look inside.

The compound was larger than I thought; I saw at least a dozen doorways on the far side, with more rooms to the right, about 30 metres away. I informed the team that there were a lot of rooms and debated whether we should wait for another team. We explained the situation to the platoon commander, who directed us to clear the compound, as the other teams were still busy clearing their primary areas.

We slowly made entry and did our best to scan all the rooms—we needed to cover three or four doorways per person. I approached the first door and shone my infrared light into the room. On the floor lay twelve people, all completely still. I am unsure what they were hoping to achieve, as the infrared light of our NVG shone on their eyes, illuminating them like cats' eyes in torchlight.

Nobody moved when I ordered them in Pashtun to show me their hands. I was stunned. Chucky came over to my room when he heard me ordering the occupants, as his rooms had been empty.

'What the fuck are they doing?' he asked as he stood beside me in the doorway.

'Mate, I have no idea,' I responded. Chucky then tried his hand with his dubious Pashtun and ordered them to raise their arms—still nothing.

Chucky looked at me, and we both started laughing, finding humour in this bizarre predicament. In the middle of southern

Afghanistan, we were in a raid where people were being killed less than 50 metres away, and we were playing hide and seek with a bunch of people pretending they hadn't noticed an assault force sweep through. We were both in hysterics.

A string of shots in the compounds to the south brought us back to reality, and we decided to get an interpreter to our location while we stood in the doorway, our guns trained on the room's occupants. I was concerned about those whose hands I could not see, and focused on them as they posed the most risk. The interpreter entered the room, and we soon had everyone up against the wall, searching and cuffing the fighting-aged males. Still, to this day, I am unsure exactly why twelve grown men were lying together in the dark.

Afterwards, a call came over the radio asking for assistance with the site exploitation (information collection) of the compound the platoon HQ team had cleared, and I moved over to lend a hand. This was the compound with the two enemies KIA, and it was the first time I saw the dead bodies up close.

One of the fighters had been shot in the abdomen numerous times and had part of his intestines protruding, with his PKM machine gun next to him. A few metres away, his mate was lying face down in the dirt, his arms underneath his body with his legs twisted behind him. The first dead enemy still had his eyes and mouth open, which I found bizarre. I can't recall having any emotion outside of morbid curiosity: 'This is what a dead body looks like.'

The other thing I found strange was the smell. I had read about 'the smell of death' before, but having been killed in such a traumatic way, the stench of the bodies was palpable, and I would best describe it as a sickly-sweet smell. One had shit himself, a common event in the last stages of life, but the sickly-sweet smell overpowered even the smell of faeces. I was jealous of the lads who had cleared that compound. I am not ashamed to say that I too hoped to get my chance to kill the enemy at close range in a compound, as the assault platoons had.

This feeling was common among SF operators. We had spent thousands of hours on the range mastering our weapons, shooting paper, steel and robots. We were trained to kill the enemy at close range, and we all wanted to test ourselves. At that moment, there was no thought as to why we were in Afghanistan or that the enemy might have a son, daughter or mother. We wanted to kill the enemy, as that was what we had trained for—it was that simple.

One day we witnessed some disturbing elements of Afghan culture. We were on our way back to TK from a DA when we were redirected to an area near Chora to try to capture a Taliban commander. Intelligence had suggested that he was potentially having a meeting in a village in the valley. It was a time-sensitive task, and we approached the compound we hoped to find him in shortly after dusk. Once again, we were the ladder team, and as I slowly made my way up the ladder, I saw something that still disturbs me to this day.

Inside a large room in the compound, a group of grown men, some with long white beards, sat on mats drinking tea, while two young boys in bracelets and makeup stood dancing in the centre. The kids were no older than eight or nine and had a look of defeat and sadness in their eyes. I watched the assault team make their entry, and the compound was secure in a few seconds.

I wanted to know what the kids were doing, so I asked one of the interpreters after the assault. His answer shocked me.

'Sir, they are dancing boys, *chai* boys,' he told me. 'In the tribal regions, they have a saying—women are for babies, boys are for pleasure.'

I felt sick. I stared at the group of men who were now handcuffed and sitting down facing a wall. At that moment, I could have walked up and put a bullet in the back of their heads.

Towards the end of the trip, we were tasked with a company-sized ambush of a crucial transit route for Taliban fighters moving into Uruzgan province, known as a 'rat line'. The night was cold, and the walk-in from our vehicles was agonisingly long—our bodies were starting to feel the effects of a long deployment.

To get to the ambush site undetected, we had to move through rugged terrain. Tim and I needed to cut a path through thick lantana bushes with our secateurs, which was bloody hard work. I had flashbacks to cutting my way through the jungle of Atabai in Timor; I'd never expected to encounter such thick vegetation in Afghanistan.

When we crossed a running river that came up to our necks, I knew we were in for a rough night. We moved up to a series of compounds, where the owner made us hot chips, still the tastiest potato chips I have ever had. Maybe I was just happy to have warm food. We took turns to maintain the ambush position and get some rest behind the compound's wall.

We had only one pair of puffer pants and a single puffer jacket between the five of us, which we each took turns wearing for 30 minutes before passing them on to the next person. The two hours waiting for the jacket went painstakingly slowly, and time seemed to speed up when you had the jacket or pants on. Chucky and I ended up spooning to try to retain body heat. Seconds felt like hours, and I prayed for the enemy to walk into the ambush site so we could at least get moving and warm up.

The enemy did not enter the ambush site, and the sun rose over the mountains around us. The cold always intensified before the first light, and we all lay around shivering, waiting for the glorious sun to shine on us. I have spent many nights in my career wet and cold, but that ambush would have to be one of the worst nights I've ever had. The discomfort was exacerbated by our having gotten drenched from the river, and the requirement to minimise noise and movement. After sunrise, we were glad to get moving again.

CHAPTER 18

TEN SHOTS, ONE KILL

I enjoyed a long leave break from Afghanistan before returning to work to prepare for my sniper course, and then began training for Alpha Company's next deployment in early 2010. I was living in a two-bedroom unit with my girlfriend, Sarah, who had moved in before my deployment in 2008. Sarah had almost no idea what we had been doing in Afghanistan, as she was still new to the military scene.

One night after some beers, I was showing some video of our rotation to my best mate Leithen, whom I had grown up with and known since primary school, when Sarah sat down to join us. The footage was from Operation Peeler in Mirabad, and Sarah watched wide-eyed.

'Is that training? What are you guys shooting at?'

'The enemy, Sarah—the Taliban,' I responded.

'You were fighting the Taliban?' she asked.

I am unsure precisely what Sarah thought we were doing there, but it seemed news to her that we were fighting a war. In her defence, however, I had significantly downplayed our role in the deployment, to both her and my family, as I saw zero utility in making them worry. I had told them my primary role would be training the Afghans in the safety of the base.

On 3 April 2009, 4 RAR (Cdo) had suffered its first serious combat casualty—the unit's luck on continuous vehicle operations could not have lasted much longer. On a Bravo Company patrol heading towards Sultan Rabat, where I had been with Alpha Company the year before, Damien 'Iceman' Thomlinson's SRV hit an IED, causing him significant injuries, including the loss of both his legs. Private Scott Palmer came to his aid and provided lifesaving treatment. When the IED struck Damien's vehicle, cheers could be heard from the nearby village.

Thomlinson was the first commando to be seriously injured, but Bravo Company had also lost Sergeant Brett Till, an engineer from IRR who stood on a pressure plate IED during a clearance, on 19 March. IED strikes were beginning to take their toll on Bravo Company. After the death of Brett, and Damien's injuries, vehicle operations would take longer, as IRR and the drivers approached every inch of their route more cautiously.

Bravo Company's rotation would also slowly transition from continual vehicle operations to more RW helicopter insertions. 'It was a relief, after losing Brett and Iceman. We were happy to be flying over IEDs rather than driving over them,' recalled Dave Parker, a TL on the rotation. We'd hit three IEDs in three weeks in soft-skin vehicles. We were over it.'

The regiment had decided to remove the recon teams from each company and replace them with an extra sniper team. The rationale was that a sniper team could perform the same function as a recon team and also use precision fire. Our entire team was panelled on the SF sniper course in early 2009. The only person who would not be joining us was Tim, who would be returning to an assault team. He was replaced by Anthony, with whom I had completed my reo.

I met Anthony Dimov around 2005 at 3 RAR and we became close; we are still close today. Anthony's parents are Macedonian, and he speaks with a slow drawl, never one to waste words. Over the years, I would make a sport out of mocking his slow speech, calling him 'a simple cunt'. Anthony is very intelligent and an excellent soldier, but people would mistake his laissez-faire attitude and unhurried speech for slowness. I never got over how surprised people were to realise his high intelligence as they got to know him.

Anthony was a welcome addition to our team, and our constant banter and sledging provided endless entertainment for the rest of the group. The pranks we played on each other were endless, dating back to the 2006 Timor trip in the recon/sniper platoon. Anthony's favourite was fabricating stories about me during trips outside the wire.

After my bike was shot in Mirabad, Anthony told our 3 RAR mates on their regular army rotation at TK that I had accidentally discharged my rifle into it. There had been no gunfight at all. The story spread quickly. I called a mate in Charlie Company back home, and the first thing he asked was about the bike. 'Mate, what the fuck?! How did you shoot your bike, you shit-fight?' It infuriated me, and I plotted my revenge on Anthony. This cycle continues to this day.

Despite never really having an interest in being a sniper, I looked forward to learning a new skill, and particularly to deploying on our next rotation as a sniper. The SF sniper course contained two key elements: green roles, which were like the RAR basic and supervisor courses; and black roles, which qualified snipers to be employed in the sniper platoon on the TAG, where I would end up a few years later in one of my three TAG-E rotations.

We spent weeks on the range mastering the basics of the SR98 sniper rifle,[28] and spent countless hours in the classroom learning about ballistics and all the laws of physics that are in play when a bullet travels through the air. We learned how to camouflage and prepare our equipment and approach a target without being seen, as remaining undetected and getting close enough to taking a shot are essential for a sniper's survival on the battlefield.

We enhanced our critical infantry skills—judging distance in the field and scanning and observing the bush—and learned how to interpret and accurately report what we saw. Sniping is not all about the shooting, although that is a crucial component; a lot of the work involves observing an area, accurately recording it, and reporting what we see.

The sniper is the commander's eyes and ears on the battlefield, and we needed to know how to report accurately to commanders so they could make critical decisions. The cost of getting it wrong could be catastrophic for the assaulters we were supporting.

For the black role component, we learned how to make hides in rooms and buildings, and to support a TAG assault by setting up our guns to take shots into buildings with hostages. Additionally, we learned how to use specific communications and image-capture equipment that would provide real-time intelligence to the commanders planning the recovery of hostages. This training occurred in rural areas, as well as in buildings, planes, buses and trains all around Sydney, and I thoroughly enjoyed it.

Towards the end of the course, we learned how to use more sniper weapons, including the .50 calibre Barrett, which I carried as one of two primary Barrett shooters in the team for the next SOTG. It was a big gun, weighing 16 kilograms, and each ten-round magazine weighed close to 2 kilograms, every gram of which I would soon feel in the mountain ranges of southern Afghanistan.

We worked on shooting at longer ranges, which is more guess-work than anything else, at least at first. It could only be mastered through constant training in varying environmental conditions, particularly wind.

In the old days, when snipers would shoot, they would record the environmental conditions in a shooter's log, providing a reference for the next shooter to use later. This was problematic for several reasons. Firstly, there was the presumption that when a shot was to be taken operationally, the conditions on that day would exactly replicate the data collected in the shooter log. This was short-sighted due to the constant variations in environmental conditions.

Certain variables, such as the adjustments for bullet drop[29] at shorter ranges, could be recorded and applied with a level of accuracy, as the variations are minor. But accurately calculating at ranges above 800 metres was more problematic, and so snipers were required to capture 'data' every time there was a significant change in temperature, altitude and surface pressure.[30] This would have to be repeated for every bullet variation.

The sight, or scope, of a sniper rifle was the brains of the gun, and was used to angle the sight either closer to or further away from the line of the barrel, depending on the distance of the shot, and to angle it on the horizontal plane to adjust for wind. Once the firer determined the shot's distance, they would input changes to the scope, known as 'clicks', which would sometimes be predetermined for specific environmental conditions. Alternatively, if the scope couldn't be adjusted, the firer would physically move the barrel, known as 'aiming off'. This was less accurate, and typically used when there was no time to adjust the sight.

A sniper must consider numerous factors, categorised as deterministic or non-deterministic variables. For example, the distance to the target, ammunition type, muzzle velocity, cant (angle of the rifle), station pressure and temperature can all be determined with accuracy, as can the wind at the location of the firer. Variables that cannot be determined accurately mainly come down to the wind conditions beyond the sniper's location, the archnemesis of the long-range shooter.

Even if the wind were consistent, the sniper can only ascertain wind speed and direction from the firing point; the further the shot, the less the sniper's ability to judge what the wind is doing and its effect on the bullet's flight. Only experience and practice, therefore, can enhance a sniper's ability to read and understand wind. Shots at longer distances, particularly in the terrain found in Afghanistan, add further complexity.

Wind travels differently over flat ground than it would a feature such as rolling hills or mountain ranges, and it's even harder to judge on a flat open desert, with no trees or leaves to indicate the wind speed and direction.

As I would find out in my next deployment, wind direction can change every few hundred metres, and making a first-round hit is almost impossible. Add a moving target, and your chances are even lower. Hollywood movies where a sniper takes a headshot at 900 metres on a vehicle travelling at 60 kilometres per hour just make me laugh, it's so unrealistic. An experienced sniper and good luck could, however, make it possible.

In my experience, an excellent long-range sniper is not someone who gets a first-round shot, although that is a crucial test at a shorter distance to qualify as a TAG sniper. A good sniper is someone who can adjust rapidly from their first miss, which tells them everything they need to know about the environmental conditions of the bullet's flight path for that moment in time.

In 2014, the sniping trade was revolutionised when Bryan Litz, an American aerospace engineer and avid competitive shooter, collaborated with Todd Hodnett, a Texan competitive shooter, to develop arguably the most comprehensive long-range shooting course in the world. Their Accuracy 1st teaching has been adopted by every Western SF unit, and has filtered down to most conventional army snipers too.

The core of their teachings encourages shooters to move away from the 'hard data' in a shooter's log. It instead incorporates a more scientific approach, leveraging long-known principles of flight and rocket science to create a system that mimics the flight calculations made using density altitude to ensure aircraft have enough lift to remain airborne. For sniping, the formula is a combination of temperature, station pressure and humidity.

The operator inputs these variables into a ballistic calculator or solver that uses this formula for density altitude. The calculator provides solutions for shooting at two specific ranges. The firer shoots at the provided ranges until they hit the target, then adds the density altitude to the solver. Once the gun is 'trued' in this way,[31] the firer can calculate the density altitude at any spot on the planet, then feed those inputs into the solver. The solver provides precise bullet drop measurements for that environment, meaning only wind will have to be accounted for if the sniper has to fire.

The truing method means that snipers no longer have to carry around shooting logs with hundreds of data variables, but instead have a workable scientific solution for sniper calculations. I attended the second Accuracy 1st course in Singleton delivered to 2 Cdo Regt and SASR snipers, and despite some of the formulas taking time to sink in, it was revolutionary for me.

The rifling, or twists, inside a barrel cause the bullet to spin as it leaves the muzzle, providing it with the stability necessary for accurate shooting. Having longer barrels allows sniper guns to increase the 'spin' of the bullet, and the spinning of the bullet also must be accounted for in long-range shooting. As the bullet spins continually in one direction, it will also start to shift towards the direction of the spin. This is known as the 'Magnus effect'.[32] The effect the wind has on the spin of a bullet—known as 'ballistic jump'—must also be accounted for. A strong enough wind at right angles to the direction of the shot would cause the round to go either high or low, depending on the wind direction, adding more variables for the sniper to consider.

It was a long course, lasting more than ten weeks, and despite enjoying it I was glad it was over. We spent time long-range shooting in the Hunter Valley at the Singleton Military Area, where we got trigger time behind the primary guns we would employ on the deployment, and went through the usual pre-deployment build-up training.

During the Afghan campaign, usual regimental training was almost non-existent outside the TAG-E rotations, as was our attendance at extensive ADF exercises. Our sole focus was the TAG-E and Afghanistan.

Everything we did was to prepare, deploy, take leave, and deploy again. Many operators changed companies to get as many trips as possible. I even tried to jump ship to Charlie Company, but Garry had convinced me to stay in his team to do the sniper course.

In September 2009, we headed back to Cultana to complete our MRE. Like last time, we trained mainly for vehicle operations and with Black Hawks from the 6th Aviation Regiment, which was based at Holsworthy. I got plenty of time behind the Barrett, and was growing in confidence at hitting targets at further ranges.

SF training is inherently risky, conducted on the edge of what is acceptable by common ADF standards. SASR, Australia's long-established SF unit, had suffered numerous training deaths and had averaged one fatality per year since its inception, most of which occurred during training.[33] Every operator prepares himself for the reality of war and the likely chance that some of them will be killed. But nobody ever expects it to happen on the training field.

Our sniper teams were on a different training roster from the assault platoons, and we were back at our accommodation one evening cleaning our weapons when someone from CHQ came running down to us: 'Where's Garry? We have a no-duff [real-life] priority-one casualty—a gunshot wound to the head. Grab your bikes and get ready to head out to the range to help.'

We were stunned. What the fuck had happened? We all ditched our guns and ran to our bikes while Garry dashed to the command centre for further directions. A few minutes later, he ran out and yelled at Lance and me to ditch our bikes and grab one of the army ambulances, as all the medics were already out on the range.

Still unsure of where we were supposed to go, I grabbed my map while Lance jumped in the driver's seat, and we made some calls to find out which gates were open so we could get out to the range. We believed the casualty was at the 'kill house', a wooden structure built in the Cultana desert for us to train live-fire CQB. We didn't have a key and decided to drive through a gate if necessary.

We got hold of Garry, who told us there were two casualties and we needed to get the ambulance to a southern gate, as the casualties had been moved, adding to the confusion. I then got a call from one of the assaulters asking where we were. He told me it was Mason Edwards from Alpha Company who had been shot and that he was in a critical condition. I told Lance, who responded with a look of shock. What the fuck was going on?

After driving in the desert in the dark for a while, trying to figure out where we needed to go, we saw a helicopter with its lights on coming in to land a few hundred metres away and raced towards it.

The civilian CareFlight helicopter landed as we arrived. Meanwhile, the regimental medical officer (RMO) was conducting chest compressions on a casualty—it was indeed Mason Edwards.

It was a confronting site. The doctor talked to Mason as he continued his chest compressions, aided by medics and the civilian CareFlight team. I remember it like it was yesterday. 'C'mon Mason, come back to us, mate. C'mon, mate.' Mason had been shot in the head, and compressions weren't working, as he'd had no signs of life for a significant period. The decision was made to stop compressions, and he was pronounced dead by the RMO.

Two of Mason's close mates, who had been by his side, broke down straight away, and we all stood around in the dark, utterly stunned by what had just happened. Mason was dead. What the fuck? This was just supposed to be training.

It was an accident that should never have happened. Mason had found himself at the back of the wooden structure when an assault team made entry on the other side and engaged targets set up inside the rooms, unknowingly shooting him.

It is natural to want to blame individuals when training accidents like this occur, but multiple failures on the evening leading to Mason's death were uncovered, resulting in a complete review of how ADF conducts range practices.

As I would soon find out, though, the ADF's main aim is always to hold someone culpable and absolve itself of any wrongdoing.

The day after Mason's death, Chucky and I were tasked with assisting the AFP with the first stage of the investigation, which involved taking photos of everyone's guns and equipment, including Mason's. It had all been left at the exact spot it was in when Mason was killed.

As we got close to Mason's kit, flies buzzed around his helmet. The AFP officer asked me to pick up his gun, unload it and count the rounds, while they took photos. The officer then asked Chucky to pick up Mason's radio microphone, which was sitting in the dirt. I knew Chucky was close to Mason, as they had previously lived together, so when he hesitated, staring at the earpiece that had been in Mason's ear when he died, I offered to do it for him.

Amazingly, the ADF hierarchy's main concern at this stage was what type of helmet inserts Mason had. Back then, the issued lightweight helmet inserts, which included internal padding and chinstraps, were less than ideal, forcing most of us to purchase commercial, off-the-shelf options to increase our comfort, as we would spend much time wearing them in hot conditions. Despite everyone doing this, modifying issued equipment was not formally allowed. This is why the hierarchy was eager to find out what type of inserts Mason had in his helmet—they feared reprisal if they weren't as issued.

As Chucky and I returned to the camp, an officer approached us, frantic to find out about Mason's inserts. Chucky and I had been silent on the drive back, and he was visibly upset by the tasks we just completed. The officer stood there, eagerly awaiting a response, as Chucky stared at him, shaking. The officer looked at me, and I just shook my head as a warning not to push it. Chucky was a nice guy, but as strong as an ox and a great Muay Thai kickboxer. If he were pushed in this state, it would not end well for the officer. Reading Chucky's face, the officer nodded and stormed back into his office.

The mood on the MRE changed instantly, and all training stopped for the time being, to be continued later in northern New South Wales before our deployment. For most of us, the shock would turn to anger, then disbelief. Ultimately, the Commonwealth would be found culpable for Mason's death.

The year 2009 would also be significant for another reason. On 19 June, 4 RAR (Cdo) was officially renamed to the 2nd Commando Regiment (2 Cdo Regt). This signified the official rebirth of the newest special operations unit in Australia's arsenal, and the start of its rapid growth to the point where, at the time of writing, it's rated among the finest SF units in the world.

CHAPTER 19

SIERRA ONE-FIVE

The death of Mason had brought home to our friends and families the risks of the job, and I noticed a distinct difference in the farewell this time, as we boarded the bus for the airport from Tobruk Lines. Sarah had come to the base to see us off, and I recall sitting on the bus next to Chucky as we waved goodbye to Sarah and his girlfriend, Tess.

We flew via charter plane to the United Arab Emirates (UAE), where we would prepare and be issued ammunition before flying into TK. The UAE camp would later be named Camp Baird in honour of Corporal Cameron Baird VC, MG, who would be killed in action on 22 June 2013 and later be awarded Australia's hundredth Victoria Cross.

The base continued to grow exponentially and was home to hundreds of ADF personnel supporting operations in the Middle Eastern Area of Operations. After a few days of briefs and prepping our kit in the UAE, we boarded a C-130 for the flight to TK. Again, the aircraft came at a steep angle, and some of the guys who had not been before eagerly looked out the window, probably thinking the same thing I did on my first trip.

We arrived in TK and walked into Camp Russell, marked with a small sign of a kangaroo with a boomerang, and it occurred to me that some operators from SOCOMD would never get the chance to walk back through those gates after a job, as we would do hundreds of times over the course of many deployments. Still, I was excited to be back here, and despite the twelve months between deployments, it felt like I had only just left.

Unlike our previous rotation, this time we would see a gradual increase in the use of helicopters for insertion, as the IED risk and the number of Australians severely wounded or killed had increased to the point that it was difficult to justify using vehicles outside the wire. The decision to deploy the Australian-designed Bushmaster PMV had also saved many Australians' lives.

The politics inside Camp Russell were fraught, with an increasingly tumultuous relationship between 2 Cdo Regt and SASR. Although this is not the case now, back then it had a major impact on our rotations. At the start of the tour, the CO of the SOTG, an SASR officer, gave us a briefing. 'I have two Ferraris and only one set of wheels,' he said to the crowd of commandos as he attempted to justify why most of the air assets would be going to SASR. The moment that came out of his mouth, we knew 2 Cdo Regt was going to be stuck with the vehicles. SASR often referred to themselves as Australia's 'tier one' unit, using the US term that denotes specific capabilities within US SOCOM. When referring to commandos, they would generally dismiss us as 'just like the US Rangers', an attempt to minimise our role within SOCOMD.

SASR moved away from its traditional role as special reconnaissance, and took the lead in targeting Taliban leadership in Uruzgan province, leaving 2 Cdo Regt to continue disruption and vehicle operations. This eventually backfired on them, however, when FE-B, which was made up of commandos, picked up the counter-narcotics task with the US Drug Enforcement Agency in Helmand province against a tough and hardened enemy, and saw some of the most intense combat of the entire war.

Meanwhile, FE-A, the SASR fighters, continued to target the Taliban leadership in Uruzgan province. They weren't the only ones playing name games. We called them 'the TK police', playing on the fact that most of their operations were still in Uruzgan province, where the Taliban leadership were beginning to dwindle due to years of targeting by the SOTG.

Despite us living in the same compound, a cultural line in the sand had been drawn, which neither side crossed either socially or on the job. I can only recall a very few instances where joint operations were conducted. SASR's primary goal seemed to be to ensure they took any role they wanted—which they did for a significant period of time, as most of the SOTG COs were from SASR.

I can understand the SASR perspective. They had been at the apex of the ADF as the only special operations force for decades and, I suspect, viewed commandos as the new kids on the block who had no right being on the same rung of the SF ladder. But they should have recognised the exponential growth that had occurred since 4 RAR (Cdo), now 2 Cdo Regt, had broken away from the conventional army and slowly matured.

Each rotation on the TAG-E and SOTG helped our regiment grow in experience, structure and martial skills, as lived experience on the battlefield was directly injected into the companies' training cycles and CRTC. A culture of ruthless self-criticism and continual pursuit of excellence, where junior soldiers would have three or four combat rotations before they began their commando trade and promotion courses, cultivated fertile ground to review and change the content of our courses, tactics and procedures.

I do not wish to speak ill of SASR, as I believe they are the best strategic reconnaissance SF unit in the world, with a long and proud tradition stemming from the UK's 22 SAS through to operations in Vietnam and beyond. Nor do I wish to perpetuate the friction between the two regiments.

But I would be lying if I didn't outline the frustrations I feel at what I can only describe as decades of systemic stonewalling by the operator ranks and SASR leadership. As 2 Cdo Regt grew, we had to find our own feet through trial and error. Despite our partner unit on the west coast—the SASR—having vastly more experience in most skill sets, we didn't get to leverage their experience through either training or teamwork, and lost much time as a result.

Our regiment's relationships with Five Eyes (FVEY) special operations units—a multilateral agreement between the US, Canada, the UK, Australia and New Zealand—were jeopardised by SASR. Its members would denigrate 2 Cdo Regt as a conventional force at every turn, failing to acknowledge our capabilities and increasing combat experience. Even inside Camp Russell, despite living a few buildings down from us, they had a culture of never interacting with 'dos'. On this 2010 rotation, SASR had a carton board to keep track of a form of punishment through payment of beer that an SASR operator would incur if seen talking to a 'do'.

I was disappointed with the culture that developed between the units. And our operators weren't all innocent either. Stories of alleged fuck-ups on jobs by SASR would be spread with glee, regardless of their truth or validity.

How powerful SOCOMD would have been if this animosity had never existed, and how much information sharing and joint training would have benefited both units. If we had put the same time and effort we spent undermining each other into collaborating on developing tactics, techniques and procedures, SOCOMD would have been all the better.

Thankfully, this has changed. Selection for both SASR and commandos is now a joint course, and a re-alignment of priorities for both units has seen increased cohesion and interoperability, further strengthening Australia's special operations capability.

On this rotation our sniper team would operate independently, inserting up to 48 hours before the assault platoons to gauge patterns of activity and identify enemy movement in target areas. It was a classic recon/sniper task, and it was bloody hard work. Carrying everything we needed for three days on our backs as we made our way to an OP on the hills surrounding a valley, our packs were bursting at the seams. Countless times we spent the night walking around the mountains after a helicopter insertion to get to our OP unseen. Some of the most arduous walks I have ever done have been around the mountains of Kandahar province, where our sniper team would be placed on the high ground in support of the assault teams operating below us.

It was usually mundane work at the OP site, rotating between lying in hide locations, scanning the area below, and recording what we saw in a logbook or calling Garry forward if it needed attention immediately. We would then crawl back to the admin area, out of view of the hide site, and eat, sleep and complain about the heat or cold. The weather was unpredictable and never seemed to be anything in between the two extremes.

On one OP task supporting the assault platoons, Chucky observed a fighting-aged male moving along the top of the ridgeline behind us. He was reporting on the assaulters' position below and had yet to see our OP location. We got behind our guns, ready for a shot, but he kept ducking and weaving on the ridge, and at 600 metres with high winds, the chances of a hit were low. Garry tasked Chucky and me to grab our guns and follow him as we chased after the spotter.

For the next hour, we played a game of cat and mouse, moving fast enough to keep up with the spotter but also aiming not to give our positions away, as even with minimal kit, we were too loaded down with equipment to catch him if he saw us and fled. I was gasping for air the entire time, and carrying the Barrett, I struggled to keep up with Chucky and Garry.

Finally, we cornered him on a hill with a sheer cliff face on the other side. I was just behind Chucky as he slowly approached the spotter, gun to his shoulder, and flicked off his safety catch, ready to take a shot. I only had my Barrett, so I slung it over my shoulder and drew my pistol, moving to support him. The spotter still hadn't seen us. Because he had his back to us, we couldn't see if he was carrying a weapon, so we moved to get a better view as I took up the first trigger pressure on my pistol.

'Show me your hands,' Chucky commanded in Pashtu as the spotter nearly jumped a foot in fright, dropping his radio in the process. He didn't have a weapon.

We searched him, took him back to the OP site, and then walked him down to the assault platoons to be questioned and processed. He had an old brown wallet with a photo of his wife and three kids, and I wondered if this was a hardened enemy fighter or a farmer making a few dollars for his family. To me, he just looked like a scared young man.

Under the ROE, lethal force could be used against spotters if it was supported by signals intelligence, or if we saw people digging in IEDs, which was categorised as 'direct participation in hostilities'. Even though intelligence had confirmed the spotter before we left to catch him, Chucky and I decided not to kill him.

I have thought about that day for a long time. One part of me wished we had, as spotters were used to indicate our position for the enemy to lay IEDs, which would go on to kill numerous Australian soldiers in the war. The other part of me is glad we didn't. Moments like these played over in my mind as coalition forces withdrew from Kabul years later, leaving me to wonder what all the death and destruction had achieved. If we had killed him, he would have left a widow trying to raise her three children in the harsh tribal regions of southern Afghanistan. Chucky and I never spoke about it, but I know he felt the same way, and was glad we let the man live.

Combat Outpost Mashal, in the Chora Valley, north of the Baluchi Pass, was occupied by 6 RAR at the time. They had noticed a significant increase in IED activity in the area, which they had been unsuccessful in deterring through a constant program of patrolling and searches of buildings. A request was made to the SOTG to provide a clandestine sniper team to observe the valley and report on IED activity to increase security around the base, followed by the insertion of an assault platoon to support 6 RAR in a dismounted clearance of the surrounding valley.

We inserted via US Black Hawks on a feature a few kilometres to the south of Combat Outpost Mashal, which almost ended in disaster. The US Task Force No Mercy Black Hawk inserted on the face of a hill, with only its left wheels managing to touch the ground, which allowed us to throw our packs out and jump off. Lance, as the 2ic, was last out, and as he went to jump, the chopper lost lift and smashed into the rock shelf, tearing a hole in the bottom of the fuselage. It was pitch black, and the downwash from the rotors rendered our NVG useless; the only thing we could do was to get as low as possible, hoping the blades didn't cut us in half. With Lance still on board, the chopper lifted off and re-attempted the landing, eventually getting Lance off. This very hairy insertion was the first strike in a string of helicopter incidents that plagued us in Alpha Company.

I felt every step of the walk to the OP. I was pouring with sweat and had snot dripping from my nose when we finally arrived before dawn. We then rushed around getting things set up before it got too light.

We spent the next three days observing the valley, but couldn't see anything. Then, the signals operators at Mashal confirmed our radio operator's reports about enemy bomb placements, and the decision was made for our team to collapse off the OP and head into Mashal for further taskings.

As we had only prepared for an OP, we hadn't brought our body armour, only helmets for us to use our NVG; we would have been almost ineffective with the extra weight of armour. This meant we had no ballistic protection if we were to get in a gunfight in the valley. A 6 RAR patrol had only just returned to base without incident, though, which increased our confidence in the walk-down.

As the five of us approached the base, the 6 RAR lads were very surprised, not used to seeing a five-man patrol walk around the valley without body armour, wearing baseball caps and a different uniform. We had opted for multi-cam uniforms over the issued pattern, as it offered us greater concealment in our OPs. We greeted the 6 RAR boys, met the senior team leader and officers, and began coordinating movements for the following day.

As we were working, a signals operator ran up to Garry excitedly and told him he had reason to believe an enemy was in a cluster of compounds a few hundred metres away. Garry grabbed his map, ran to one of the towers on base, and began scanning the area, identifying a fighting-aged male on a handset on the roof of a compound. 'Get fucked, that's him,' Garry exclaimed. We ran back to our kit to grab our sniper rifles and get into position in the towers.

Garry's plan was to have three snipers in towers, then wait for the right moment to synchronise our shots, increasing the chances of a hit. Our radio operator kept giving Garry updates as we needed to meet certain thresholds of confirmation to apply lethal force within the ROE.

Once we were set, Garry sent for the platoon commander in charge of the base and updated him on his intent to engage the enemy on the building. The officer was shocked, claiming we did not have the authority to engage from his base. Garry replied that this was precisely what we were here to do. The officer then claimed we didn't have multiple sources reporting; our radio operator corrected him and said the criteria had been met, so it was ultimately Garry's call.

Garry explained that by engaging from the base, we would put the enemy on the back foot, which would then deter them from placing IEDs in the areas 6 RAR were patrolling. It was outside-the-box, proactive planning—precisely what we had been tasked with providing. A mate of mine from 6 RAR told me later that the key reason the officer was so resistant was that he had been spending much time in meetings trying to win the 'hearts and minds' of the locals, hoping this rapport would lead to intelligence on bomb makers in the area. Killing a local would complicate his efforts, which was a fair point. But all those meetings had done nothing to minimise the Taliban's effort to kill the 6 RAR men, and a more vigorous approach was just what was needed to disrupt the dynamic that had developed in the valley. Garry decided to go ahead as planned, leaving the officer to storm away to his command tent while we got behind our guns and waited for the right moment.

A few moments later, our target appeared on a wall outside the compound, shouting into his radio, giving orders for other fighters to move 'equipment' to the north, and asking where the other guys were. I already had the distance to the compound dialled in, while I looked around for wind markers that would indicate the wind-speed and direction. Wind wasn't too much of a concern, however, as the compound was only 500 metres away, and I had a .50 cal. This would be an easy day's work.

The man appeared to be in his early forties, with a thick black beard. He was slightly overweight, which was unusual in these parts. He was squatting down against a wall, still shouting into his handset, when two kids ran up the roof behind him and sat down, busily playing with something. 'Fuck,' I said out loud. 'Chucky, give me the exact distance to the cunt.'

My concern was getting the stability of my gun and the distance exact, to avoid the round going high into the children. Garry also spotted the kids and jumped on the radio, reminding us to check our range and ensure we had a stable firing platform.

Chucky confirmed the range, and I double-checked my data and dials, then got into position for the shot. Garry waited a few moments, hoping the fighter would move away from the kids, then, not wanting to waste the opportunity, began his calls for a co-ordinated shot. 'All callsigns, ready-ready, ready-ready.' I flicked my safety catch off, began my breathing cycle, went through my pre-firing checklist, then aimed the centre of my sights in the middle of the fighter's chest. But the radio went silent and I never heard the 'fire' command. What the fuck was going on? Chucky grabbed the radio and tried a radio check but only got feedback, unable to transmit.

We needed Garry to give us the command to fire, as he had indicated it would be a command-initiated shot. He had the radio operator with him, which provided us with the requirements to use lethal force. What the fuck was happening? I took my finger off the trigger as the enemy fighter sat up and walked out of sight around the corner of the building. Garry walked over to our tower and told us to pack up and head down. He looked furious, and stormed off towards the command post.

We had no proof, but our signaller thought the electronic countermeasures on one of the 6 RAR Bushmasters might have been turned on, rendering our radios and his specialist signals equipment useless.

I want to believe that a fellow Australian officer would not have done that. But as I would learn later when I conducted PSD tasks where we relied heavily on the conventional army, internal rivalries can undermine operations. It was a disappointing end to what would otherwise certainly have been another enemy fighter off the battlespace.

CHAPTER 20

TO KILL OR NOT TO KILL

The next day, November platoon, who had driven in from TK, left their PMVs inside Mashal to conduct a joint clearance in the green belt that Mashal was located in. The 6 RAR platoon would be separate from the 2 Cdo Regt teams, providing support while November conducted aggressive patrolling; the teams had specific areas of interest to clear. Our team would move out well before first light and occupy an overwatch position to the south, supporting the clearance from the north of the patrol base.

We moved out on foot under cover of darkness, using the vegetation to cover our walk into the most suitable position. Picking a spot at night that is also suitable by day can be difficult, so I moved a few times at the last minute, but I had my Barrett stabilised and my range cards filled out well before first light. For snipers, this is an imperative task so that you know precisely where your friendly troops are. Even ricocheted rounds from the Barrett can be fatal. If there is any risk, only in the most extreme circumstances would you shoot in the proximity of friendly troops.

In the first few hours, the assault platoon killed three fighters and one team chased an armed fighter into a compound. The shots alerted the valley to their presence, intelligence indicated the enemy was about to lay an IED, and was frantically trying to pinpoint the location of our patrols. I got on the radio and got a grid to the southernmost callsign, then began scanning for anyone digging in their path.

Around 500 metres away, I spotted a fighting-aged male running through a series of compounds before squatting down and peering around the edge of a wall. He was unarmed, but if he began digging in a road or pathway, and this observation was supported by intelligence, I could use lethal force. I lasered the exact distance, dialled in, and prepared to take the shot.

I looked at my map, called in the suspected fighter's location, and again asked for the southernmost location of our assault teams. The grid I was sent placed them less than 200 metres from the squatting man—I must have been too preoccupied with him and lost track of them. I got behind my gun and saw him in a clearing with his back to me, busy doing something on the ground. I did not see a weapon or him digging, so I could not be sure he met my ROE for lethal force.

Had I got the grid location wrong for the fighter digging? Was I walking the assault teams into the path of an IED? I turned to Davis and asked him to double-check the grid. As he pulled his map out, shots rang out in the green belt; one of the teams was in contact. I scanned to further up the valley and could see movement, but I couldn't identify if they were friendlies; I now faced a dilemma. Had the assault platoon become too preoccupied with its TIC and lost track of the grid I'd given them? I could not allow them to hit an IED.

I placed my crosshairs on the squatter's back and took up the first trigger pressure. 'Turn around, cunt, show me a shovel—give me something,' I thought. Again, I scanned to the north. I could see an assaulter moving through the green belt, gun at his shoulder. I jumped on the radio and asked all callsigns to stop, as they could be walking into an IED, but the teams were busy on their radio network, and I couldn't get my message through.

Never in my life have I been so conflicted. Should I kill the suspect only to find out he was a farmer and that I'd taken an innocent life? Or should I let him live and risk another Australian dying from an IED? My mind was racing. I had to decide.

Suddenly, an explosion right in front of the squatting man echoed through the valley and his body disappeared in a cloud of black smoke and dust, with limbs and ripped clothing flying 6 metres high.

He was a Taliban fighter, it turned out, and he had accidentally set off his own IED. I breathed a sigh of relief and relaxed my shoulders, not realising how tense my upper body had been. I called it in on the radio, then there was another explosion to my north a few moments later. What the fuck was going on?

On the radio, one of the assaulted teams reported that they had come across another blown-apart body—own goal number two. 'Better them than us,' I thought. 'They must have the B team out today.' Still, watching a human body get ripped apart so violently was unsettling.

The drive out of the patrol base and back to TK the next day sticks in my mind the most. The four enemies killed the previous day were being buried in a ceremony at the local cemetery beside the road out of the village. As we approached, hundreds of locals paused and stared at us. I distinctly remember the men who stared down the convoy—they gave us a look of pure hatred I had never seen before. I want to say I wasn't intimidated, but I knew it wouldn't have taken much for a suicide IED to hit one of our cars, they were so close.

Sitting away from the men was a huddle of women and children. The kids were all crying, and the women stood and joined the men staring at us. Usually, when we entered compounds, the women would cover their faces and turn away. On this day, however, they stood there staunch, with disdain in their eyes.

Not a word was spoken on the radio or in our car; everyone was thinking the same thing as me.

I didn't feel guilt, but I did question our purpose in serving here. Yes, we had killed 'the enemy', as occurs in war. But to witness the aftermath—a funeral—somehow brought home the gravity of it.

Weren't we there to make their lives better? I am sure our presence in the valley for those few days created more Taliban fighters, which would be a barrier to improving the locals' quality of life.

One other sniper OP task sticks with me. Our team had inserted via chopper into an area in Kandahar province one night, and we had our electronic warfare radio operator and his interpreter with us. The terps were either Afghan nationals who had been security-vetted, or US citizens who spoke fluent Pashto, also with the high-security clearances needed to work with SOTG.

Our usual male terp had gone home on leave on this job, so we were provided with a woman at the last minute. She was a 23-year-old of Afghan descent from California who had worked in the headquarters building for the past eight months. We were initially concerned about her experience outside the wire, but were informed there were no more terps available, as this was a last-minute task, and that she had been vetted and was more than capable. It was a 48-hour task, and, as usual, our packs were heavy with water, food, ammo and equipment.

Chucky was tasked with keeping an eye on her, and after a few movements, they began falling behind and slowing the patrol. A helicopter insertion lets the entire area know where you are, so getting as much distance as possible between you and the aircraft is essential for a small team. I kept watch to our front as Garry returned to Chucky and the terp to find out what was keeping them.

Chucky indicated that she kept falling over, and the boys soon realised that she had never used NVG before. Aside from learning where all the controls are, it takes some time to get used to the depth perception and narrow field of view they provide.

Regardless, we were on the ground now, so we had to give her a quick lesson on the NGV and then start the walk up the hill. Walking up steep hills in a full pack never gets any easier no matter how often you do it, even with our 'pack fitness' acquired from repeated foot insertions. For the young woman, it was all too much. She slowed us down to the extent that Chucky ended up grabbing her pack, throwing it on top of his, grabbing her arm and dragging her up the hill.

She was nervous and utterly unprepared for the task. On the second morning, after shivering through rain and sleet, I spotted three fighting-aged males leave the cluster of compounds we were watching and disappear into the valley below the hill we were on. We couldn't be sure they weren't armed, and if we were compromised, we would have to extract anyway, so we moved into a defensive position, waiting to grab the men if they discovered us or kill them if they had weapons.

As we lay there in wait, the terp hit her limit and went into a panic attack, hyperventilating as she curled up behind a rock. The signaller tried to console her, but we had bigger fish to fry. After twenty minutes or so, we spotted the men on a feature to the south. They were unarmed and had been moving to a group of sheep they were herding.

The incident so shook the girl that she refused to move from behind the rock, even going so far as to urinate in a bottle in front of the team rather than walking back to the clearing we had been using.

The young woman was sent back to Operations Room. The situation wasn't her fault, but she would have significantly compromised the team if we had broken contact.

We continued our routine of short-duration missions for the next few weeks leading into April. There was little action except for an insertion into the town of Gizab, north of TK in Daykundi province, in a combined operation with FE-A. The locals, fed up with the Taliban, had begun an uprising, and political allies of the coalition had asked for assistance. The SOTG was stood up to insert via US Black Hawk helicopters. We needed more time to prepare, and we were told that FE-A had inserted and were gathering local PRC troops to plan a defence of the town.

As FE-A inserted, their helicopters were engaged by small-arms fire, which ceased once they landed. But when the remainder of FE-A and FE-B landed in a wheat field, in place of the hordes of enemies we were expecting, we disembarked to the cheers and waves of thousands of locals who had gathered to repel the Taliban. It was more a strategic play than a tactical action.

Another time, weeks of vehicle-mounted missions led the company to hit another IED, injuring three soldiers, and fighter jets were called in to destroy the damaged vehicle. Fatigue was starting to set in, as is typical on a deployment. Each trip has a particular time, before halfway, when the novelty rapidly wears off and the end seems so far away. This period can be dangerous, as repetitive missions that lead to no meaningful outcome wear thin and complacency sets in. During such a low-tempo period, I did something on the range at TK that would be one of the lowest points of my career in the army.

CHAPTER 21

THE BACK DECK

Live-fire ranges in the ADF are not what people would expect when they think of military training. The movies have people running around shooting guns with bombs exploding everywhere, which could not be further from the reality. Live-fire training is a highly controlled, detailed and planned training event, with all the usual risk-mitigation strategies and qualifications necessary to run a safe practice.

SF range control courses are done in the SOCOMD through the SAS or commando trade module, but SF operators must also attend the regular ADF range safety supervisor and OIC courses for the varying types of ranges, ammunition and ordinance. There is a perception among conventional ADF that SF conducts unsafe range practices that are free from rules and regulations; this could not be further from the truth.

SF training is different from regular ADF training, as SF are required to maintain an advanced skill level. For example, the infantry battalions on a typical training cycle may live-fire a few times a month, at best. They do this on typically highly controlled ranges and not in complex environments, such as rooms and buildings, as there are no suitable facilities for such training. That, however, is slowly changing.

On a TAG-E rotation, on the other hand, we would live-fire multiple times a week, dedicating an entire year to counterterrorism and hostage rescue (HR) training. This requires a high skill level in varying environments with multiple weapons, which can only be mastered through time and repetition. Despite this, even on a TAG-E build-up there is a progression of training, where operators and TLs are validated, then allowed to progress to more advanced training, such as multi-team live-fire under NVG or shoot reduced angles.[34]

All coalition forces used the range at TK, which was just a point on the outer HESCO walls of the base where we could fire into the empty desert. We would shoot everything from 9mm pistols through to our 84mm rockets, but the range didn't have any of the things a range back home required, such as blast- and splinter-proof cover or specific firing bays for grenades.

Some practices for platoon training were run along the same lines at TK as at ranges back home, with a safety brief, a safety vehicle and a medical plan. For operational reasons, however, the boys would also just go up and shoot from the wall by themselves. If, for example, we had a short time between jobs and the armourers had just repaired one of our weapons, we would quickly drive up and test-fire our guns before rolling out on a mission.

On 10 April, our team was pencilled in to conduct aerial fire support training with the Americans in a few days, so Garry directed Davis, Lance and me to go the range to dry zero the sights required for aerial fire support, which involved fitting and aligning a secondary, non-telescopic sight, and said he would be up later for us to live-fire. The three of us prepared our sights and waited for Garry, but after an hour we decided he must have been held up at HQ, as TLs often were.

Still, we wanted to get our guns ready for the next day's training. I was confident in the dry zero of our sniper rifles, but I wanted to make sure the 40mm grenade launcher was also prepared, as we planned to fire it from the choppers. I then made a decision that will haunt me to this day, one that I have played over and over in my head, trying to understand what I was thinking.

I told the boys I was going to fire a few rounds of 40mm, to which I received no pushback. Then I picked up the launcher, chambered one round of 40mm, and stood up on the HESCO. Lance jumped up and joined me, and we discussed what range I should shoot at, agreeing on a range appropriate for the aerial fire support training. I flicked the safety catch off, took aim, and fired.

The 40mm round exploded around 15 metres in front of us, throwing debris and dust over the firing point. On the other side of the HESCO, piles of ammunition liners and rubbish had been thrown over the wall and had built up over the years. The 40mm round had clipped the top of a pile of ammo liners. I then turned to my left and saw Lance, clearly injured by shrapnel from my round, drop to the floor holding his face as blood poured out of him. My heart skipped a beat.

Lance was bleeding profusely from his face, but he was still breathing and talking. All that mattered was getting him to the medical facility at Camp Russell. To our rear, a team of SOER were conducting some dry training with their Minelabs, and we screamed at them to bring the Bushmaster over as we had a priority-one casualty. My hand was still on Lance's face as he lay there stunned, unsure what had just happened.

When we drove to the medical aid post, the RMO and medics were ready for Lance and began treatment immediately. They asked me what happened, and I told them it was fragmentation from a

40mm grenade at the range, then the RMO told me to get out to make room for them to work on Lance. I left the medical post, found a quiet spot, knelt and wept, praying that Lance was okay.

Garry and HQ soon asked me what happened. I told them I had fired a 40mm launcher, and that no qualified OIC had been present. For Alpha Company, which had already suffered a fatality with Mason at a range incident, and with his death still fresh in everyone's memory, there was zero appetite for another range-related incident.

People were appointed to begin an investigation immediately, and I spent the next few days being questioned. Right then, though, all I cared about was that Lance was okay.

He was taken to the Role 2 Hospital at the Dutch camp next door, then evacuated to Germany for further treatment, where he spent some days before being flown back to Australia. He had two pieces of shrapnel in his head, and he developed an infection in his gums and mouth that required medication and stitches. We learned the day after the accident, though, that he was stable and his injuries were not life-threatening. It was a miracle he was not killed, as the fragments could have penetrated his brain.

The next few days marked one of the lowest points in my career. The ADF Investigative Service (ADFIS) arrived, and I was appointed a legal officer who attended all my interviews and talked me through the process of what would happen next. The day after meeting the legal officer, I called Sarah, and she knew something was wrong as soon as I spoke.

'Scott, oh my God, what's happened?' she asked.

'I fucked up big time—Lance has been hurt. He's on his way back home. I can't say much more,' I told her.

There are two types of charges in the military for illegally firing a weapon. A negligent discharge (ND) occurs when a soldier accidentally fires a weapon—while unloading or cleaning it, or walking around the base. An unauthorised discharge (UD) occurs when a soldier has full knowledge that he is firing but doesn't have the authority to do so. An example may be at a rifle range, where he shoots at a target but hasn't been given the command to start firing by the OIC. For some reason, the definitions of ND and UD always get mixed up when people explain these incidents. In SF, where a high level of weapon proficiency is required, having an ND is a guaranteed way to lose your reputation—the one thing no one ever wants to lose.

News of the incident soon reached home, and people's general confusion about the difference between a UD and an ND didn't help. A mate from the unit who was in TK for another task for a few weeks told me that my name was dirt, the story being that I had accidentally fired my 40mm while walking around Camp Russell. My lawyer had advised me not to say anything about the incident, further fuelling speculation about how it occurred.

My round had hurt a mate, and I took full responsibility for it. Even worse, my other mate's comments echoed—'Your name is dirt'—and that cut deep. For the first time in my career, I just wanted to go home, wished I had never joined the army, and wondered how I would return from this.

Being in Camp Russell can feel like being in prison; you have guns and better food, but sometimes when you leave, people try to shoot you. We were always able to make our own fun, though. We could leave the base and make fun of the Dutch in the base gym over the fence, where the men always wore Lycra bike pants when they trained. The Dutch girls weren't bad to look at either. Next to the gym was a small café called The Windmill and Green Beans Coffee Shop, which was never short of a line-up.

Most commandos had come from the infantry battalions, which were located over the fence at the main camp, and we would regularly visit the lads over there or meet them for a meal at the Windmill. Sometimes, we would invite them to Camp Russell to have dinner with us, as the food at Russell was substantially better than what was on offer next door.

On this rotation, fresh seafood was flown in from the UAE; one night, we even had grilled crocodile. The chefs, typically Indian or Nepalese, would cook up some of the best curries I have ever had, and snacks and cold drinks were offered 24 hours a day.

The stark contrast between the living conditions for the regular army and the SOTG was the best recruiting tool for SOCOMD you could get. Many regular army soldiers put in their SF applications after interacting with SF operators in TK. Overly strict command teams and meaningless tasks added fuel to the degradation of morale, thanks to the ADF's and the government's unwillingness to put a highly capable and professional infantry fighting force in harm's way, despite that being their core role—a stark contract to life in our camp.

The infantry would walk past Camp Russell and hear parties and loud music while they were prohibited from drinking altogether. One day I was sitting on the wall in the sun in the FE-Bravos' drinking area, shirtless and wearing a pair of shorts and baseball cap, having a beer. One of the 6 RAR lads from the HESCO walked past and told me he was getting charged for having his sleeves rolled up.

On one Charlie Company rotation, the boys took it a bit too far, covering golf balls in the fluid from Cyalume sticks and driving them into the multinational base next door one night, leading to smashed cars and broken outside lights on buildings.

FE-A, with their smaller numbers, could turn one of their rooms into their drinking hole, which they named the Fat Lady's Arms, giving them the luxury of drinking behind closed doors. They were also not immune to drunken antics: one operator on Rotation XX in 2013 decided to ride a motorbike up and down the hallway of their building.

At this time, alcohol was provided by the chain of command. The task group's allocation of alcohol would be kept in a shipping container and given to each unit, with the platoon sergeants responsible for ordering and issuing alcohol.

The CO, Lieutenant Colonel Burns, when questioned on providing alcohol to the task group, was recorded as saying, 'If I've got the right to send a man to his death, I think I've got the right to give him a beer.'[35] We only drank during downtime, however.

One night, when no part of the company was tasked, a few beers in the afternoon turned into one hell of a party on the Back Deck, our pub of sorts—the night would become the catalyst for tighter alcohol restrictions for the remainder of the rotation and those that followed. For me, still unsure of the fallout from the range incident, for which I was told I would soon be formally charged, the party was a welcome distraction.

Two female medics from the camp next door who had attended were not used to drinking on the deployment, slept in the next day and were charged for being absent from duty. When questioned, they informed their chain of command that they were drinking with 'the SOTG boys'. Phone calls were made early the next day to our head-shed (HQ), who began an investigation.

The command team was now in damage control—the range incident and the two medics being charged for drinking with us only added fuel to the fire. ADFIS officers were on the way to investigate the incident, despite the fact that the booze had been supplied to us openly.

We were given a cut-off time to clear the booze out of our rooms, which I missed as I had a meeting with my lawyer about my charge.

But I had a few cartons of beer under my bed, and Chucky told me to get rid of them ASAP.

I grabbed some large black garbage bags, filled them with my contraband, and walked to the skip bins from the front. The CSM, Mick, was out there. Mick and I had a tumultuous relationship, and the range incident meant I was already in his sights. And as I walked past him, the garbage bag split, spilling dozens of beer bottles on the concrete, in full view of Mick and the HQ. Of course, this would only happen to me. I looked at Mick, who was fuming. Behind him, Mali Gray, one of the assaulters, was in hysterics and still says it was one of the funniest things he has ever seen.

Before the end of the day, I would again be in Mick's crosshairs.

The decision was made to drug-test the entire task force, and my initial urine test returned a positive. I wasn't too concerned, as I had been taking cold and flu tablets, which the medics had given me. But Mick banned me from leaving the wire on operations, pending results from the more sophisticated drug test, and threatened to relegate me back to 3 RAR. This seemed unfair, but I couldn't argue.

The rumour mill again began: the shit-fight who had fired an ND was now also a drug addict. It seemed I couldn't put a foot right, and I spent my days in bed, watching movies and wishing it would all go away.

A few days later, the company got ready for a RW insertion in Kandahar province, and I prayed my test results would come back in time, which they did not. I helped the team prepare as much as I could and sat in on the orders for the operation. It sounded like it would be a good one.

CHAPTER 22

BATTLE OF SHAH WALI KOT

Operation Tavara Sin VII in Shah Wali Kot, northern Kandahar, saw one of the biggest battles SOCOMD faced during the war. Both FE-A and FE-B engaged in such fierce fighting that the operation came to be recognised with Australia's first battle honour since the Vietnam War.

FE-B was inserted on 10 June 2010 into the town of Chenar Tu via US Chinooks for a five-day operation. The aim was to increase security around Kandahar City by conducting disruption operations to the city's northern approaches. The intelligence had been promising, and the OC briefed the company that they should expect a decent fight.

I was livid I was missing out, yet I did my best to hide my disappointment and support the team before they left. The boys geared up, and I walked them out the gate to the waiting aircraft and watched them fly off. The selfish part of me hoped it was a fizzer, and that they would just spend a few days chasing shade, as we had done many times on this deployment. Another part of me hoped the boys gave the enemy hell, though, and I moved into the command centre to keep tabs on their progress.

The company would be working out of their packs, and the combination of three days of food, water, ammo and specialist equipment would prove back-breaking in the 51-degree heat of an Afghan summer. Regardless, the boys were fit and trained when they inserted into the valley, ready for a fight. The snipers would see some of the heaviest fighting in their exposed overwatch position, their first shots the catalyst for the entire battle.

Anthony, who carried the Barrett for this operation, recalled that his pack was so heavy he needed help carrying it to the chopper, as he had his Barrett and three days' sustenance. Including his body weight, he was at 150 kilograms. As soon as the snipers landed in the valley, signals intelligence increased drastically. The team began a strenuous walk up to their OP location that night, at one stage on their hands and knees, so steep was the feature.

As Anthony and the team arrived at the OP, Anthony spotted a male in white sneakers running a few hundred metres away on the edge of the village beneath them, but he didn't engage as the male was unarmed. This, strangely, was consistent with what the boys knew enemy fighters had done in the past before fighting.

Garry called the team to run after him, as his capture would provide real-time intelligence on the enemy picture, and he tasked Anthony and another sniper with stripping down their kit and giving chase to cut the male off. They used the terrain to their advantage to come up from a slight ridgeline on to the enemy in white sneakers. But they lost sight of 'white sneakers', and as they approached the top of a slight hill, Garry saw an enemy fighter and engaged him with his .338 sniper rifle from less than 10 metres, with Dan supporting him by engaging him with his M4.

Anthony followed up and completed a search of the dead

enemy, finding a satellite phone with batteries sewn into his clothes and a Soviet-era grenade. The phone would later be searched, and it provided invaluable intelligence on the enemy network in the region. Anthony explained his search of the body:

> I used my issued knife to cut his clothes, as I could feel something stitched into his shirt. I realised how much my hands were shaking, and I took a moment to look at the face of the dead enemy. I felt impartial. I didn't have much time to think, as a lot was happening. I remember thinking how dark his beard and eyebrows were compared to his skin, and thinking to myself, for the first time, that we are at war; this is the real deal.

As Anthony finished his search, he looked down into the green belt and saw 'white sneakers', who was now armed and running with two other armed fighters. Anthony engaged them with his M4, killing one, while the other two ran out of sight. The fighter in the white sneakers had got a weapon from a compound that must have been a cache. Anthony recalls that the enemy weapons had coloured tape, which they often used to decorate the AK47s. The battle had not even been going for an hour, and enemy bodies were already littered around the village.

After Anthony's engagement, Garry and another sniper, Davis, moved up the ridgeline to cut off the fleeing enemy. Anthony stayed in his position, but when he began to be engaged by enemy machine gun fire, he ran 50 metres to take cover behind a large rock. With tracer fire landing all around him, he was pinned down for a full ten minutes.

As Anthony scanned his surroundings, he saw two more enemies moving towards him from the green belt and he engaged with his M4, before having a significant stoppage of his gun.

Unable to rectify it, Anthony had to strip his gun completely to get it working while being shot at, tracer fire landing all around him. Anthony explained:

> I was getting hit hard. Every time I looked up, I could see the tracer fire approaching me. I wanted to focus on getting my gun working, but I couldn't help looking at the rounds landing all around me, wondering if one of them was going to get me finally. The timing of my gun stopping was terrible. I thought I was going to die on that hill that day. Strangely, I was reminded of the feeling you get when you are going through training, and an instructor is watching you strip and assemble your gun while you fumble about knowing you are being watched.

Back at the primary OP location, James Connor, a member of the second sniper team who was also on the OP, and an assault team who was there to support the snipers were joined by the platoon JTAC, who immediately set about calling in fixed-wing air support on known enemy locations. At that moment, the snipers, down behind their scopes, noted something. Intelligence completely died off, and we started to see different enemy positions with coloured flags. 'The pricks were using flags to communicate,' James explained.

The use of flags had never been seen by Alpha Company on their previous two SOTG rotations. It gave insight into the sophisticated command and control the enemy was employing.

Mid-afternoon, the battle quietened, and the primary OP team used the opportunity to get some rest as the temperature continued to soar. James looked at his Kestrel weather station,[36] which read 55 degrees Celsius in the shade. Then, an hour or so later, the team spotted more movement below. Viv Hunt, also on the sniper team, engaged with his Barrett, causing dust to kick off around him and allowing the enemy to pinpoint their exact position. The second wave of attacks then began. James, spotting for Viv, confirmed a hit on an enemy fighter just over 1620 metres away.

A barrage of fire hit the OP location; the automatic fire was constant, followed by half a dozen RPGs in 30 minutes. One RPG landed next to Viv, causing him to move from his cover, completely coated in dust because the rocket was so close. The snipers tried to fight back, but every time they tried to get their rifles down to get a sight picture, incoming fire pushed them back behind cover. 'I looked over at one of the boys, who was low behind a rock, and a dozen rounds smashed into his cover and all around him. He was completely pinned down,' James recalled.

There seems to be a threshold in combat where the mood transitions from adrenaline-charged excitement to a realisation that a particular situation is quite dire, and the thrill of combat is replaced with the realisation that you may not get out of this one unscathed.

You can look at a person's face and tell if they are hyped up on adrenaline or genuinely afraid for their life. No training in the world can minimise the fear a person feels when their life is at risk, but selection and training provide an operator with the tools to still achieve the mission. To my mind, this is what characterises SF.

Anthony recalls crawling at one stage over to his Barrett, a few metres away, while rounds landed next to him. Numerous times during this battle, he came within inches of being shot; the fire was accurate and relentless. Anthony began calling in mortars, but was cautious about calling them in too close, as the chaos of the battle meant the precise location of the assault platoons was unknown.

The assault platoons also saw fierce fighting that day. Oscar platoon inserted into Chenar Tu and commenced their clearance before first light.

Later that day, the sniper position was continuing to receive fire from multiple locations; they were unable to fire back, however, as Oscar platoon was fighting in the area and the risk of blue-on-blue was too high. Snipers would see the enemy for a split second, followed by gunfire in the area, but even suppressing rounds into likely locations was not feasible. But as the JTACs began their barrage on the surrounding hills, and Oscar platoon's fight in the green belt became more sporadic, the fighting slowed down for the rest of the day, giving the boys a well-earned rest.

CHQ and the mortar platoon had taken up a position in a large compound and got shot at whenever one of them tried to leave. At one stage, everyone in the compound was crammed into one room. They were in a valley, with high ground all around them, the plunging fire aimed at them rendering the compound walls useless. The mortar team nevertheless worked tirelessly under fire to support the assault teams who were in a fight for their lives.

Around 10 a.m., Mali Gray and elements of his Oscar platoon took position behind a small wall, between compounds down in the valley, already tired from clearing dozens of compounds while carrying all their kit. 'There was a massive fire hitting the wall I was resting behind, kicking dust into my eyes, and I was disorientated from the start,' Mali explained. 'An RPG detonated above my head, and I could feel the heat of the round on my back, making me throw myself into a small hole in the ground.'

The battle in the green belt had begun for Oscar platoon. Mali came under attack as he crossed a creek line. He moved into cover and aimed at a father and son digging something 50 metres away, but he couldn't identify where the fire targeting him was coming from. As he moved into a better position to observe the father and son, machine gun fire cracked around him, and he threw himself into an orchard. Mali described the ambush, for which he was later awarded a Commendation for Gallantry in the battle:

I threw myself into a slight depression in an orchard and looked at the trees above me. It was like someone was cutting [them] with a whipper snipper; the fire was so intense. The PRC, who ended up near me, ran away and hid, I couldn't see them. I got up and started firing my M4 and 40mm grenades at where I thought the machine gunner was. As I did so, I was engaged by a gun on the other side, and the fire never stopped. I tried to engage both sides, but realising I was alone, I knew it was hopeless . . .

I got down low into the small ditch and started building a fighting bay. If they came for me, I wanted to give myself the best chance possible. Every time I went to get my pack, which was sitting a few metres away, I would be engaged and throw myself back down . . . Eventually, Damien ran over to me in a lull in fire, covering me as we broke contact towards the nearest compound, the mortar position. It was the most fire I have ever received. I don't know how I didn't get hit.

Our team was low on ammo. After the initial ambush in the green belt, I only had one magazine of M4 and two 40mm rounds left. I was also nearly out of water, with a few litres getting shot up in my pack and the rest keeping me going in the morning heat.

Once Mali and his team had resupplied in the compound, Damien, the PRC mentor, asked Mali for help finding his partner force. As Damien left, he was pinned against the wall by fire, unable to move, while Mali did his best to cover him, going through a few of the freshly resupplied M4 magazines and finally getting him to safety. Their trust in each other, forged through years of training in the regiment, got them through.

Around lunchtime, Oscar platoon cleared some compounds in the area they had been engaged in but found no dead bodies, only blood trails. Mali and his team were then tasked to move up on the high ground to support the snipers, as intelligence indicated the enemy were looking to target the sniper position. As they moved, they were again engaged by automatic fire. They could also hear the enemy talking, but couldn't pinpoint where they were.

Dale McGuire, who was a team leader in November platoon, also remembered the enemy tactics in the valley, which he had not seen on either of his two previous SOTG rotations: 'We could see snipers moving around on the high ground, but it was hard to identify them, so we refrained from firing. When the enemy engaged, it was well coordinated, and we could see vehicles dropping them off. Then they would use flags to communicate—something I had never seen before.'

The sporadic fire continued to land around the sniper position for the rest of the day, but died down as it got dark. Apache gunships came on station to support the company and blasted known locations around them. The next morning, Anthony was on watch and, through his optics, spotted a pack of wolves, who seemed to be following a scent in an area where the team had killed some enemies. He zoomed in and could make out a wolf eating at the leg of a dead enemy fighter. 'I couldn't believe it; they usually take their dead away immediately. A wolf was eating the dude's leg; it was crazy,' he recalled.

Anthony then spotted about 30 figures on a distant feature who were moving in tactical formation. Mortars and Apache fire were called in, but the fighters dispersed after the first mortar round landed short of their location. Tracer fire could be seen targeting the Apache. At one stage, the boys thought it had been hit, so close did the fire come. Anthony reported the group over the company net; it seemed the enemy still wasn't done with Alpha Company.

Unbeknownst to Alpha Company at the time, the Taliban leadership had converged on the village of Tizak, a few kilometres west of Chenar Tu, with dozens of other fighters. 2 SAS Squadron, from FE-A, was spun up after signals intelligence located an enemy commander in the village, inserting via RW early in the morning of 11 June. Earlier that night, FE-B snipers had been warned they would be moving from Chenar Tu to the high ground to the east of Tizak to support the FE-A insertion. Still, they were called off at the last minute, despite Chenar Tu having significantly quietened down, as the enemy regrouped and formulated a plan to attack.

Task Force No Mercy, from the US 101st Airborne Division, who were allocated to the SOTG as our insertion platforms, received fire as they landed, and all the FE-A operators in multiple positions began receiving effective enemy fire, soon realising they were facing a numerically superior enemy. From Chenar Tu, FE-B watched the battle unfold, frustrated that they weren't there to assist, despite being perfectly positioned to do so. Realising their vulnerable position, FE-A attacked the enemy positions to regain the initiative. Multiple teams were in contact, neutralising the enemy with grenades, small arms and heavy weapons.[37]

By the end of the day, FE-A had fought into the village of Tizak and held key terrain. More than 50 weapons were recovered and dozens of enemies lay dead. Corporal Ben Roberts-Smith, MG, would later be awarded the highest award for valour, the VC for Australia, for his actions that day in Tizak. The fighting seen by FE-A and FE-B in Chenar Tu has become part of Australian military history.

Overall, the Battle of Shah Wali Kot severely diminished, for years to come, the insurgents' ability to use the area as a haven. After suffering such a large loss of life, the insurgents would never challenge the SOTG in Chenar Tu or Tizak again. Only more minor skirmishes were reported in subsequent rotations. Enemy losses in the battle were said to be more than 100, with no casualties suffered by either FE-A or FE-B. The battle honour citation for the Battle of Shah Wali Kot, awarded to Alpha Company, 2 Cdo Regt, and 2 Squadron, SASR, reads:

> The Australian Special Operations Task Group Rotation XII, which included combat elements from the 2nd Special Air Service Squadron of the Special Air Service Regiment, Alpha Company Commando Group from the 2nd Commando Regiment, and supported by the Incident Response Regiment and the United States 101st Airborne Division, Task Force No Mercy, is awarded the Battle Honour Eastern Shah Wali Kot in due recognition of extraordinary heroism, exemplary combat performance and the relentless destruction of a highly trained and fanatical Taliban enemy of numerical superiority within the extremely inhospitable region of Eastern Shah Wali Kot, Afghanistan, during the period May to June 2010.
>
> Tasked with a mission of vital operational importance within Regional Command—South, and of strategic significance for the International Security Assistance Force, from May 2010 the task group conducted a series of daring daylight helicopter-borne raids, deep into enemy territory, to destabilise local insurgent networks and to identify key Taliban leaders. Often resulting in fierce engagements with the enemy, these deadly shaping raids created fractures throughout the command-and-control architecture of the Taliban.
>
> During the early hours of 10 June 2010, immediately realising a tactical opportunity, Alpha Company Commando Group audaciously established an attack by fire position inside the insurgents' strong hold of Chenar Tu. Shortly after first light, the enemy surrounded the commandos and employed sophisticated tactics to overrun the commando positions throughout

the day. Holding their exposed positions doggedly under heavy and sustained attack, the commandos, determined to regain the initiative, launched several aggressive counter attacks against the assaulting enemy. Surprised by the ferocity of the commando response, combined with having lost significant numbers of fighters, the enemy withdrew to the village of Tizak to conduct deliberate planning for the destruction of the isolated commando company.

Receiving intelligence that a high-level Taliban commander had now been drawn to the village of Tizak, a troop from the 2nd Special Air Service Squadron deployed by helicopter to conduct a kill or capture mission on the morning of 11 June 2010. Upon landing in Tizak, the troop was immediately engaged by a maelstrom of small arms fire and a stream of rocket-propelled grenades from insurgents in the village and the surrounding high ground, resulting in two friendlies being wounded in action and four helicopters sustaining battle damage. Despite being outnumbered four to one and suppressed under a hail of machine gun fire, the troop inched forward until they were again checked and fixed by the interlocking fire of three machine guns. Drawing on the deepest reserves of collective courage, combined with notable acts of individual valour and gallantry, the initiative was regained, allowing a subsequent break-in of the enemy's defensive position. Exploiting a tenuous tactical foothold, the troop unflinchingly cleared the remaining depth positions in close-quarter combat throughout the remainder of the day while being relentlessly supported by U.S. AH-64 Apache helicopters from Task Force No Mercy. At the conclusion of the battle, late on the evening of 14 June 2010, a significant number of high-level Taliban commanders, [as well as] a significant and disproportionate number of enemy fighters were killed, and the remaining enemy were routed and fled from the region.

The extraordinary heroism and exemplary combat performance displayed during the Shah Wali Kot Offensive resulted in a major enemy supply line from Pakistan into Kandahar being destroyed and the Taliban in eastern Shah Wali Kot being rendered ineffective. The battlefield orchestration, courage, gallantry and determination displayed by the combat elements of the Special Operations Task Group Rotation XII, under extremely adverse and hazardous conditions has set them apart, and by their achievements, they have brought distinguished credit on themselves and the Australian Defence Force.

CHAPTER 23

LONE RANGER

My contribution to the battle occurred late on the evening of 12 June. That day, the drug test results came back from Australia and confirmed that I had only consumed cold and flu tablets. I was given the green light to insert into Shah Wali Kot with the ammunition and water resupply scheduled for that night. There were two CH-47 Chinooks tasked with landing in two different landing zones. The first would land near CHQ, and the second would land on a plateau near my sniper team, who had elements of Oscar platoon with them.

I rushed back to my room and packed my kit, stuffing it with extra ammo, water, food and snacks for the team. I knew the boys had been through a tough couple of days, and that they would appreciate some snacks—what we called 'jack rations'.

I met the storeman who was charged with loading the supplies into the Chinook. When the birds arrived, I confirmed the landing zones with him and double-checked my map. He confirmed the tail numbers and pointed me to a CH-47 that had just landed.

My orders had been rushed, and I wanted to ensure I was landing in the correct spot. I checked my radio frequencies with the signallers to ensure I was on the same net, but something still didn't sit right with me. I was being inserted into an area that had seen constant fighting for the past 48 hours, so I suppose it was natural to be apprehensive.

I got my pack, grabbed my Barrett, and walked to the Chinook. The aircrew was busy fussing around the aircraft and didn't notice me at first. But then one of them saw me and walked over.

'Hey mate, can I confirm the landing zone grid, please?' I asked, pulling out my map.

He looked at the map and gave me a thumbs up. 'Yeah, buddy, that's the one,' he shouted over the noise of the aircraft engine.

A little voice was telling me something wasn't right, but it was too late to go back now. So I sat by myself in the bird and we took off. I looked at my map once again, getting my bearings to where my sniper team was, less than 100 metres away from the landing zone. I was checking my kit and reapplying my camouflage cream when the loadmaster came over and asked if he could get a photo with my sniper rifle, which I found strange, but I obliged.

When I got the five-minute call I put my pack on, ready to jump off. We landed with a thud and got the signal from the loadmaster. As I exited, I fell straight off a ledge, tripping and landing on my side, facing the rotor wash of the Chinook. For anyone who has not been under the rotor wash of a Chinook, it's like standing in the middle of a storm with gale-force winds, dust and rocks pounding you; it's even worse when you are on your back facing the chopper.

I lay there, doing my best to cover my face, and eventually, after it flew off, I wiped the dirt and dust from my eyes and got a look at the area around me for the first time. I'd expected to land on a ridge-line, yet I was in a valley with hills around me. Where the fuck was I? I slipped my pack off and adjusted my NVG, and once I got a better view, realised I was in the wrong spot. Starting to panic, I pulled out my torch to study the terrain of the other landing site in case I had been dropped off at the wrong one, yet nothing I saw on the map reflected anything I could see in front of me.

I had just turned my torch off and pressed the menu button on my GPS to get an exact fix on my position when I heard movement in the bush to my right. I went for my M4, but it was in my pack, as I'd expected to land straight onto the sniper OP. Now I wished I had it ready and in my hands. I grabbed the Barrett instead, took up a position in a slight depression and tried to identify what the noise was.

I can't say I was scared, more confused. It wasn't the fact that I was possibly alone in the middle of Shah Wali Kot, more that I could imagine the headlines in the news: 'Australian Special Forces Soldier Missing in Southern Afghanistan'. Why did this always happen to me, I wondered. I would be the only person in the history of the SOTG ever to go missing and be declared an 'isolated person'. Of course it had to be me.

I could hear someone walking, and I wanted to make sure there was no 'blue-on-blue', so I checked that my infrared strobe was on and lay in wait. I slowly reached for the push-to-talk button on my radio and tried to contact any friendly callsigns. 'Any callsigns, radio check, over.' I heard nothing. I tried again. Still nothing. Fuck. I repeated the radio check several times. 'Surely the signallers would have given me the correct frequencies,' I thought to myself.

I needed to check the channel on my radio but didn't want to turn my torch on and lose sight of the area I'd heard the noise coming from, so I decided to take my M4 out of my pack slowly, leave my Barrett, and move away from the landing zone. If the enemy were coming for me, they would go straight for the landing zone, and I would have a better chance if I sat away from it to ambush them when they came.

I lay there for another ten minutes, ready to ambush, wondering what the fuck I was going to do. I had no radio communications with the team, I still hadn't had a chance to check my GPS to get a fix, and enemies were possibly coming my way. I went through the escape and evasion plane in my head; I had my escape map, GPS, water, ammo and NVG. If I had to bug out, I had enough on me to at least get me to first light, and then once I identified my location I could walk to some high ground where the boys would see me.

Just then, I spotted an infrared strobe walking towards the landing zone, then another one. I flashed my infrared torch and got a response. I let out a big sigh of relief, stood up and walked towards them. 'Is that you, Scotty? What the fuck are you doing here?' asked an operator with November platoon, who was in a defensive position a few hundred metres away. I had been dropped 200 metres from the proposed landing site. Apparently the CH-47 crew didn't want to land on the grid they were given, as they were concerned about the height of the trees hitting their blades. The JTAC, who had been coordinating the resupply, hadn't been told about the change of plan until after they had dropped me off.

The following day, being too far away to join my team, I was tasked with moving up to November platoon's headquarters to provide sniper support. Snipers had already been resupplied, and the command team wanted me to stay at their location. The walk up to their spot was horrendous—I'd filled my pack with so many extra supplies, I could only take a few steps at a time before needing to rest. Once I got to the top, I was briefed by the platoon commander and caught up on the past few days with Peter Rudland, one of the team commanders.

I had set up the Barrett and started sketching some range and gathering data when intelligence got a fix on an enemy location. I was given the direction, and through my scope, I could see the enemy. He was wearing traditional black robes, had a thick black beard, and was unusually overweight, walking back and forth and talking on his radio.

After tracking him for an hour or so, the platoon commander gave me the green light to engage him. He was 1400 metres away and was now walking around a series of compounds in the valley below me. It was already approaching 48 degrees on the hill, and I assessed the wind. There was a slight quarter-value wind from two o'clock at my position, and I could see bits of paper and rubbish moving from left to right down at his location.

I tried to imagine what the wind was doing between my barrel and his chest, and adjusted my wind dials accordingly. Again, as had occurred in Mashal, kids were playing outside a compound 50 metres away from the target, but this wasn't close enough to concern me. Pete Rudland, who was spotting for me through his range finder, confirmed the range. I checked my data card and got ready for the shot.

I waited until the fat man was still, controlled my breathing, and then increased pressure on the trigger until the rifle fired. The time of flight, although slight, felt a lot longer as I waited to see where the round would land. My elevation was perfect, the bullet exactly level with the middle of his chest, but I missed by a few sideways metres—the wind was more substantial than I'd assessed. He initially froze, stunned, then, realising he was in a sniper's sights, dropped his radio and sprinted for the nearest compound— well, his version of a sprint. I adjusted for the wind and his running direction and fired again.

The second shot landed between his legs as he ran. I fired again, the shot landing just to his front—he was running out of steam and must have slowed down. The third shot landed on a wall above his head as he dived behind it. 'Fuuuck!' I yelled to myself.

For a few minutes he lay behind the wall, which was part of a smaller compound separated from the primary set.

He stuck his head up briefly above the wall, and I fired again; this time the round must have gone high, as I couldn't see the splash where it landed. A few moments later, I could see the top of a head on the other side of the wall, but it looked different from the fat man's, so I refrained from firing again. Then the fat man appeared again, with three kids he was using as human shields to get to the primary set of compounds. Once he got into the cluster, I had almost no chance of seeing him again.

The kids looked petrified, and I immediately felt sorry for them. I cursed the fat fuck for putting them through this; it was not a fair fight. I took my finger off the trigger and watched him ditch the kids at the opening of a compound, pushing one of them over as he made his own escape behind a wall, never to be seen again. I was annoyed that I had not killed him, especially as he'd been willing to put kids' lives at risk to save his own.

The remainder of Shah Wali Kot was uneventful. There were a few shots here and there, but after the action at Tizak, the enemy had essentially been decimated and had lost the will to fight. We had another long walk out and arrived back at Camp Russell for 48 hours of rest. Not that I needed it after my short duration on the ground.

We sat on the Back Deck and did our usual debrief, and the full picture of the battle became apparent to me as I listened to the boys' stories from the first few days. Of course, we didn't interact or socialise with FE-A, so we only heard a second-hand account of the fight in Tizak.

The day after we arrived, Major General Cantwell, the commander of all Australian forces in the Middle East, met us for lunch and told us in no uncertain terms that the battle of Shah Wali Kot would go down in history. He had somebody coming to officially record the events, which we found strange but thought nothing of at the time.

Every day when I woke up, I wondered if this would be the day I'd find out what the fallout from the range incident would be. Lance was now back in Australia; the metal was still in his head, as the risk of surgery was too high. Yet nothing was said to me, and after our two-day rest we received orders for another few nights of strikes and clearances around northern Kandahar.

Our team was to insert into overwatch positions near the village of Doab, again being inserted by Task Force No Mercy, where we would support an assault platoon to conduct a village clearance. It was a relatively small green belt surrounded by high features. It was suspected that Doab was being used to store weapons and IED components; the intelligence brief, however, didn't indicate that anyone was expecting a gunfight.

This would be the second of a series of back-to-back, short-duration jobs where we would insert at night, conduct a clearance, and then return to TK in time for lunch. The last four and half months were starting to take their toll, and we only had another week or so of our operational window before we left—the advance party from the next rotation was already in Camp Russell.

We inserted on a flat hill surrounding Doab, with Davis and me to the east, and Chucky and Anthony in a pair on the same feature, 60 metres away. As the sun rose, the assault force began its first-light clearance. The pattern of life in the village was nothing out of the ordinary, with women and kids running to hide in their homes as we landed. I did note a distinct lack of fighting-aged males, but that wasn't unusual either, as they would typically be out with their animals or tending their crops.

I checked some ranges, recorded them on my sketch, and then sat up to get some water. A string of shots rang out in the village, and

I jumped behind my Barrett to identify where the assaulters were. Over the radio, one of the teams reported they had shot a dog. A few moments later, automatic fire echoed through the valley as 'Contact' was broadcast on the net. Through my rifle scope, I could see the lead elements of the assault forces running to cover, returning fire to their front, which gave me an indication as to where the enemy was.

As Anthony opened from the left with his Barrett, I scanned the area. In front of the assaulters, who were now pinned down next to a series of compounds, I saw three fighters dressed in black robes and carrying AK47s. They were manoeuvring to flank the team as Anthony's Barrett rounds smashed into the rocks behind them, narrowly missing them.

The three enemies, unsure of where exactly Anthony was, began a mad dash towards a bend in a dry creek bed. I fired three or four rounds quickly, but they went high, and I hadn't added enough lead to account for the men running.

Anthony was still shooting, and I watched the lead enemy trip over and fall just as one of Anthony's rounds hit the rock, exactly where his head had just been; luck plays a huge part in combat. The enemies disappeared behind some thick vegetation, and Davis, behind me on his spotting scope, tried to pinpoint where they were.

There was a large rock next to the bush they had disappeared into, and I fired into the rock to get my adjustments for that distance, which would also serve as suppression; .50 calibre bullets landing around you is a great deterrent from running into the open.

I felt surprisingly calm as I engaged the enemy. To apply fire accurately enough to support the boys in the green belt, I needed to stay composed, focusing on where our team was while ensuring I had accurately applied the adjustments to my rifle—which shooting the rock had confirmed. I kept my sight on the area of the bush where

I had last seen the enemy and asked Davis to get a fix on the assault teams so I knew where they were.

Suddenly, two of the Taliban fighters started sprinting from the bushy area towards a bend in the creek line that curved around a hill, out of sight. I fired another five or six rounds but again missed, not allowing enough lead for their running speed, and they ran behind the feature, out of my view, leaving to fight another day. 'Fuck's sake,' I said to nobody, annoyed at myself for missing again.

There was still one more fighter though, and surely he would follow suit. Maybe he hadn't joined his mates out of fear, or maybe he was injured.

I imagined what I would do if I was pinned down by sniper fire, and ascertained that my best bet would be sprinting out of sight behind the hill. As I scanned, Davis spotted him: 'I see him! He's in the aqueduct—he's crawling in the aqueduct!'

At first, I didn't see him, as he was moving low and slow in the aqueduct, which must have been bigger than I initially thought. Then I saw him, a fighter in traditional robes, with a black beard and short hair, carrying chest webbing, with grenades hanging off the front strap.

He must have still been confused about where he was being shot from, as he frantically looked around him. He was now in direct line with the rock I had been firing at to get my adjustments— exactly 1080 metres away. I went through my breathing cycle and slowly applied pressure to my trigger; the fighter paused and turned around, looking in our direction. I could see his face and a grenade in his hand. His eyes were wide, he looked scared, and it seemed like he was staring straight at me for a split second. It was as if, at that moment, he knew he was in the last seconds of his life.

I waited till he turned around again so I had the entire width of his back, then pressed the trigger. I knew before the round left the barrel I had him; you can feel it when you have a good shot. The round hit him in his lower right back, the impact completely spinning him and landing him face-first in the aqueduct, filling the watercourse with blood.

If he had joined his two mates and sprinted around the bend, he would probably still be alive today.

'SC', who was the team leader engaged by the enemy fighters I observed, recalled of that morning: 'On initial contact, I was excited—I had a drive to kill these fucks who had shot at us.' SC and his team fought through the village and came across the fighter I had shot, stopping to search his body.

'He had an entry wound above his right ass cheek which had exited up the back of his neck,' SC explained. 'The bullet had created a massive canoe shape in his back. During the search, we found a Russian grenade with the pin half pulled ready for use, radio, batteries and IED components—to be honest I was annoyed that snipers killed him before we got to him, but glad there was one less enemy. I was proud of how my team reacted—they went straight into hunter mode, solely focused on killing the threat—it's what commandos do.'

I have read many books where soldiers are asked what killing is like. A typical response seems to be that nobody took pleasure in it: it was kill or be killed, it was just the job, and so on. Now, I am not saying the Afghanistan conflict came anywhere remotely close to the levels of death, killing and combat in previous conflicts such as Vietnam or the two world wars. But I do feel that I can speak for most for modern SF soldiers, who spend their professional lives learning how to kill, when I say we have a different view.

It may sound psychotic, but I can best describe it as elation. Hundreds of hours spent on a sniper rifle, training for just this moment, and finally getting to put it into practice—I felt like I had validated myself, particularly given my misses on this rotation up to this point. This dude had shot at my mates and was quite happy to send them home in body bags, so I had no issues with killing him. I felt no guilt then, and I still don't. If I were placed in that situation again, I would do the same thing.

CHAPTER 24

FALLEN ANGEL

Certain pivotal events in a person's life define them, altering both their life and their families' lives forever. What happened on the morning of 21 June 2010 was one such event. It would bring the most extensive loss of life and combat injuries for Australian soldiers since the Vietnam War, and would alter the DNA of Alpha Company for good.

The fallout from the Battle of Shah Wali Kot provided a mountain of intelligence that led to a series of operations by FE-B in northern Kandahar, supported by Task Force No Mercy, which would see platoons rotate every 24 hours to strike different locations. So far, nothing relating to a charge for the range incident had been mentioned to me—and I certainly wasn't going to remind anyone.

As we had done in the weeks after Shah Wali Kot, our team geared up early in the morning for a night-time insertion and a first-light clearance. This time, however, we would have Pete Rudland's assault team to support us in our overwatch position—Shah Wali Kot was still fresh in everyone's memories. This was the second-last job of the rotation, and as our alarms went off at 2 a.m., we could all feel it, dragging ourselves out of bed and getting our kit together as we had done countless times over the past few months.

Every team had its routine before a job, and for us it involved heavy rock music and Red Bull—sugar-free, of course. The end of a trip usually feels monotonous, where even a job that we thought might lead to a gunfight felt less exciting and was approached with fewer nerves than it may have been in the first few weeks. Still, the loud music and Red Bull soon had us in the zone.

We did our radio checks, and trucks drove us to the waiting aircraft. Our team comprised Garry, Chucky—who was filling the role of 2ic since Lance was back in Australia—Anthony and me. Davis was dropped off this job to make room for the assault team to manage the aircraft's weight. The assault team comprised Peter Rudland as the team commander, Matty Compton as his 2ic, and privates Scott Palmer and Tim Aplin. We also had our electronic warfare operator Gary Wilson and his interpreter.

We would be in the lead aircraft, with the remainder of November platoon in the second and third. As we got on board, there was not much room to move around, mainly due to our team's sniper rifles and packs, and we were crammed in like sardines for the 40-minute flight south.

In our previous two jobs, Garry had placed me in the rear right-hand seat of the aircraft, known as the 'hurricane seat' because it copped the total weight of the rotor wash of the blades. Flying with the doors open made for a very uncomfortable ride, and this seat was hated by everyone, so this time I asked Garry to swap me with someone else, which he did. Regardless, the seating somehow became a clusterfuck, and everyone just found spots where they could—we were all getting off at the same spot anyway.

Once on board, we had a slight delay taking off and I nodded off. When the bird started to lift, I quickly checked my kit to ensure everything was in place, paying particular attention to my pistol and magazine for the Barrett—anything that could be bumped by an arm, a leg or someone else's kit.

Despite seatbelts being mandatory, we didn't bother with them on some jobs, particularly on nights like this with a Black Hawk at capacity and zero room to move. The aircrew would sometimes have them folded back up behind the headrest so we could access them, as trying to find the male and female ends once on board was near impossible in the dark, but I don't recall seeing them—or maybe I didn't look. But as I was checking to make sure my pistol hadn't been dislodged on my right side, I happened to feel the male end of the waistband portion of the seatbelt, so I pulled it up. Then I tried to find the female end. I felt around on my left side and couldn't find it and was about to give up when the tips of my fingers caught it between the seats. I pulled it up, rested my Barrett between my knees, and tightened my seatbelt. And, as it happened, I had nowhere to put my helmet if I took it off, so I left it on. Plus, the helmet provided a natural pillow on the cargo net behind my head. These actions may have resulted in me surviving the night.

On a moonless night, at 0330 local time, on the open plains of the Kandahar desert, the 'five-minute' call was given by the crew chief, Brandon Silk. A few moments later, Brandon asked the pilots on his headset, 'How low are you going?'[38] Seconds later, the US Army 101st Airborne, Task Force No Mercy, UH-60 Black Hawk crashed into the desert, travelling at more than 200 kilometres per hour.

The aircraft, flying just above the desert floor, had hit a slight embankment then flipped over, rolling for more than 180 metres before coming to a stop and bursting into flames. The remaining two aircraft, believing they were receiving ground-to-air fire, banked hard and gained altitude, conducting an evasive manoeuvre but not knowing exactly what had happened.

'I was adjusting my NVGs when I had a complete whiteout,[39] then my chopper banked hard to the right,' said James Connor, who was in the second chopper behind us. 'We had no idea what was happening, but I knew it was bad. Our bird then circled back around, coming in to land, when the loadies started screaming that we had a Fallen Angel.'[40]

My last recollections before impact are of looking out the door and seeing the ground rush by. At first I thought my NVGs were out of focus, and I recall trying to adjust them, as what I saw was confusing—my view should have been in focus. I also remember looking at the horizon out the right door and wondering why we were so low when we were still five minutes out.

Those of us who survived all vividly recall the impact, but nothing more, due to our head injuries. I recall sitting on a seat for one minute, and then everything around me erupting into a violent spin before I lost consciousness. The next thing I remember is lying on my back, with somebody's hands holding the side of my face, and being in immense pain, the area lit up from what I thought was a bonfire but was the wreckage in flames. These memories are vague and fleeting.

It felt the way it does when you have just been tackled or had a bad fall, and you're waiting for the worst part of the pain to subside. But in this case it never did. Bizarrely, I remember tasting dust and dirt and wanting a water bottle to wash my mouth out.

When Dale McGuire arrived at the crash site, he came across Tim Aplin, who had a nasopharyngeal airway in his nose but was already dead. Ryan Walker was working on Chucky, who was still alive. Dale then saw Garry Robinson, who was lying awkwardly, and moved him onto his back. 'Garry's leg was completely mushed,' Dale says. 'When I moved him, the bottom half of his leg and knees went a different direction, but he didn't feel it—his eyes were rolling around in the back of his head.'

The second and third aircraft landed on either side of the crash site and November platoon established a cordon while everyone else rushed towards the site, running past one of the blades that had managed to land upright in the sand, making it look like someone had thrown a dart into the ground.

James came across one of the pilots screaming in pain and began providing first aid, remaining with the pilot until he was evacuated. All the bullets in the aircraft were now on fire, causing them to explode, adding to the chaos. I have vague memories of what I thought were gunshots, the smell of aviation gas and lots of people screaming as the teams frantically searched for survivors. Some of us had been flung more than 20 metres away from where the aircraft had crashed.

'It was chaos, rounds were cooking off everywhere, and it was dark,' James said, 'but our training did kick in. I just went into auto-pilot mode; we had so much to do. The crews of the second and third Black Hawks ripped their seats out. They threw them on the desert floor, turning them [the Black Hawks] into medical evacuation birds to expedite our arrival to Kandahar.'

'It was very confronting,' Dale explained. 'Seeing your mates dead and injured, screaming in pain around a burning helicopter. We did our best but felt helpless. The whole situation was chaos. It was pitch black, and the only light we had aside from our head torches was the burning wreckage.'

Ryan and Dale moved over to treat me, and Ryan suspected I might have spinal injuries as I was complaining of back pain. 'There were no more stretchers,' Ryan said, 'so I grabbed a piece of the chopper engine cowling, and we put you on it and evacuated you on the first bird, still on the cowling.' That cowling would be painted in commemoration by the medical staff at Kandahar who treated us that night, and it remained on the hospital walls until it was brought back home to Australia and presented to the War Memorial in Canberra, where it still sits. I didn't work up the courage to see it until I left the army in late 2023.

'You were in and out of consciousness,' Ryan recalled. 'You kept asking me how big the IED was; I had to keep explaining what had happened, and then you would forget a second later. You were in pain but in good spirits and talkative. Then you would realise where you were and ask the same questions—in the end, we just wanted you to shut up.'

The platoon medic, Darren, ran around the position, doing his best to guide the team medics on treatment. He was later awarded the Distinguished Service Medal (DSM) for his efforts that night.

Tim Aplin and Scott Palmer had been killed on impact, and the crew chief, Brandon Silk, still had not been accounted for as everyone frantically worked to keep those of us who were alive stable and ready for evacuation. The team CFAs began to rip open their medical kits, doing what they could for the casualties.

Dealing with high-pressure, high-stress environments was our bread and butter—what we were trained to do. If it weren't for the quick-thinking actions of the boys on the ground that night, many of us, including me, would not be here to tell this story, and I am eternally grateful to and proud of them for everything they did. I only hope that if it was them who had crashed, I would have displayed the same courage and clarity of thought. I am immensely proud to be included in their ranks and will be indebted to them forever.

Oscar platoon, which was the quick reaction force for our mission, was woken up not long after we crashed and told there was a Fallen Angel and to get ready to move to the crash site. Their orders were short and sharp: secure the site and help with treatment if we were still there. At first light, Oscar platoon lifted off from TK south to Kandahar, and as they approached the crash site were shocked at what they saw. 'It was completely flat, and we could see pieces of the chopper and equipment strewn across hundreds of metres,' explained Mali, who was on the quick reaction force team. 'I have no idea how any of the boys survived.'

As Oscar dismounted and approached the site, they saw Viv and James, completely covered in blood, with open medic kits, bandages and ampoules of drugs everywhere. All the wounded had already been evacuated to Kandahar, and the platoon went about looking for equipment such as guns, radio equipment and NVG, to ensure nothing could be left for the enemy.

Oscar platoon also placed people in security and searched for the body of Brandon Silk, which had still not been located. He was eventually found in the wreckage once the fire had died down—he had died in his seat. As the platoon went about their work, they got news on the radio that Ben Chuck had also been pronounced dead. 'The mood immediately went dark; it was hard for everyone,' Mali recalled.

Back at TK, people were tasked to head to Kandahar Airfield, to the hospital where we had all been taken. Davis, the only team member back at Camp Russell, was fast asleep when he heard someone calling his name in the hallway. An officer from head-quarters told him there had been a Fallen Angel but he didn't know the details, and to make sure our team's hospital bags were packed. As Davis left to pack, he was told to grab Chucky's toothbrush. 'As soon as I heard, I was so angry I had missed out,' Davis said to me. 'I had no idea how bad the accident was or who was injured. The fact that they asked for Chucky's toothbrush told me he must have died and they needed his brush for DNA. I grabbed the bags, and they flew a bunch of us to Kandahar, and I finally got to see you guys. You were being looked after very well. Not being on that chopper is the best thing that happened to me and easily the hardest thing

I have ever had to deal with. I was so riddled with guilt but grateful I wasn't killed or banged up like you boys.'

Back at the crash site, Oscar platoon waited for the downed aircraft recovery team, a US unit whose primary role was to respond to downed aircraft in Afghanistan, and loaded the bodies of Tim Aplin, Brandon Silk, Scott Palmer and the interpreter, whose name I won't give for security reasons, onto Black Hawks once the injured had been evacuated. When November platoon landed to assist, Oscar platoon flew back to TK.

I have only vague recollections of my evacuation, as I was in and out of consciousness. I recall being slid over on the floor of an empty Black Hawk as bodies piled in around me, but I can't say who they were. One memory I have is someone telling me we needed to make room for Chucky, and I tried to move over, but the pain in my legs and back wouldn't allow me to move, and then someone shouted at me to lie still. I could feel Chucky's body next to me, but I don't remember seeing his face, or maybe my brain has shut it out.

I also have vague recollections of being in Kandahar with bunches of nurses and doctors fussing over me, but no one memory stands out. Not long after I arrived, my lung collapsed and I lost consciousness.

The chopper crash decimated Alpha Company Snipers, which lost an entire team in one night. The sniper teams would never look the same again, forcing the company to run a sniper course not long after returning to Australia to fill the spots before the company rotated on the TAG-E in 2011.

Chucky, Tim and Scott were flown home on a RAAF C-130 Hercules to RAAF Base Richmond in Sydney. Their bodies lay in ice caskets, with an Australian flag draped over each of them. In TK, they had lain in the morgue, where a sentry was in place 24 hours a day. A candle was lit that was kept alight by the guards.

We never leave anyone behind or alone, even in death. Years later, I met a nurse who was working at the Role 2 hospital in TK, where the morgue was located, at the time, and she commented on how the vigil for the bodies moved her. 'No matter what time of day, in the heat, or the rain, there was a commando there to keep watch, ensuring the candle never went out. I realised then how powerful the brotherhood in your unit must be,' she said.

Davis told me of the repatriation of the bodies, 'The whole flight, I couldn't sleep. I always had my hand on one of the caskets.'

When I interviewed members of Alpha Company for this book and asked what the most challenging part of the ordeal was for them, all responded with the same answer—seeing the families at the ramp ceremony.

'We were exhausted. The last few days had taken a toll on us,' Dale tells me. 'We were home in body, but we were still on the job. Our mission became to ensure we sent the boys off properly.'

The scars from this deployment for some members of Alpha Company would never heal, and the helicopter crash on 21 June 2010 in Kandahar would claim more commandos' lives in the coming years. The next few days would be a blur of drill rehearsal, flights, lack of sleep and alcohol as Alpha Company flew up and down the east coast as the official uniformed presence for the three boys at their funerals with full military honours. Tim Aplin, Ben Chuck and Scott Palmer were farewelled in front of family and friends, escorted and carried by the men alongside whom they had slept, fought and died.

CHAPTER 25

GERMANY

As my eyes slowly opened, it felt like the lids were glued together, and I had to blink several times to try and clear them. I could feel something in my throat and started to panic, as it was stopping me from breathing. I started thrashing around to remove it, but my right arm was held back by something, and it took me several attempts to force my arm free—as I did, I could feel warm blood running down my arm. A voice beside me reassured me, 'You're okay. Stay still, you're okay.'

The woman with the soothing voice was holding my arms down, and I could feel someone else pulling the tube out of my throat. My vision slowly returned to me as I kept blinking to try to clear what felt like sand in my eyes. I could see I was in a hospital bed, with intravenous lines in my arms, and tubes and gauges all over me. I was utterly confused. I tried to speak, and when I did, I felt agonising pain in my ribs, forcing me to lie back and take deep breaths to calm myself—with each breath, the pain would force me to take shallower breaths and limit my ability to speak.

After a few moments of shallow breathing, with a creaky voice, I asked the woman, an African American with a thick Southern accent, where I was. 'Scott, you're in Germany at the Landstuhl Military Hospital.' I lay there momentarily, trying to remember what had happened and how I came to the hospital. Immediately, I assumed I must have hit an IED and started to panic. 'My legs, my legs, I can't feel my legs,' I cried, my voice still not recovered. 'Scott, your legs are fine, they're there, you're okay,' she said reassuringly. 'Show me, show me, I need to see,' I demanded, still unconvinced.

The nurse, now joined by another two colleagues, sat me up and removed the blanket covering me so I could see my legs. My left leg was wrapped in a bandage from ankle to knee, and my right leg was in a soft cast. I wriggled my toes, and they worked. Relieved, I lay back down. I tried to talk but went into a coughing fit—each time I coughed, the pain in my ribs was so intense it would cause me to cry out, further exacerbating the pain in my ribs and neck.

Still confused, I asked her what had happened.

'Scott, you were in a helicopter crash in Afghanistan. You were flown here from Kandahar.' I tried to come to terms with what she said. She must have got it wrong, I thought, as I wasn't in a helicopter—my last memory was leading my team to a compound for a DA raid.

'No, you have it wrong,' I told her, between bouts of coughing and trying not to move too much in an effort to minimise the pain. 'Go get me somebody who knows what they're talking about,' I begged her. Unfazed, the nurse walked out and returned with a slightly older woman who also had a thick Southern American accent.

'Mr Ryder, you were in a helicopter crash; you were brought here from Kandahar,' she said before going on to tell me the injuries I had suffered. I lay there, trying my best to remember, and started to recall gearing up for a night helicopter job, but that felt like months ago. As she continued with my list of injuries, I thought of the team, hoping they were okay.

'How many survivors?' I asked, interrupting her mid-sentence. She looked at the other nurse, and I repeated my question.

'Scott, there were four killed,' she said.

Surely not, I thought. 'Aircrew or passengers?' I asked, trying not to panic.

'I'm sorry, Scott, they were all passengers.'

I never knew that grief and guilt could overcome a person with such a force so suddenly that your very existence becomes worthless. I was so overwhelmed with sadness that I began to sob uncontrollably—each sob and cry matched with a pain in my neck of equal ferocity, but I didn't care. I didn't know how I was the only survivor, and my whole team was dead. I didn't think I would walk properly ever again. It all became too much.

After inferring that my whole team was dead—I had no recollection of the flight, or the fact there were other passengers besides us—I thought of Garry, Chucky, Anthony and Davis and how I would live with myself for surviving. I thought of their families—how could I ever face them? As I lay there in pain, tears and confusion, I closed my eyes and asked God to take me.

At that moment, I had no desire to live. For the first and only time in my life, I wanted to die to be with the team. As I write this, those memories are still fresh, and I still find it difficult to think of them.

I remained in despair while doctors and nurses asked me questions, fussing about my intravenous lines and taking notes, but I wasn't paying attention. I was in a different place, my mind spinning, hopelessly trying to remember what had happened, still believing that my entire team was dead. Surely not, I thought to myself. I wasn't religious, but that day as I lay on the bed, I prayed to God that the nurses had got it wrong. Surely this couldn't be right.

A few hours later, Kane, one of the company's members, walked into my room, and I don't think I have ever been so relieved to see a familiar face. I held his hand, wanting to ask him everything, but I couldn't stop sobbing. Eventually, I got it out.

'What the fuck happened?' I asked him as he held my hand tighter.

'Chucky is gone, mate. Garry and Anthony are alive, but Garry's in a bad way. Scotty Palmer and Tim Aplin are also dead,' he said. I was relieved, sad and still utterly confused.

'Tim and Scott? Why were they on board?' I asked. Before that mission, we had only ever had our team in our chopper. Garry had dropped Davis off the list for that night to make room for an assault team who were there to support us, Kane explained. I had forgotten that entirely. Kane then told me what had happened and the status of each of the survivors.

Pete Rudland, who was leading the assault team, was in a bad way. John, one of Pete's team members, was okay with a few broken bones and still conscious. Matty was fine but had fractured his spine. Anthony had suffered multiple broken bones and an open-book fracture of his pelvis. Brandon Silk, of the flight crew, was dead, but the loadmaster and pilots were alive. The signaller, Gary Wilson, was in a coma and not looking good, and his interpreter was alive but in a bad way. Kane explained to me that Chucky had been pronounced dead in the hospital at Kandahar, with Scotty and Tim having been killed on impact. The nurses had been wrong. Three passengers had died, not four. And I'd been mistaken too: I wasn't the only team member to survive. It was a lot to take in.

Meanwhile, back in Sydney, the unit liaison officers informed our families of the crash. My sister called Sarah to tell her I had been in an accident and gave her updates as my mum was on the phone to the unit, trying to gauge what had happened.

Initially, there was confusion, as the unit had called my mother and told her that her son, Anthony, had been in an accident, but not to worry as he only had minor injuries. My mum's anxiety increased immediately as she explained that her son's name was Scott, not Anthony.

Sarah, who was at work, felt sick—she knew something was wrong as soon as she saw my sister's name flashing on her phone. Sarah's boss sent her home as she frantically called around unit members and their partners, trying to find out what had happened. My family were told I had just broken my legs, and they would only fly my mother over to Germany as she was still listed as my primary next of kin, adding that this was a good thing, as they only fly two family members for those who are classified very seriously injured.

My family was inundated with calls from friends who had learned of the accident on the news—it was headlining across all channels and online media platforms. The names of Chucky, Tim and Scott had been released, but the rest of our names were not published because everybody in SOCOMD has protected identity status. Mitch McAlister, a close mate in the unit, acted as an unofficial liaison officer between the regiment and my family, keeping Sarah and my parents updated with news.

Once Sarah learned that Chucky had died, she drove straight to Cronulla to be with Chucky's girlfriend, Tess. She had thought she would not be needed for anything to do with me, as my mother got ready to fly to Germany. But that night, Sarah got a phone call from the unit asking her if she had a passport. One of my broken ribs had caused my lung to collapse, classifying me as very seriously injured, so she was now eligible to fly with my mother.

Sarah didn't have a passport at the time. But after going home to pack, she was met at the passport office by representatives from the Defence Community Organisation, who had organised a passport to be issued on the spot, then she went on to the airport with my mother for the long flight to Germany. Sarah, who is not a good flier at the best of times, did her best to control her anxiety, opting not to eat, being unable to sleep and counting down the minutes until she could get off the plane.

Meanwhile, as Sarah and my mum were in the air, the doctors were operating on me at Landstuhl. Before I went in for surgery, one of the doctors had briefed me on my injuries. Multiple fractures of my thoracic spine that needed fusion right away would see ten screws and two plates fixed to my spine, which are still there today.

I had broken two ribs, and this had punctured my lung cavity, causing a condition known as a tension pneumothorax. My left shin had a large chunk of meat missing to the bone, and I had broken my right leg in two places and shattered my right ankle, which would need surgery back in Australia; I had also chipped and broken some teeth.

Aside from the significant injuries, which took priority, I would also find out later that I had damaged my lumbar spine, torn ligaments in both my shoulders and swathes of skin missing from all over my body. We all had suffered knocks to the head, known as traumatic brain injury, although mine was a lot less severe than Garry Robinson's or Gary Wilson's—they were both in comas.

After the surgery on my spine, the pain and swelling became almost unbearable. As my lungs began healing, I would go into fits of coughing and spit up vile brown mucus—each time I coughed, my broken ribs and spine would make me feel like I was being stabbed.

At times, this cycle of pain would be so bad that I would scream for pain relief, and they would give me morphine or ketamine, which would put me out and help me get through another few hours. As I woke, my grief and pain would wash over me again, and I would wish I was back out. I would remember that Chucky was dead, then go into fits of coughing, then ask for more drugs—it was a vicious cycle.

Arriving at Landstuhl, our families were provided rooms at Fisher House, an annex of the hospital reserved for families whose loved ones are patients. When they came to the hospital, Sarah and my mum were met by the surgeon who had just completed the operation on my spine. He showed them images of my thoracic area before the surgery with what looked like spaghetti around my spine. That was my spinal cord—immediate surgery had been required to reduce the risk of paralysis.

I spent the next few days recovering from the surgery. My neck and upper back felt like they were completely locked up, and I would ask Sarah to massage my neck to try to relieve the pain. 'You would ask for a massage, then the moment I would touch you, you would cry out that it was too hard, even though I was barely touching you,' Sarah says.

As much as I was relieved that I had not lost the use of my legs, the doctors were uncertain how much mobility I would have once my back healed. The fractures to my leg weren't severe enough to warrant external fixators, but I would have to wait until my back had healed to find out if I could get back on the tools. My immediate concern was keeping my job. I did not want to leave the army, and the anxiety around my uncertain future would continue for the next two years.

Sarah stayed with me the entire time I was in there, only taking short breaks to leave the hospital. One afternoon I woke up, and Sarah was next to me. As we were chatting she asked me what the brown mark on my bedsheet was. She lifted the sheet to investigate and was met with my shit completely covering the bed, my clothes, and the sheets. I had shat myself and not even known about it. She called for a nurse, but after twenty minutes of waiting, she started cleaning me up herself. I was embarrassed and helpless. When the nurse came in, they spent the next 30 minutes doing their best to clean me while I lay there in pain, utterly humiliated.

But at least I was alive. Tim Aplin had always yearned to become a commando, but his wife Jen was against it. With two kids at home, she viewed a career in SF as inherently riskier than his job as an infantryman. He obliged, only applying for SF after they separated.

Even before becoming a commando, service life had been tough on the family. 'I always had the kids; Tim was always away from home and the kids missed their dad,' Jen said. After successfully passing commando selection, Tim remarried. It was his new wife, Tash, who had to make the difficult call to Jen about Tim's death.

'I'd just got off a plane when she called me,' Jen says. 'I was feeling very off that day. I knew something wasn't right. When she told me, I felt sick, I collapsed on the spot.' Tim's children, Josie, who was nine, and Daniel, eight, were in the car, waiting with Jen's mother to pick her up. When she got to the car, she broke the news.

'I was not equipped to tell them. I don't know what I said or how I said it. We were only going off what Tash had told us,' Jen said. To make matters worse, nobody from the ADF had contacted Jen, or Tim's mother, who discovered Tim was dead when she was watching the TV news and saw a story about three commandos who had been killed. Tim's mother called Tash, who had to break the news to her. 'Nobody called us. It's like we didn't exist,' Jen recalled.

Every commando must provide documents naming the next of kin to be notified in the event of injury or death. As Tim had remarried, Jen was no longer his next of kin, which meant that notification teams weren't required to contact her. It is a bureaucratic technicality that excludes families from critical support when they need it the most. The effects on Jen and her kids were devastating. 'When I told them in the car, they didn't understand. I think they were in shock,' she said. 'We all slept in the same bed that night. I was so upset for them—they will have to deal with this for the rest of their lives.' Jen shared with me the ongoing impact of Tim's death on the family:

Josie was already seeing a therapist to help her deal with Tim being away and our marriage splitting up. Tim's death affected her greatly, and she acted out a lot. Both kids would cry a lot every night. I had to stop working to be with them. Josie wasn't sleeping and would lie awake till 2 a.m. crying. Her bin next to her bed would be full of tissues. I didn't know how to help her. When we started seeing therapists again, she would shut down when Tim was brought up. She didn't want to hear it. Daniel dealt with it differently. Being younger, he attached himself to me. If I was out of the house and coming home late, the kids would be in a panic, and they thought something would happen to me.

After a week, we prepared to leave the Landstuhl hospital and fly back to Sydney. Garry and Gary were still in a bad way, both in comas, but the rest of us were conscious, although heavily medicated. We thanked our nurses and were met by a team of RAAF doctors and nurses. An RAAF C-17 Globemaster aircraft fitted out to be an AME platform flew all of us back to Sydney. The aircraft was impressive, with multiple beds for critical and injured patients, a team of doctors and a nurse for each of us.

As we all got wheeled out of the hospital to the waiting transportation that would take us to the aircraft, a guard of honour was formed at the hospital's exit. Every staff member from Landstuhl who wasn't attending patients clapped and cheered, and we were taken through the guard, with people randomly shouting out, 'Thanks for your service!' and 'Be well, Aussies!' It was a moving experience and elevated our mood for the journey home. As I always say, when it comes to military customs and traditions, the US does it so much better than we do.

As we boarded the plane, I saw Garry for the first time and was shocked at his condition. He was in an induced coma and had dozens of cables and tubes hanging off him. It was a stark contrast to the tall, fit TL I had last seen. Garry would never be the same again. I asked the medical team about his condition, and they told me he had severe brain damage and there was a good chance he would lose his left leg, so bad was the damage below his knee.

As we touched down at RAAF Base Richmond, seven ambulances were waiting to take us to Westmead Private Hospital in Western Sydney. The strategic airlift from Germany through to Sydney had been a remarkable exercise in logistics—the first time seven casualties had been strategically moved across the globe.

When his phone had first rung, the senior medical officer at Forces Command, Surgeon PS11, a colonel, was walking out the door for a family holiday. It was his boss, and the urgency in his voice told him this was serious. Without hesitation, Surgeon PS11 got moving.

His first task was to find a hospital that could hold seven patients. 'I rang around all the hospitals in the area. I needed to find a place that had the capacity to treat and had low visibility from the public.' The story was headlining the news, and our protected identity was at risk if the media caught wind of what hospital we were in.

The managers at Westmead Private Hospital in Sydney happily agreed, and Surgeon PS11 built his team. 'I had every resource at my disposal; I got anything I asked for,' he said. He called around, and every specialist he spoke to agreed without hesitation to come on board. Anaesthetists, plastic surgeons, general surgeons, orthopaedic surgeons and dental surgeons were assembled, an expert team of the country's best.

Before our arrival, Surgeon PS11 briefed the entire staff of Westmead Private in the courtyard. 'They have risked their lives for us and done their best; now it's our turn,' he told them. 'These men have protected identity; you don't talk about it; you don't tell anyone. We don't want the media attention making them and their families' lives harder after everything they've been through.'

Ultimately, he and his team conducted numerous surgeries on all of us. Remarkably, not one of the specialists asked to be paid.

Surgeon PS11, who still runs a private practice in Sydney serving the veteran community by helping them with their Department of Veterans' Affairs medical claims, cites the project as one of the proudest moments of his career, and has nothing but respect and admiration for everyone involved. 'It was a team effort. It had never been done before. More should have been done to recognise people's efforts.'

Surgeon PS11 recalled another significant event from our treatment at Westmead: the time he approved a request from Garry Robinson's family to have their dog visit. The dog entered the ICU, jumped onto Garry's bed, and licked his face and arms. 'It was like the dog knew what was happening and was beckoning him to wake up,' he says.

And the next day, Garry did wake up.

I spent the next few months in the hospital undergoing many surgeries and physiotherapy sessions to regain my mobility. When the nurses went to remove the bandage on my left shin, which had been damaged to the bone but had already begun to heal, they ripped skin from the hole in my leg. It was excruciating.

After a few weeks, I was put in a room with Anthony. We had numerous visitors, including senior military officers and the governor-general of Australia, Quentin Bryce. An elegant, softly spoken woman, she had become fond of commandos after a few security details the regiment had provided her with for a trip to the Middle East, and she seemed genuinely concerned for us. She came in, sat on my bed and held my hand, asking me about my role in the unit. She asked me about my back injury, and my brain, foggy from oxycodone, thought it would be a good idea to take my shirt off, much to the horror of her entourage and the senior military officials who were present.

One day, the nurses told me that they wanted to change the catheter that was currently living in the eye of my dick, which I didn't have a problem with until they said it wasn't done under anaesthesia. I looked at the giant tube that would be inserted into my penis and told them there was zero chance that was happening while I was conscious. They argued that anaesthesia wasn't possible, and then I remembered I had a consultation with a plastic surgeon that afternoon, so I informed the nurses I would get him to do it the next day instead.

The nurses told me Peter Hayward, a highly regarded plastic surgeon, didn't change patients' catheters. 'I'll see about that,' I thought to myself.

Peter came later that day and explained about the skin graft that would be cut from my hip and placed onto my left shin. After he finished, he asked me if I had any questions. I sure did. Pulling my pants down, I pointed to the giant tube protruding from my dick. 'Mate, they want to pull this out and shove another one back in while I'm awake. There's no fucking way that's happening. Can you please sort this while I'm under for my skin graft?' I asked. He looked at me for a second, and then a smile appeared. 'I think we can sort that, Scott,' he said.

*

I was happy to be in a room with Anthony, and I was now recovered enough to spend my days tormenting him. He had horrible hip fractures, and his recovery had been slower than mine. I could sit up in bed, eventually get onto a wheelchair with some help, and get around. I would spend hours drinking coffee with friends and family at the café in the courtyard. One of my mates, Steve, visited me almost every day.

Somebody bought me a Nerf gun, so I spent hours shooting darts at Anthony, the walls, the fan and sometimes the nurses who walked past. Some found it amusing—a lot of them didn't. One day Anthony was being helped to the bathroom by a nurse. He was in a lot of pain, so to help him, I fired Nerf bullets at his head. The nurse threatened to take my gun away. I pointed it at her face while she winced and ducked.

Once I could get around in the wheelchair, I would visit Garry Robinson every few hours. He was awake, but due to his head injuries he had many memory problems, unable to recall where he was or grasp his injuries completely. One day, he asked me to get closer to him. I leaned in, and he grabbed my shirt. 'Scott, these cunts are trying to kill me, so this is what we'll do. You close the door on the nurses and help me get into my wheelchair, and we'll get out through the fire exit.' He was dead serious.

He got angry when I tried to explain that this was impossible. 'You're supposed to have my back. Why are you leaving me?' he asked. It was hard to see him like this. The next day he seemed in good spirits, and we had a normal conversation. I was surprised he was talking about the crash, as the day before, I'd had to tell him about it repeatedly. Then, out of the blue, he asked me about Chucky.

'Have you seen him around, mate? He hasn't come to see me yet.'

I was stunned. Garry looked at me, concerned.

'Garry, Chucky's dead, mate. He didn't survive the crash.'

Garry had known Chucky was gone but, in his state, had forgotten. Garry then burst into tears and sobbed while I held his hand. I spent the next hour or so talking Garry through the crash—who was sitting where, and how we had been evacuated. He was still visibly upset, so I left him alone for the rest of the day. It was hard for me to comfort Garry, as it was still very raw for me too, but I tried to remain strong for him.

The next day, Garry again asked me where Chucky was, and I once more went through the crash story and told him that Chucky was gone. Again, he burst into tears, and we spent more time reviewing the crash, the deployment and the state of the rest of the team. The day after, however, I came prepared. I had drawn a diagram of the chopper, showing everyone's seat and the survivors' names and injuries.

Once I knew this would happen each day, it didn't affect me as much. We continued this routine for a week or so, until he was well enough to remember himself.

Eventually, I was in a good enough position to leave the hospital and go home—a place I hadn't seen in more than eight months. But my battles in Australia were only beginning.

CHAPTER 26

PAYING THE PIPER

After I was finally allowed to go home, I continued to get treatment as an outpatient, primarily for physiotherapy and dental. My several chipped and broken teeth required attention, as the exposed nerves were causing me discomfort. But aside from healing from my injuries, I was in good spirits and optimistic about my future. I was soon out of my wheelchair and on crutches, but in the back of my mind was a constant fear.

The army had placed me on a medical classification that gave me ample time to recover, but there was a genuine chance I would be medically discharged, and that kept me up at night. I told myself that if I got better as soon as possible, I could begin training to get back on the tools. Then one morning, I ran into the RSM at the hospital; he was on his way out from visiting Garry and Gary. He dropped a bombshell on me that left me gobsmacked.

'Scott, just so you know, the range incident hasn't been forgotten. It would be best if you got in contact with a legal officer soon. You'll be court-martialled with grievous bodily harm,' he said, in a very matter-of-fact way.

I was so stunned I nearly dropped my crutches. Surely not. I'd expected to face some consequences for the incident, but I never thought it would be a charge as severe as grievous bodily harm. Any motivation I had for rehab, or hopes of getting back to work, were shattered instantly. The comment so totally crushed my spirit that I immediately dropped into a pit of anxiety, panic and shock. For the first time in my career, I no longer felt like a soldier but an outsider—someone the system wanted to punish.

I jumped in a cab and called Sarah. She was furious. 'They're doing what? Are you serious? They can't do that! If what you did was so bad, they should have sent you home. They can't pretend it didn't happen, then send you back out on jobs, then charge you because you survived!' She had a point. I was still on crutches and undergoing intense rehabilitation, not knowing if I could ever walk or run again due to my spinal fusion. I was on two types of oxycodone and I couldn't think clearly. The drugs exacerbated my anxiety about the charge.

On 16 September, I was officially delivered my charge notice by the director of military prosecutions. 'Following the review of the brief of evidence, I have decided to prefer charges against PTE [Private] Ryder,' the document read. The two charges were 'Engaging in conduct outside the Jervis Bay Territory that is an offence causing grievous bodily harm' and 'Unauthorised discharge of a weapon'.

I contacted legal services and was given the name of David McLure SC, an Army Reserve lawyer working for a law firm in the Sydney CBD.

Lance called me when he heard about the charge. He bore me no ill will; he knew it was just an accident. Lance also had mixed emotions about the range incident himself. As the team 2ic, had he not been injured at the range, he would have been sitting on the chopper the night we crashed.

I had numerous phone calls and meetings with David over the coming months, who was equally surprised that the director of military prosecutions was pursuing such a severe charge, where I could face imprisonment if found guilty. At one meeting, he asked me what the worse moment of the entire ordeal had been, and I broke down in tears as I recalled waking up in Germany, thinking my whole team was dead. I didn't know this then, but that answer would be used strategically at the trial.

As the trial date grew near, my anxiety would get to the point where I had trouble sleeping, so I started taking sleeping tablets and Valium. And to manage the pain in my body, I found I was taking more opioid painkillers, to which my body was steadily building up a resistance. I saw a psychologist at 2 Cdo Regt, who commented on the drastic effect the impending trial was having on me. She could see that the director of military prosecutions was taking a dogmatic view in pursuing the grievous bodily harm charge. I was mentally and physically broken, and my body quickly became a petri dish of prescription medications.

I felt abandoned and dejected and could not come to terms with the fact that I was being treated as a criminal. I didn't expect, nor have I ever expected, special treatment for surviving the crash, but I also never expected to be charged with such a severe crime.

The stress of the trial brought my deeply harboured survivor's guilt to the surface, and I sometimes broke down under the weight of it. One night, at a barbecue with some friends, I got blind drunk. Mixing alcohol with my heavy medication was a bad idea, and Sarah found me inconsolable in the shower, claiming it should have been me who died, as the others didn't hurt their mates at the range.

I was beginning to abuse my medication, but I didn't care. I spent most of December off my face; when I wasn't, I would lash out at

Sarah, my family or anyone I was with. I had developed a terrible temper, which everyone attributed to post-traumatic stress disorder (PTSD), but I knew it wasn't that. I was tracking fine till I was told I might go to gaol for grievous bodily harm and therefore might never be a commando again.

On the weekends over that Christmas break, I began partying even harder. I figured I already had a bunch of drugs in me that the army had given me, so what was the harm in increasing my dosage? The combination of opioids and booze took all my pain away and the stress of the trial vanished. I also found it healing; when I was off my face, I would openly talk about my experience and how I felt to my mates or whomever I was with on a two-day bender.

I am in no way advocating for abusing prescription medication, but for me, then, it seemed to help. Still, I was on a slippery slope, mixing pain medications and booze. I began to lose weight, and my skin turned a strange yellow.

Sarah bore the brunt of the worst of my behaviour. I would tell her I was going out for a few beers on a Friday, promising her I wouldn't drink too much as I was still on medication. But I had already planned how fucked up I would get. Sometimes I wouldn't stumble back in through the front door for days.

One weekend, my phone died shortly after I went out on a Friday night. All weekend Sarah was frantically looking for me, calling all my mates. Then, not knowing what to do, she decided to drive around my usual haunts in the Hills on Sunday morning.

When she found me, I'd been walking home from some dude's house where I'd been having an all-weekend bender. I had passed out on the side of a road that happened to be next to a hotel where a wedding had just taken place. Driving past the hotel, Sarah noticed a group of people looking and pointing at the ground, and she knew it was me. I was angry at the world because of what was happening to me, and I didn't care who I hurt, including myself.

One day in late February 2011, I hobbled into work to get my polyester service uniform, still unable to place too much weight on my right ankle, which had been operated on weeks before, undergoing a complete reconstruction. The consensus at work was in line with Sarah's—nobody could believe the scale of charges laid against me.

A few days later, Sarah and I drove to Victoria Barracks in Paddington, Sydney, not saying a word the entire way, my feeling of trepidation growing with each passing minute. We were met by David, who explained the process, and stepped into the courtroom. Lance, who had now fully recovered, and Mitch, with whom I'd been living before Sarah moved in, his partner, and a group of workmates and family were all there in support. I hadn't been able to eat anything that morning, and my medication was making me feel nauseous—or maybe it was the nerves.

The first day was anticlimactic, debating whether my name would be released to the media. David fought against it, citing that I still had a protected identity; the prosecutor argued it was in the public interest to do so. The day was also noteworthy for another reason. Sarah had contacted a respected investigative journalist, Chris Masters, who was the only Australian journalist ever allowed to be embedded with the SOTG.

On arrival, Chris met resistance from the court staff, but they could not stop him, as this was still classified as a public hearing. 'I think David thought having me in there would keep them honest,' Chris explained. After endless complex legal debate, the first day ended, and I was happy to get home and into bed.

On day two of the trial, I gave my testimony. I felt dizzy as I walked up to the stand, and I could see the anxiety in Sarah's face; she was barely able to contain herself. David asked me about the day it had happened and my decision to fire the round. I explained the culture on range practices at TK to date, and the prosecutor grilled me on my decision to fire the round despite knowing it was illegal to do so.

Interviews with those involved, representations of the range layout, and images of the range, the weapon and everyone's position when I fired were presented. It was long and exhausting. I constantly tried to gauge where the verdict was heading, but the legal talk and continual references to documents I had never seen made it difficult.

Then David asked me the question I'd been dreading: 'Can you tell me what the worst experience has been for you in the past few months?' Hesitating, I looked at David, and he gave me a slow nod as if to say, 'You know what I'm asking; go on.' As soon as I started to speak, my voice was muffled, I could barely get the words out. 'When I woke up in Germany, I wasn't sure where I was. The nurses told me I'd been in a helicopter crash, but I didn't believe them,' I said. I paused; my chin started to tremble. 'The nurses got the details wrong; I thought I was the only survivor,' I sobbed. 'I wanted to die,' I said before burying my face in my hands, not wanting the court to see my crying.

The judge was also in tears, as was Sarah and half of the gallery. It was decided to drop the grievous bodily harm charge. When David told me, I was relieved, but he said not to get too comfortable; we still had the UD charge to hear. We were ushered outside to await the verdict, and then within an hour I was found guilty with no conviction, and the trial ended. The prosecuting lawyer came up and shook my hand. 'Congrats, mate, a good result,' he said.

I hugged Sarah. It was finally over. A giant weight had been lifted off my shoulders.

Within a few days, Chris Masters published a special report on page two of the *Daily Telegraph*, titled 'Australian War Hero Court Trauma'. The article described me as 'Private S' and outlined the range incident, crash and injuries. 'As his fiancée, I want to know, if he did do wrong, why was he allowed to go on an operation?' Sarah is quoted as saying, under the name 'Tracy'. My psychologist was also interviewed and paraphrased: 'Soldiers were trained to deal with combat-related trauma. What they were not prepared for was a perception the institution they trusted to look after him had turned against them,' she said. My lawyer, David, was even quoted as saying the decision to prosecute me was 'callous and demonstrating a weird lack of empathy'.[41]

The reaction from the public was strong. Talkback radio stations and other publications picked up the story, and the public seemed outraged that I had been charged, given that I had been put in a life-threatening situation and was only charged after surviving the crash.

I learned a valuable lesson from the experience. If I stayed in the army, it would be for my reasons. The experience taught me that I could never expect loyalty from the organisation, and that no matter who you were, you were ultimately just a number that could be easily replaced.

As I was medically downgraded after the crash, I could not hold a position in the commando teams, so I was sent to work with the unit's PT instructors while I continued my rehab journey. I was slowly coming off my pain medication but was now placed on antidepressants. They made me nauseous for a few weeks, but they did help to a degree.

My issue wasn't that I was depressed; I just wanted my job back. I knew that to get medically upgraded, I would have to take the commando annual fitness test, so I set my sights on training. I was only working one or two days a week, helping the PT instructors run activities, so I had plenty of time to devote to it.

My first training program consisted of walking out to the cul-de-sac in front of our unit in Castle Hill in the Hills district, walking up and down the fire exit stairs, and doing five push-ups, five air squats and five sit-ups. That was one round, and I would do as many rounds as possible in twenty minutes. It was challenging work and had me sweating profusely. My sweat smelled toxic, with all my medications pouring out of me, but it felt good to sweat. Then on the weekends, I would go out and get shitfaced, ruining all my good work through the week.

My motivation for training would come in peaks and troughs. Some days I was confident I would get back to the boys and be on the tools, which would keep me pushing hard; other days, I would wonder why I was bothering, then sit around the house popping pills and playing Xbox. There had never been a commando with metal in his spine who had been deployed again, and I knew my chances were slim.

Matty Compton, one of the boys in Pete Rudland's team from the crash, had also suffered a spinal fusion to his cervical spine, but had opted for a medical discharge as soon as we got back. He had fallen in love with one of the nurses he met in Germany, which may have influenced his decision. I needed something more concrete to work towards.

A mate of mine, Steve McKinnon, an eight-time world champion Muay Thai kickboxer, suggested I get back into training, as I had attended some classes in the past. My fitness needed a lot of work, and nothing gets you fitter than kickboxing. As soon as I started, I became obsessed, quickly increasing my private sessions with Steve and moving from the beginners' class to the fighter class run by his brother Stuart, the owner of the gym where the classes were.

The fighters' classes were challenging and run like a traditional Thai gym. Stuart expected prospective fighters to do a 5-kilometre run before the class started, then we would do a few hours of work on the pads, clinching, hitting the heavy bags and sparring. I loved the sparring element, and always sought learning opportunities from the more experienced fighters.

Within a few months, I had my fitness back, and the goal of getting in the ring had me drop all my pain meds. I found physical training a more beneficial way to manage my injuries than lying on my back taking tablets. To this day, I don't take any pain medication apart from an anti-inflammatory now and then. I still stayed on my antidepressants for no other reason than I didn't want weaning off the drugs to affect my training.

For me, fighting training felt like when I was training for selection or getting my fitness up and ready for deployment, as it gave me a clear goal to work towards. I also enjoyed the intensity and nerves during sparring; there is something primal about standing in a ring and using your fitness and skill to beat an opponent physically.

After months of hard training, I entered the ring for my first fight.

My mates from Alpha Company and many civilian friends from the Hills came to watch my fight at the Roxy Theatre in Parramatta, and I was surprised at how nervous I was. Finally, after hours of anxious waiting, I stepped into the ring for three two-minute rounds of K-1 rules (no elbows) kickboxing, where I won on points. I was fit but exhausted after the first round; the nervous energy you experience before a fight takes away so much of your physical capacity.

I had found the same thing to be true in combat. In training, carrying the same amount of gear, you could run around for hours clearing buildings and rooms, but in real life, the nervous energy and adrenaline reduce your physical capacity to the point that you are gassed after clearing a few compounds. I found many similarities in the physical and mental responses in kickboxing and armed combat, and I was hooked. In a small way, I was preparing myself for the chance that I would never be a commando again, and was looking to fill the inevitable void. At the time, I thought kickboxing may have been what would do it.

The week after that match, I booked a two-week trip to Thailand to train at a local gym. And if I thought training in Sydney was hard, the Thais took it to the next level. Two three-hour sessions a day while I tried to acclimatise was hard work, but I relished the training and fell in love with the Muay Thai culture. In my spare time, I would go to every local Thai boxing match, and on the way home, I watched the locals battle it out in the famous Lumpinee Stadium in Bangkok.

I had my second fight in Canberra a few weeks later, which I also won on points, and booked another training trip to Thailand for my third fight in a few months. But I broke my rib (again) in Thailand while sparring with one of the trainers, and had to take a break from sparring and fighting for the rest of the year. I didn't mind, as I had completely neglected my rehabilitation and was starting to get constant pain and tightness in my back.

In addition to Muay Thai, I also got into CrossFit. Again, I enjoyed the style of CrossFit, as it replicated the physical movements in combat. CrossFit isn't just slow, long-distance runs or powerlifting, but a combination of nearly all styles of training, using both aerobic and anaerobic energy systems. Running, then dragging, then a bodyweight activity followed by a rope climb in a weighted vest is by far the best form of training you can do for combat, and I thoroughly enjoyed it. I probably could have gone a bit easier on my back, though, as deadlifts and muscle-ups certainly didn't help my injuries.

But while I was working on my new physical endeavours, Charlie Company, 2 Cdo Regt, was in some of the heaviest fighting they'd seen to date, which would take the lives of two commandos and an engineer within a few weeks of each other.

CHAPTER 27

THE LONG ROAD BACK

Helmand province had been a heavily contested part of Afghanistan due to the vast networks of opium production directly linked to funding and resourcing the Taliban insurgency. In Helmand, 2 Cdo Regt was exposed to a level of intense combat unparalleled by anything seen by any other Australian unit in the entire Afghanistan war. It would cement 2 Cdo Regt's reputation in the international SF community.

A SOTG plans officer, Major Tristen, had strongly advocated for TF66 to build relationships with the US Drug Enforcement Agency and Afghanistan's National Interdiction Unit, which was a higher calibre of unit than the PRC, with whom the TF was already partnered.[42] Approval was finally given, and TF66 prepared for its first 'counter-nexus' operations into Helmand, given the codename Makha Niwel.

There was constant jostling for jobs between SASR's FE-A and 2 Cdo Regt's FE-B. FE-A had taken the role of targeting critical Taliban leadership within Uruzgan province, while FE-B conducted larger-scale offensive operations in Uruzgan and neighbouring provinces, targeting known high-activity enemy zones to eliminate Taliban networks and generate further intelligence.

Commando Adam Smith recalls Charlie Company inserting into Helmand province via chopper during the night for a walk into a cluster of compounds and built-up areas. 'My team leader and I were both lying in this shallow hole in the ground in the open, while accurate tracer fire and RPG fire landed all around us. Never have I been shot at with such accurate fire at night; they must have had night vision, because it was pitch black.' Over the following days, multiple operators would be wounded.

As teams fought through Keshmesh Khan to target key IED facilitation nodes, they discovered fortified enemy positions, wall keyholes, escape holes and tunnel systems—something not typically encountered inside Uruzgan. This highlighted the sophistication of the Taliban in Helmand province.

During another clearance, Adam walked past a compound that had a large metal door with padlocks, and he could hear the enemy talking inside. The team threw grenades into the compound with little effect, then one operator fired a 40mm grenade at the door to breach it. The grenade initiated an IED next to the door; blood from the enemy was all over the floor as the team cleared it, but the wounded man had escaped through a mousehole.

Multiple teams were in heavy and close contact. Sergeant Brett Wood, a well-respected veteran and mentor to many at the regiment, was the Tango platoon sergeant and attached himself to a team led by Matty Bourne. An enemy PKM gunner who had ambushed the platoon moments before had fled through a maze of compounds; Matty's team began clearing compounds, using aqueducts and jumping from roof to roof to minimise their chances of stepping on an IED.

It was high-level urban warfighting at its core. 'Throughout the clearance, we used high-explosive grenades when clearing rooms and over compound walls,' Matty recalled. As Matty slowly moved around the corner at the end of an alleyway, he was rocked by a massive explosion. It was an enemy IED. 'I remember screaming and realised I had landed metres away from where I'd been standing,' he said.

Another operator, Tyson, realising Brett was missing, under accurate machine gun fire grabbed another commando and they moved into the location of the IED strike, with complete disregard for their own safety, as there was a high change of another IED. They found Brett and Matty, and dragged them into a compound. Realising their precarious position, Matty pulled his pistol out to cover the rear door of the compound—injured or not, the Taliban could take advantage of the blast and attack at any moment. Then, over the company radio, a call for help went out: 'We need a fucking medivac right now—we've got a triple amputee.'[43] Tyson would later be awarded the Medal for Gallantry for his actions that day.

Brett Wood had stepped on an IED; he lost three limbs and could not be saved. He would be the eighth commando killed in Afghanistan—a tragic loss that was felt by every member of Charlie Company and 2 Cdo Regt.

Within a few weeks, Charlie Company and the US Drug Enforcement Agency were back in northern Helmand in an intense battle with a hardened and well-prepared enemy. On 6 June, multiple teams were in heavy contact, and Sapper Rowan Robinson from IRR was shot in the throat in an overwatch position on a ridgeline, the second Australian claimed by Helmand. The counter-nexus operations were taking a heavy toll on TF66.

On 4 July, FE-B returned to Helmand, south of Keshmesh Khan, to the village of Mahyan. In a company-sized task, the platoons held

positions in the village while the sniper team took overwatch positions, where they came under intense small-arms and rocket fire. One of the snipers, Heath Jamieson, was shot through the neck. Somehow, Heath was alive and stable, but he needed to be evacuated immediately.

Sergeant Todd Langley, an experienced and well-respected member of the regiment, moved onto the roof of a compound with his binoculars to call in mortar fire to help the snipers withdraw from their position. At that moment, a single Taliban marksman's bullet shot him in the head. Todd died instantly. After that shot, the village erupted, with both platoons receiving accurate small-arms fire.

On hearing the snipers had sustained a priority-one casualty— Heath's bullet wound—Adam Smith, an assaulter, and his team moved to a position to support the team's withdrawal, pouring machine gun fire onto likely enemy positions. Moments later, he heard over the radio about Todd. 'When we heard Todd was killed, it was a shock, but you must get on with it,' Adam said later. 'You suppress any emotion and focus on the job. Your mates depend on you not to fall apart. They rely on you.'

Matty and his team moved in to where Todd had been killed. Every time they reached up to try to get Todd's body, they would be engaged with accurate fire. They eventually had to place an explosive charge on the ceiling next to Todd to blow a hole to extract him. JTACs called in 2000-pound bombs onto the enemy, who was dangerously close, only a few hundred metres from the platoon positions, to help the team break away to the helicopter landing zone. They were under fire the whole time, engaging and killing the enemy at only 25 metres.

The enemy pursued them the entire way as Charlie Company moved with Todd's body back to the helicopter landing zone. 'Todd was a big boy. It was a bloody tough stretcher carry, and lots of people took turns in carrying him, and we were getting chased up and engaged the whole way,' said Adam. 'The trip took a toll on everyone.'

In the following few months, my emotions were like a yo-yo. Knowing operators in the regiment were fighting, getting injured and dying in Helmand while I sat around marking time, I again sank into a deep depression. I have never been one to get depressed; on the contrary, things never seem to faze me as much as they do others. But the uncertainty of not knowing if I would get my job back cast a long shadow over anything positive that was happening to me at the time.

And there were a lot of positive things happening. After asking permission from her father, Pete, I took Sarah to Taronga Zoo, as she loves animals, and I proposed. I tried to get on one knee, but I was having a horrible day with my pain, so I did it standing. I had just received a small payout from the Department of Veterans' Affairs, so I splashed out on a 1.5-carat princess-cut ring imported from Israel through a mate of mine who was a jeweller. She said yes, and we set about organising an engagement party and wedding for the following year.

Back at work, I was employed in the regiment's sports shop, known as the Regy Store, which was the responsibility of the unit's PT instructors, to whom I was still attached. The shop sold various running shoes, military equipment and sports supplements. I grew to resent being there. I had gone from being a commando sniper in Afghanistan to selling water bottles, and I was deeply frustrated.

I started partying hard again on the weekends as an escape. As I awoke from each bender, I would feel hopeless; everything became an effort, and I would grind out the weekdays until I could get shitfaced with booze or anything else I could get my hands on. One day I ran into Mark, the team leader who had been injured when his Bushmaster hit an IED, and I vented my frustrations to him. 'Why the fuck am I selling shirts and protein powder? I'm a sniper—surely I would be better helping on a sniper course or doing something else more worthwhile?'

Mark, a motivated, experienced and competent soldier, reflected on my situation, and the 2 Cdo Regt Human Performance Optimisation cell was born. Injured operators would manage the unit's numerous Human Performance Optimisation initiatives and support commando core courses and training. It was another few months, however, before it was fully in place.

In the meantime, I felt like I was just going through the motions, and I even started wondering if the psychologists were right—maybe I did have PTSD and should look at getting out of the army.

Sick of my endless self-pity, Sarah sat me down. 'What do you want?' she asked.

I just looked at her.

'If you want your job back, stop moping around, start training and fight for it. Prove to them you can do this. Give it 100 per cent or get out,' she said.

It was time to decide. Did I want this badly enough? Could I get my job back? I walked inside to write my training program. I told myself I would prove them wrong. Yes, I was injured, but I wasn't done with the army yet. I still had a lot to give.

I regularly visited Garry, who was now in a rehabilitation hospital in Hornsby, in north-western Sydney. His wife would spend all day with him there, so I would drive to Wattle Grove, where they lived, next to Holsworthy, pick their kids up from school and drive them over to the hospital. Only their oldest, Bec, was out of school and now working full time. I wanted to help in any way I could. I knew if Chucky were alive, he would be doing this, so I told myself I had to do it for him. I grew close to the family and taught Garry's middle daughter, Carly, how to drive. Garry's son, Josh, would later follow in his father's footsteps and join the army, serving in 2 RAR in Townsville.

Garry's leg hadn't healed, so the decision was made to amputate it. It is brutal news for anyone to take, let alone a commando sniper and TL who was also a triathlete. He took it hard. To help him, I called my friend Paul de Gelder, the ex-navy diver who had had his arm and leg amputated after being attacked by a bull shark on a diving exercise in Sydney Harbour. I thought if Garry saw Paul and spoke with him, it might help him come to terms with it. Paul visited within the week, and the conversation helped Garry immensely. His leg was amputated the following week.

During the day, I would work out in the gym, pack march or hit the cross-country track. I knew what to do physically, and my training consumed me. In the ADF, when you are medically downgraded, you are restricted from doing certain activities based on your reasons for downgrading. My restriction would stop me from doing everything except swimming and light walking, which was futile, as the benchmark to assess commandos' suitability for the job was the commando annual fitness test—a 15-kilometre pack march in less than two hours and fifteen minutes; a 3.2-kilometre run in webbing, cams and runners; chin-ups; and a 400-metre swim in clothes and runners. So, I trained for that.

Towards the end of 2011, one of the companies was conducting its annual fitness test before another SOTG rotation, a requirement at the time, and I decided I would join them. I knew I had a medical board evaluation coming up soon, and as the first SF operator with metal in his bones who was aiming to get back overseas, I wanted to give myself the best chance possible.

Once I got there, the PT instructor, a mate from 3 RAR, told me I wasn't allowed to participate as I was medically restricted. 'Mate, there are 80 other people here. Let's just say you didn't see me.' I gave him a look that told him there was no way he could stop me, and he turned around and walked off.

My training had paid off, and I achieved a pass in all events. I waited until the PT instructor wasn't looking and wrote my details down on the sheet of paper that would be used to input the scores into the system. I might have taken a few minutes off the time and added a few chin-ups—anything to improve my prospects of getting back to the teams.

I stopped taking all other medication but stayed on my anti-depressants; I no longer suffered any side effects. In some way, I thought they might help me deal with it if I was medically discharged. The end of 2011 also saw a change in ADF-classified medical injuries. Previously, it was relatively black and white: you could either do the job or you couldn't, with a bit of room to undergo rehabilitation and be assessed for suitability for your role. But now there was a rehaul of the system, with allowances made for various medical conditions.

I tried not to build any false hope, as I realised having ten screws and two plates in my spine would be a big hurdle to overcome, but I stayed as optimistic as possible. I continued to avoid partying and drinking, and pored over my course booklets and pamphlets to keep my mind on the game. If I got the chance to get back after being off the tools for so long, I didn't want to blow it.

Before the Christmas break, my case went in front of a central medical board in Canberra. I was the first SOCOMD member to try to get upgraded with a spinal fusion and my case was conten-tious, given the board was still coming to terms with defining and categorising cases, and given my long list of injuries. The board had mixed opinions, as allowing me to deploy would set a precedent for all those with thoracic or other fusions.

After much debate, the question was asked about the physical fitness requirements for deploying commandos. My records were analysed, and there sat my results for the latest commando annual fitness test. The decision was made to upgrade me to deployable status. In a strange twist of fate, my blatant disregard for the rules was what got me over the line. I am eternally grateful to Sarah for pushing me to train and fight, and to the 2 Cdo Regt RSM, WO class one Paul Dunbavin, for fighting for me in person at the medical board.

Sarah and I married in February 2012 in front of family and friends on the New South Wales Central Coast, then spent our honeymoon in Thailand on Koh Samui island. While we were there, I had a phone call from Paul. 'Scott, how's the honeymoon?' he asked. 'Enjoy the break. As soon as you get back, you're going to Charlie Company who are on the TAG. You're back.'

I ended the call and sat on the bed, still taking in the news. I had done it.

Sarah didn't need to ask what was said—she could see it on my face. From that moment, I went cold turkey on my antidepressants and all other medications. I was a commando again.

CHAPTER 28

SLOTH LIFE

The Black Hawks sat in a holding pattern in a slow circle hundreds of feet above the bush off the coast of Wollongong, south of Sydney. I adjusted my NVG and tried to stretch my leg, which was starting to get pins and needles as I had been kneeling on the floor of the chopper for more than 30 minutes. The straps of my gas mask were already starting to give me a headache from being pushed into my head under the weight of my ballistic helmet. Finally, over the radio, we got the green light. 'All callsigns, go, go, go!'

My aircraft, Black 1, the lead chopper, banked hard to the left, dropping over the cliff and the beach, screaming in low and fast over the Pacific Ocean on a warm summer's evening, the moon glowing brilliantly on the horizon. The doors were thrown open, and the rotor wash rushed into the cabin as I strained to look over my TL's shoulders to try to make out our target vessel.

More than 48 hours earlier, an extremist group based in Western Sydney had hijacked a civilian cruise ship, the *Spirit of Tasmania*, with 80 hostages on board. One hostage had been executed and it was broadcast on Facebook Live, forcing the Australian government to ask the governor-general to approve legislation handing over responsibility to the ADF.

I was at home and had just thrown some steaks on the barbecue when we were called in to work. It was 6 p.m. on Saturday. As I was on call, I hadn't had any beers, opting for a few Coke Zeros instead.

After rushing in to work and grabbing gear, guns, ammo and cars, we were up at the 6th Aviation Regiment at Holsworthy, standing in our gear-up next to the Black Hawks as the helicopter assault element. Having drawn the short straw, the other platoon would make up the boat assault. They were also waiting for authorisation to launch the assault from Port Kembla, south of Wollongong.

Intelligence had told us that there were four terrorists on board, armed with pistols and assault rifles, who were now attempting to flee Australian waters. My team's task was to assault the ship's bridge; the Facebook Live video had shown this was where the execution of the hostage had occurred, and was a priority for the assault.

The other helo and boat teams would clear the remainder of the ship in a planned assault where each team had their areas of responsibility. In our briefing, our mission statement was read out: 'Save the lives of the hostages' (SLOTH).

The ship was in sight, and I could see the rigid-hull inflatable boats laden with assaulters speeding towards their ladder points. The *Spirit of Tasmania* was a decent-sized vessel, and the teams in the boat assault force would have a long climb up their caving ladders in the high swell as the rigid-hull inflatable boat drivers did their best to steady their craft. It was a long fall from the ladders into pitch-black water, especially risky when carrying that much gear. But if someone did fall off, the assault would still go on—hostages' lives were at risk.

I checked the strap of my helmet and sling of my M4 rifle, ensuring nothing would get caught when I roped out of the chopper. The loadmaster turned to us and yelled, 'One minute!' and we yelled the timing back to him with our index fingers raised, ensuring everyone had heard and seen the timing call.

The loadmaster gave us the signal to go, and the team leader kicked the coil of rope out the door, watching carefully to ensure the rope had touched down—a metre or so off, and we would be roping straight into the ocean.

The team leader grabbed the rope, swung out the door and started his slide down. As soon as he made room on the rope, I reached out and grabbed it, swung out the door and slid down. My legs missed the rope at the start, forcing me to hold on with my hands to try to slow my descent.

I landed on the deck, keeping my eyes on any threats, and grabbed my weapon from the side of my body. The light in the bridge was off, but the glow from the dials and instruments gave me plenty of light to see through my NVG. The team leader made entry and hooked to his right, calling out, 'Show me your hands!'

I pushed past him, identifying an open space, and pressed my laser on as I moved around the corner. A terrorist was kneeling behind a makeshift barricade, pistol aimed at the head of a petrified woman who was holding her face, screaming.

I rested my laser on his face and squeezed off three rounds, hitting him just under his eyes and throwing him back against the wall. 'Don't move. Remain calm. You've been saved,' I yelled at her; I didn't want her running around in panic, complicating the assault and getting shot in the crossfire.

The rest of the team flooded in, and we secured the bridge in less than a minute. The TL had also engaged a terrorist who had been kneeling behind another door with an assault rifle, killing him before he could fire.

We waited another twenty minutes while the rest of the teams cleared their areas, then were given 'Ship secure' over the radio.

'Ryder, you're a fuckwit, you shot me in the head,' the terrorist said as he stood up, pointing to a golf ball that was starting to
develop above the protective glasses he was wearing. 'Sorry, mate,'
I said, laughing. 'I saw it was you and couldn't help myself.'

The 'terrorist' was my mate Steve from Delta Company, which
was the enemy role player company for the training scenario. It was
one among hundreds I completed on my three rotations with the
TAG-E as an assaulter, sniper and assault TL.

My medical restrictions at first seemed tight, but I used the failed
medical bureaucracy to my benefit. The first restriction was black
and white: 'no land parachute jumps'. There wasn't much I could push
back on there. My other restrictions, however, were more vague, and
allowed me to argue my case to participate in key activities on the
TAG, such as fast-roping and rappelling from buildings.

Instead of stating 'no rappelling, fast-roping, or any other form
of helicopter insert/ extract techniques', which would have essentially made me useless in the team, my restrictions said 'no abseiling,
hang-gliding or paragliding'. In 22 years in the army, I never encountered anyone who had completed a hang-gliding course, but that
was the medical policy's generic restriction on me according to my
injuries.

For our first roping activity in the platoon, I came prepared with
my restriction document and record of attainment (ROA) for my
military roping course. The OIC bailed me up as soon as he saw me.
'Hang on, Scotty, no way you can rope with your restrictions, mate.
I'm sorry.'

I pulled out my documents to show him.

'What the fuck is this?' he asked.

'Have a read of my ROA. Can you show me where it says I can't rappel or fast-rope?' I asked. 'My restrictions say abseiling. I'm not qualified in abseiling, I'm qualified in rappelling and helicopter insertion and extraction. I don't hold qualifications in abseiling, therefore, I'm not breaking the rules by participating in regular platoon training.'

He looked at me, and a smile slowly appeared on his face. 'Well played, Scotty. Get kitted up for the next load,' he said as the Black Hawks landed behind him.

The sole reason I could be employed in the TAG-E in its total capacity was a technicality on a bit of paper. The flawed bureaucracy in the army rarely works in your favour, but it's sweet when it does.

The regiment's HR (hostage rescue) capability is a crucial reason it's so well-funded, and the TAG capability is unparalleled in the Western SF community. In the US, Tier Units,[44] which are commanded by the Joint Special Operations Command, do not have a domestic counterterrorism mandate. That falls to state police tactical groups or the FBI's Hostage Rescue Team, which provides a response capability at the federal level.

TAG-E was initially based on Charlie Company and was located at the company's compound and offices at the 6 Aviation Regiment, where the Black Hawks SOCOMD uses are held. A trickle system was put in place to select and train operators from the 'green' companies—those not in the TAG—to hold a position in Charlie Company, and the roles were highly sought after. The additional training to qualify as a TAG operator, as well as other specialist skills and the extra pay, made it an attractive option for the other companies; TAG operators were taking home almost $25,000 more, with the TAG disability allowance making up for the continual disruptions holding a short-notice capability made on our personal lives.

SASR and 2 Cdo Regt arguably have the world's best training facilities. The SFTF, built in 2007, is located at Holsworthy Barracks, a five-minute drive from 2 Cdo Regt's headquarters at Tobruk Lines. It provides the regiment with almost everything it needs to conduct its training, including multiple indoor and outdoor live-fire ranges for various weapon types and calibres. The SFTF also has numerous villages, a 24-metre roping tower and a mock-up of a Boeing 747 capable of facilitating live-fire aircraft recovery training.

The SFTF also has two indoor ranges and two levels of room floor combat ranges that can be adjusted to create any layout imaginable. During the Lindt Café siege in 2014, the TAG built a mock-up of the entire Lindt Café to conduct rehearsals, but of course, the TAG was never used to resolve that incident. These are only some of the facilities the SFTF provides, but there are tens of dozens of other facilities that I can't mention in this book, where operators can hone their sensitive and unique capabilities.

Outside of deployments, that first year in the TAG-E assault team was probably my best year in the army. Aside from having my job back, as a private in a team, you get the benefit of constant training without having any of the paperwork or responsibility that comes with being a TL or training supervisor. Every day, you focus on a core skill needed in HR: shooting, driving, roping and breaching. As the months go by, your skill level compounds, and you become more proficient all the time.

The regular training was broken up by critical activities used to validate the entire TAG-E task force, which included maritime recovery on static and moving vessels, and entry to complex land-based strongholds such as high-rise buildings, planes, trains and buses. Each TAG operator is also required to conduct training in chemical, biological, radiological and nuclear environments, a critical capability the TAG provides the Australian government with. Outside these activities, the TAG regularly trains around Sydney in various buildings and structures such as sporting stadiums, shopping centres and theatres. This access to non-military facilities for training is unparalleled outside of SOCOMD, and is essential for the teams to adapt their training to a variety of real-world environments.

Any possible location where Australians could be taken over by a terrorist threat group, or that could be used to hold hostages or seen as valuable for a terrorist attack, is used for training. Most of this training occurs at night to keep prying eyes away, but some activities are conducted in broad daylight, and I never got sick of seeing the look of shock on people's faces when half a dozen Land Cruisers went dashing past a café or pub with gas-mask-wearing armed commandos standing on the back.

When an old building is earmarked for demolition somewhere on the east coast, there is a good chance you will find an element of the TAG assaulting it, sometimes with explosives to breach a point of entry, or manual tools to smash or cut their way in. Getting to consolidate skills on real-world targets is an essential tool in the development of a TAG operator, and I had a smile from ear to ear every time I took part.

HR requires extremely high standards of shooting, assaulting and other core skills, often in uncertain and ambiguous situations and in varying environmental conditions. This capability is therefore only held in SASR and 2 Cdo Regt. During selection, candidates are put through activities to assess their ability to make decisions in high-stress environments under high cognitive load.

No single element makes somebody a good CQB HR operator. Of course, technical skills such as shooting at varying ranges day and night, and learning how to use your equipment, are essential, but anyone can be taught to do that with enough time and resources.

A good HR operator can identify a problem and rapidly adapt and apply their skills to it, regardless of the size of the structure or complexity of the situation. It's about everything from assessing the room layout, to identifying who poses a threat, to always maintaining spatial awareness (particularly at night, as using your NVG over a gas mask significantly reduces your field of vision—it's like looking through two toilet rolls).

Regular army infantry units typically conduct live-fire training every few weeks, at best, and this mainly occurs on a simple rifle range, with the firer at one end and the targets at the other, at varying ranges. Some ranges have mechanical targets, and some have cardboard targets in various shapes and sizes.

Infantry units are getting a better understanding of 'room combat' and fighting in urban areas, but the conventional army doesn't have the infrastructure to allow each infantry soldier time in a purpose-built, indoor room–combat training facility. Facilities exist for urban training, but the ammunition is restricted to blanks or Simunition (paint bullets).

The first course of the CRTC is the SF weapons course, where trainees learn the weapon systems they are required to employ on the remainder of the reo. Trainees often comment on how much they live-fire on the course, which is just a qualification course. Most of them fire more live ammunition on the SF weapons course than they have in years in their previous ADF roles.

On a TAG rotation, an assaulter would live-fire two days a week, from 9 a.m. till 4 p.m., going through thousands of rounds. Two other days would be taken up with scenarios against role players with Simunition, or working on specialist skills such as driving, breaching or roping. Fridays would typically be administrative days, where guns were cleaned, vehicles were washed, and everything was checked to ensure it was in working order.

A lot more training is focused outside the core skills I have mentioned—I'm using broad brushstrokes and only focusing on generic skills, as the remainder of the TAG's capabilities are compartmentalised and classified as secret. The TAG holds many more roles and capabilities that, for obvious reasons, I can't disclose in this book. Just be aware that there is always a group of commandos from the TAG-E ready to go, 24 hours a day, and that they are the best strategic-strike, HR and crisis-response unit in the world. If the army is ever called to an incident on Australian soil or surrounding waters, rest assured that you will be in good hands.

Adam Smith, a former infantry soldier who completed reo in 2012 and was posted to Charlie Company, completed multiple rotations of Afghanistan as well as the TAG. He left in 2016 to become the first direct-entry, lateral-transfer applicant to the Victoria Police Special Operations Group (SOG).

Charlie Company had solely held the TAG-E role since its inception in 2002, only rotating off in 2009 when the TAG-E changed to a rotation model. Adam explained his perspective on how this shaped the culture of Charlie Company. 'I went straight into a company where guys had been doing nothing but the TAG-E for years,' he says. 'They were all very professional and had this aura of confidence, as they were all excellent operators who had mastered core commando skills to a high level.'

Like most operators, Adam loved the routine and consistency of the TAG: 'The whole year is planned out; we used to work long, weird hours, but you could plan your year, knowing you would be pulled in a dozen directions.' In 2016, talking to people he had got to know in the SOG through a climbing course he had attended a few years earlier, Adam expressed interest in moving back to Melbourne, where he'd originally come from, and joining the SOG. A likeable and competent operator, he was given a letter of offer. He left the army for his recruit training in the police academy. He was told he would go straight onto the SOG reo and not have to complete the SOG selection course, as he had already completed commando selection.

Adam received a phone call while he was at the academy, telling him the letter of offer would be amended, and a place on the SOG reo would only be offered after he successfully completed the selection course. 'I was shocked,' he says. 'The selection course started weeks after I graduated the academy, and I had no time to train.' A mate of Adam's already in the SOG informed him that the change of plans was solely due to senior SOG members' conversations with SASR members in Perth.

Despite his lack of preparation, Adam relied on his experience as a commando corporal to get him through. 'You see straight through the games. I'd done it all before and run similar programs myself as a DS on commando selection,' he explained. 'Once we got through selection and started the reo, I had zero issues. One day on the range, one of the senior SOG officers apologised to me for making me complete selection, as I was doing well on the reo, which was a basic version of what I had been doing for years as a commando.'

After seeing the high standard commando trainees were at during SOG training, Victoria Police opened a lateral-transfer program for any qualified commandos who wished to become SOG operators. At the time of writing, there are half a dozen former commandos in the SOG, and I regularly smile when I see the SOG on the news, with the commandos I know instantly recognisable.

People often compare the SOG, the New South Wales Tactical Operations Unit and other police tactical groups with the TAG. But, Adam says, 'It's hard to compare. Individually, the SOG are good operators, but they don't have the luxury to train as often as the TAG. If you dropped the SOG into Uruzgan province, they'd be out of their depth, as it isn't what they're used to. Similarly, if you dropped a TAG team into the Melbourne CBD for a vehicle pursuit or armed robbery, their specific skillsets would see them not perform as well as the SOG. The SOG also have the luxury of working the same areas for years, so they get intimate knowledge of the area. Overall, it isn't easy to compare. However, the capabilities the TAG has, with numbers and insertion platforms, are unmatched by another police tactical group in the country.'

Meanwhile in Afghanistan, SOTG Rotation XVIII, Alpha Company lost another two operators. Back in Helmand province in the Kajaki Dam, on 31 August 2012, Private Nathanael Galagher and Lance Corporal Mervyn McDonald were sitting next to each other on a US UH-1 Super Huey helicopter when the pilot became disorientated in a brownout and flipped the aircraft. Merv and Nate were trapped under the rolled aircraft and died at the crash site.

For Alpha Company, memories of the 21 June 2010 Black Hawk crash came flooding back.

I volunteered to be part of the official honour guard at the ramp ceremony at RAAF Richmond. We held a ramp ceremony for every fallen commando from the Afghanistan campaign, and it never got any easier. At the time, I was in Charlie Company, holding the TAG-E role for the year. As much as I loved being on the TAG, I was still crushed that the company in which I had spent five years was deploying back to Afghanistan without me, and I wanted to contribute somehow.

The C-130 Hercules taxied slowly to its stop point as the escorting members of Alpha Company carried the two bodies off the aircraft. I was on the side of the guard of honour with my back to the families. As the two boys' bodies appeared from the ramp, Merv and Nate's families let out screams of grief and pain, some collapsing. The other side of the guard facing the families was doing their best to remain stoic, but tears trickled down their cheeks as they witnessed the families' grief.

Merv's brother, Percy, who served in 3 RAR with me, would leave the army and later join the Australian Federal Police. I would see Percy at times—not as a colleague, but as a family member of the fallen in events with the regiment. Tragically, in December 2023, Percy was diagnosed with terminal cancer, and he passed away in May 2024. Two brothers; two veterans—two amazing Australians, taken too soon.

CHAPTER 29

THE RETURN

After our year on the TAG, we took some leave, knowing that we would have a busy start to the year in preparation for our deployment in July 2013. We had been living and breathing 'black roles' on the TAG, and now it was time to get ready for the last rotation of TF66.

The company was filled with many guys who had only completed their reo in 2011, while Charlie Company had been in the thick of the fighting in Helmand.

Weeks out from our deployment, however, the regiment was rocked by the news that Corporal Cameron Baird, MG, had been killed, and another highly respected operator seriously wounded. Cameron's life and the legacy he left in 2 Cdo Regt are the subject of the book *The Commando: The Life and Death of Cameron Baird VC, MG* by Ben McKelvey, who recounts Cameron's life and the circumstances leading to him being awarded the VC for Australia.

Cameron epitomised what it was to be a commando. Fearless, competent and respected by all, he led from the front, never expecting his team to do anything he wouldn't do himself. The charity

Cam's Cause was founded by Cameron's friends and family to support the regiment and their families in his honour. In 2023, the charity became the Zero79 Foundation.

For Rotation XX in early 2013, I was put into an assault team in uniform platoon as the team medic (CFA), and we spent a few months preparing for our MRE, which was to take place at Holsworthy at the SFTF. We had long been questioning the utility of still conducting the MREs in Cultana, South Australia, as the rotations now focused heavily on RW insertions, reducing the need to spend weeks away from home and countless millions of dollars getting the whole TF, as well as vehicles and Black Hawks, down to Cultana.

My own experience of the importance of team CFAs, who were the first responders to most casualties, made me want to ensure that if somebody in my team were injured in combat, I would give myself the best possible chance at saving them.

I studied our medical training manuals and spent hours online, looking at videos of surgeries, gunshot wounds and traumatic amputations. Although I never had a problem with blood, I wanted to ensure I was adequately desensitised to trauma injuries.

Before our deployment, I also spent weekends at St Vincent's Hospital Emergency Department in Sydney. An agreement was in place for us team medics to attend shifts for additional treatment exposure, which I found extremely valuable.

We would arrive in plain clothes, introduce ourselves as 'army medics under training' and assist in intravenous cannulation and managing airways, as well as observing the trauma teams as they treated patients. I would leave there with the utmost respect for trauma nurses and doctors. I saw a likeness between the high-pressure, high-stakes job and special operations, and was impressed by their ability to think and remain calm under pressure.

The MRE for this rotation was by far the most realistic, relevant MRE to date. More importantly, it was the shortest. The main activity was conducted at the SFTF at one of the Middle Eastern villages, and Defence pulled out all the stops to create realism for us. More than 80 Afghan people from Western Sydney were contracted as role players, and lived in the village for days before we conducted our assault.

A mix of all ages, from teenagers to retirees, turned the training area into a realistic Afghan village. They set up bazaars, tea rooms, fireplaces and mosques, and if it wasn't for the numerous shipping containers littered around the training area as makeshift rooms, the sights, smells and sounds took those of us who had been to Afghanistan right back to a village in Uruzgan. It was powerful training that everyone benefited from immensely, and I wondered why it had taken so long for Defence to move away from the far longer but less effective training in Cultana with subpar facilities. In fact, after Mason Edwards was killed, I'd thought we would never return to Cultana, but I was wrong.

As I was in the hospital when the funerals of the three boys killed in the Black Hawk crash occurred, I never felt like I had any closure. I would get my chance weeks before I deployed back to Afghanistan. After years of petitioning from Chucky's father, Gordon, the local council had finally approved the creation of the Avenue of Honour near the site of Chucky's funeral, on the shores of Lake Tinaroo in the Atherton Tablelands. Sarah and I attended the opening on 22 June 2013 by the chief of the ADF, General David Hurley, which was attended by more than 5000 people, including Prime Minister Julia Gillard and opposition leader Tony Abbott.

The memorial is dedicated to everyone who served and was killed in the Afghanistan campaign, but for me it was a way of saying goodbye to Tim, Scott and Chucky. Sarah and I had lunch with Chucky's family, and they took me down to the site of Chucky's funeral.

As soon as I arrived, I was overcome with emotion. Years of not dealing with Chucky's death and the crash came bursting out of me. I knelt on the ground and wept, telling Chucky I was sorry I survived and he didn't, and that my upcoming deployment was for him. I felt like a weight had been lifted off my shoulders; I had never expected the trip to be so instrumental in my healing. I felt renewed and energised to return to the country that I had left so abruptly from the desert of northern Kandahar.

As the deployment date drew closer, the anticipation started to build. This was to be the last SOTG, and we didn't know what to expect. There seemed to be no political will to have another Australian come home in a coffin, so we got the feeling there may not be too much fighting going on, and the US's announcement of the war's end did nothing to minimise that. All operations had to have an 'Afghan face', where the PRC SF teams would be the ones to interact with the locals and be the first to enter a compound, having us in the background to aid where needed.

Complicating things, a rule had been brought in where we were restricted from bringing suspected insurgents back to TK, as the pipeline to process detainees through the International Security Assistance Force had been abandoned, to force the Afghan legal system to be used. Of course, this was wishful thinking, as any insurgent captured by the SOTG had been released and returned to their village, sometimes in a matter of weeks, without any due process being followed. Risking Australian lives to capture insurgents only for them to be released within days created some frustration in the teams, and was the first sign for many of us that this war was not going to end well.

The counter-nexus line of operations had been binned weeks out from our arrival as part of the Australian strategy to shrink back towards TK in preparation to hand over the province to the Afghans. This disappointed me greatly, as I had missed out on those jobs while I was in rehab. I hoped that we would still see action around Uruzgan itself.

The last few days at home before deployment are by far the hardest. People probably think that you spend as much time as you can with your partner, to make up for being away for so long, but with Sarah and me, with our experience of the chopper crash, it was different. The last time I left her for a deployment, she had to fly to Germany to nurse me back to health, so I can understand her anxiety about me returning. But if she hadn't pushed me to fight to regain my job, there was a high likelihood that I would have left the army by now.

My friends and family thought I was mad to return. My best mate growing up and my best man at my wedding, Leithen, summed up most people's sentiments on me going back over. 'Mate, you've done enough. Just take a pension and find a cruisy job. Why would you risk your life again?'

It's hard to explain why I wanted to go back over. I felt like I had unfinished business; I never got closure from my last deployment. Strangely, I felt robbed of the usual post-deployment routine of flying into the UAE, handing all my gear back, catching a chartered flight to Sydney, and walking out of the arrivals gate for a few weeks of well-deserved leave.

I also felt like I owed it to the boys who were killed in the crash not to pull the pin and get out just because I had been injured. I felt as if getting out of the army and sitting at home with a pension was the weak way out. And there was a lot more I wanted to achieve before I left, too. I knew, however, having the injuries I had at just

24 years of age, a lifelong career in the army was out of the question. Each day I spent on the tools would slowly worsen them, and I had no desire to leave the army at 60 in a wheelchair. I knew it would come to an end one day—just not now.

After waking up in a hospital in Germany to spending months in the hospital completing numerous surgeries, being court-martialled and spending two years in rehab, the moment I never thought I would get to experience again was almost upon me.

Almost three years after losing Chucky, Scott and Tim in the desert plains of northern Kandahar, I touched down at the airstrip at TK and walked off the ramp into a brilliant summer morning in Uruzgan province.

As I walked through the gates of Camp Russell, I was overcome with emotion. I was so happy that I was finally here. All the tears, pain and uncertainty were behind me now. I'd never thought I would set foot in TK again, and I was so grateful to be given the opportunity—I needed this more than people knew.

I was also sad, though. As I walked through the camp, I remembered all the good times I'd had with Garry, Chucky and all the other lads who never made it back, and in my head, I told them that this was also for them.

CHAPTER 30

RETROGRADE

Rotation XX had a rocky start. Within a week of our arrival at TK, it was decided that the TF66 footprint needed to be reduced, and an entire platoon would depart within days. FE-A would also downsize, 3 SAS Squadron working with a minor element from 2 SAS Squadron to see the end of the rotation. Some from TF66 would remain in the country on other security tasks in Kabul, and some would be going home altogether. The TLs locked themselves in a room to determine who would stay. I was told I would stay; they knew how much I had fought to be here.

Our focus was mainly on Patan, Langar and the Khod Valley. All with RW insertion, they would be short jobs, less than 24 hours, with the PRC. Some of the PRC police officers had been working with TF66 for years, and I hoped that this meant they were battle-hardened and experienced, and not requiring constant supervision on the ground.

We would work closely with the PRC, sitting next to them on the choppers and patrolling with them in the green belt. But given our requirement to let them be the first to enter compounds for clearances, our main aim was to ensure their targets were appropriate when the firing started.

The trip was relatively slow compared to my previous rotations, but still enjoyable—and a lot easier on the body than extended vehicle operations or night DAs. We would typically insert before the sun came up and be back at the mess for lunch or dinner, depending on the size of the clearance.

It soon became apparent that neither the Taliban nor the PRC were willing to fight. For the insurgents, it was a waiting game. Why risk getting killed now when they knew we were leaving soon? For the PRC, there was an uneasiness about what the future would hold once we left—as it turned out, with good reason.

Despite the narrative of the politicians who had declared that Afghans were ready to take responsibility for the region by themselves, the reality on the ground was very different. The ANA checkpoints littered through the region were only able to operate due to the coalition patrol bases nearby. The ANA outposts in areas without constant coalition presence were continuously attacked and overrun.

Even this late in the war, I was still trying to figure out exactly what impact we were having here. We would fly or drive into an area, fight, kill a bunch of dudes and then head back to base. I had learned years ago that the tribal regions of southern Afghanistan were far removed from the halls of power in Kabul—most people in the areas we cleared wouldn't even have known who the president was, let alone partaken in any democratic process.

Despite the term 'Taliban' being used to identify the enemy, I thought it was misleading. The idea that unified enemy forces with a country-wide command-and-control structure filtered down to remote villages in Uruzgan province was mostly inaccurate. These areas were ruled by tribal warlords, and had been fighting with each other for centuries for power, land and resources. Coalition alliances with regional warlords would generate false intelligence, the warlords using the coalition to maintain their power base; essentially, using the International Security Assistance Force to enact their proxy war.[45]

For some jobs, myself and Jason, an infantryman from 2 RAR off the 2012 reo, would insert ATVs in the back of the US Chinook helicopters to catch fighters running off as we landed, as even with a light assault order[46] we would never catch them on foot. At one job in Langar, we drove our bikes off and were hiding in a creek line, waiting for our TL, Matt P., to direct us to any areas suspected fighter were seen fleeing, when he vectored us onto a location on a hill a few hundred metres away.

We raced up the hill, and soon had to dismount our bikes as it was getting too steep. We cleared the hill with our guns up but couldn't find the squirter. 'He's to your right; you are next to him,' Matt said on the radio. As I turned back down the hill, the suspected fighter hid behind a rock with his back to us. As I couldn't see his face or hands, so I aimed my M4 at the centre of his back and took off the safety catch, ready to engage if he decided to try to shoot us or detonate a grenade as we got close.

Jason and I closed in, and when we were 15 metres or so out, I started to see the suspected fighter's right arm move in front of his body. We both stopped and took up the first trigger pressure, only a millisecond away from killing him. After a few seconds, he stopped moving, and we walked in slowly to search him.

He was in his twenties, with a thick black beard, and was shitting bricks. I needed to know if he was just a scared farmer or a local fighter who had suddenly decided he wasn't keen on martyrdom and had a change of heart as our choppers flew into his village.

We searched him and the area around him for a weapon or radio, but found nothing. We were about to let him go when Matt got on the radio and said the PRC wanted to question him, so I threw him on the back of my bike, took him to the PRC TL, then drove off on another task.

The PRC had decided he was Taliban and took him into a room for questioning. Our job was to give the Afghans the lead, as they would soon be here by themselves, so we left them to it and continued searching compounds with another team from the PRC.

A few hours later, the Chinook landed in a cloud of dust in the desert, away from the village, and Jason and I drove our bikes up the ramp to the front of the chopper while the rest of the teams piled in. I asked one guy what had happened to the suspected fighter I had taken into the PRC; he said he had no idea.

I looked over at the PRC commander, and he stared at me, smiling, giving me a thumbs-up. At that moment, I was suddenly unsure who the good and bad guys were.

Compared to previous SOTG rotations, as I've said, this final one was tame. On a combined operation with SASR, we got into a gunfight, but my team was away from the action. The mortar team, on the other hand, found themselves in the thick of it.

Jimmy Hammond, who completed his reo in 2007 and four SOTG rotations before leaving the ADF in 2017, was the mortar team commander for this last rotation in 2013. 'Our smaller mortars provided us with the ability to get closer to the action and re-role as an assault team if required,' he said.

During an operation in Patan, a combined clearance with FE-A, our assault teams sequentially cleared the high ground surrounding the valley. In contrast, Jim and his mortar team were positioned at the end of the valley, providing fire support and acting as a pseudo-blocking force. The plan worked well.

As we in the assault teams began clearing the high ground, we found it was almost deserted. This was a signal that contact was imminent—a key indicator we had learned years ago in the war. The sniper teams in overwatch began engaging the enemy moving towards Jim's position at the bottleneck to the south. Jim's scout, Chris, saw a fighter manoeuvring towards the sniper overwatch positions, which had been unmasked by their shooting. Chris and another team member approached the fighter, killing him with a burst from Chris's Mark 48 machine gun. Further past him, they saw another fighter laying IEDs, and killed him too. The morning was starting to heat up.

From the empty compounds, we knew our clearance was squeezing the enemy down the valley, and we could hear the shooting and constant updates on our radios. Mortars began firing down the valley, supporting our clearance and pushing the enemy further south.

Snipers informed Jim they had seen the enemy approaching the mortar baseplate position, moving tactically to flank them. Jim decided to split the team and launch an assault. He took two other operators and shook out in an extended line towards the last position snipers had seen the enemy fighters.

'We started a slow assault through the green belt,' Jim said, 'clearing compounds as we went along. I knew the enemy was in front of us somewhere. We moved into some light vegetation, and I saw a fighter lying on his side with his AK pointed at me. I shot him several times and launched a 40mm grenade that landed right next to him.'

The fighter had been previously engaged by snipers and had moved into cover to ambush anyone following up. It was his final, failed stand.

That same afternoon in Patan, our team was patrolling down a road in the village when a single sniper round landed right in the middle of the team, narrowly missing Matt, the TL. We all threw ourselves under any cover we could find, waiting for more fire, but none came. We deduced from studying the terrain that he must have been in the hills, which would have made it at least a 600-metre shot—not bad. We called an Apache to have a look, which identified him and finished him off with a rocket.

In Langar, the company was spread out all over the valley on another short RW insertion, and multiple teams had small engagements throughout the day. As our team moved along the edge of the green belt, we separated, and I found myself with a team PRC. Not wanting the PRC to get too far ahead, I stayed behind and ushered them along when we started receiving fire. It wasn't a large volume of fire, but bullets still shot up the trees above us, showering leaves onto us.

We all took cover and, realising we were in a shit spot, I tried to get the PRC to move into a building. Staying in the open was serving zero tactical purpose, and I thought it would be better to get into cover and find another way forward into the lower ground, which would shield us from the fire coming from the high ground.

Despite being in a shit spot, however, the PRC didn't budge. I asked them, then yelled at them, to move, sporadic rounds landing all around us the whole time. If we stayed, one of the rounds would eventually find its mark. Still the PRC didn't move, falsely assuming the fire was coming from a different direction. I didn't want to leave them here, as I didn't want to go by myself to link up with the rest of the team—the golden rule was always to have someone with you. Or as we say, 'Two is one, one is none.' If you were alone and got shot, it drastically decreased your chance of surviving.

A burst of fire, now more accurate and seemingly a lot closer, cracked over my head, making me dive into a compound. Annoyed at the PRC, I got on the radio and said that I was 'pinned down'.

As soon as the words left my lips, I regretted using that term, as being 'pinned down' wasn't the issue so much as the PRC refusing to move.

Matt and the rest of the team doubled back to my position, by which time the fire had stopped entirely, making me look like a complete dickhead. One of the team commanders, Joel, never let me forget it.

In another team, Adam was engaged by the Taliban from 50 metres away, returning fire and engaging two fleeing enemies with rifle and automatic fire, killing two insurgents. Other teams were caught in the open by enemy positions from the hills, which kept our snipers and JTACs busy pouring fire onto the surrounding hills.

One morning back in TK, the medics came through our building asking all CFAs to head over to the Role 2 Hospital next door, as they had just received two category A casualties from an IED blast, and he had permission for the SF CFAs to watch so that we could get some exposure to their treatment, similar to what we'd done at St Vincent's in Sydney. I threw on cargo pants and a T-shirt, grabbed my pistol, and followed him out the gate.

In the trauma bay, two nationals injured by a vehicle-borne IED lay on gurneys. One casualty had already died, and I watched the blood drain from his face, leaving him pale and wax-like, something the movies never get right.

The other, the one closest to me, was having a sternotomy, his ribs being sawn open for the doctors to access his heart so they could manually compress it to keep the blood flowing. I was utterly fascinated. His entire chest cavity was exposed—I had never seen a beating human heart before this.

The trauma teams were doing everything they could to keep him alive and using almost all the blood in the trauma bay. At the same time, the doctor continued the cardiac massage, the only reason the casualty's heart was still pumping blood and oxygen around his body.

Eventually, the surgeons, out of options, decided to stop heart compressions, and everyone fell silent. The doctor took his hand off the young Afghan man's heart, and we all stood and watched as it stopped.

Watching a human heart take its last beat was surreal. I recall thinking what a waste of life this was. These two men had mothers, fathers and people who loved them, and now they were dead in front of a room full of strangers for no reason.

Afghanistan wasn't just the graveyard of armies but the graveyard of Afghans dying needlessly. I had a sudden realisation that no matter what we achieved during our time here, this land was never going to change.

<hr />

As it was the last SOTG, Camp Russell was being prepared to hand over to the Afghans—'retrograding' in army vernacular, aka packing shit up. Each week, another part of the camp would be ripped down or demolished in preparation for the final week, including all the furniture in and around the accommodation buildings. Since the camp was constructed in 2008, each rotation had seen another wooden structure added, which would be improved yearly. By 2013, the buildings at the camp were almost unrecognisable.

Wooden walls were built between each building, with steps and 'tanning' decks a feature of most. In the rooms, teams had built little boxes around each bed space. On one rotation, we'd even built a tiered, two-level theatre in the rooms to watch our flat-screen TV in.

SASR had built a full bar in the Fat Lady's Arms, and the Back Deck was constructed during my first rotation in 2008. It all had to go.

We were told that anything that wasn't the original building had to be burned before we left. A fire was started behind the Back Deck that burned for weeks. At one stage, the base fire truck contractors parked their truck behind the camp, tired of the dozens of phone calls telling them the Aussie SF base was burning.

In mid-October, we were told that the ADF would hold a closing-of-the-war ceremony organised by the regular army next door, to be attended by families of men who had been killed during the war.

At first I thought I had misheard—they were doing what? But I hadn't misheard at all. Dozens of family members would attend the ceremony in TK itself, including families of SOTG members killed. We were then asked to nominate ourselves if we wished to host families of any operators who were close to us. I volunteered to host Chucky's parents.

On 2 November 2013, an RAAF C-17 Globemaster touched down at TK carrying 57 family members of the fallen, along with senior defence and government officials, and dozens of 2 Cdo Regt operators who provided personal protection to the VIPs and families. It was a risky move, given that some of the families' loved ones had been killed by 'green-on-blue', or insider, attacks, and nobody wanted family members of the fallen also killed, which would be a catastrophic failure for everyone concerned, let alone any remaining political will to continue a presence in Afghanistan.

I had trouble sleeping the night before due to my mixed emotions about the visit. On the one hand, I was glad to be part of it, given that I had been with Chucky when he was fatally injured. On the other hand, I felt guilty that I had recovered to the point that I was back over here while their son had died.

I decided to downplay my feelings about being back here and focus on showing Chucky's family as much as possible of the base and telling them stories about him. But his parents, Gordon and Susan, were such lovely people that any apprehension I had quickly disappeared. As soon as they saw me, they embraced me. They told me how glad they were to see me and how happy they were that I was back here. I did my best not to cry.

After showing them around Camp Russell, which was already mostly packed up, we attended the ceremony at the main base. The folk singer Fred Smith sang 'Dust of Uruzgan', a song he had written about the death of Private Benjamin Renaudo, but for me, it was a song about Chucky. Looking at his parents, I knew they were thinking the same.

Despite my anxiety, it turned out to be a cathartic experience for the families. Gordon Chuck told me, 'Ben never spoke much about the army. We knew Ben as a boy and a young man—but not as a commando. We got to see where Ben ate, worked, slept, and got a glimpse into his army life, and we're grateful that we were given the chance.'

<hr />

Back in Langar, we conducted another RW insertion with the PRC. No matter how often you do it, the thrill of hanging out the side of a Black Hawk as it flies low over Taliban villages never diminishes. Scanning every compound below, looking for a threat as you approach the landing site, and then sprinting off to clear the rotor wash was always exciting.

With the PRC in the lead, we cleared a series of compounds in the green belt, staying in the rear to ensure the PRC cleared the correct areas while we coordinated our positions with the other teams.

Jason—the other scout in our team—and I were clearing a compound that the PRC had missed when a series of shots rang out to our front. We moved onto the road and jumped on the radio, trying to figure out who was shooting, but nothing came over. Matt grabbed the team. We started making our way to where the PRC was and saw a few of them standing over a fallen motorbike and some bodies. As we approached them, Matt told the PRC to push past the road they were standing on and ensure we'd secured our permitter, which they begrudgingly did. Next to the motorbike were two men, one no older than his late teens and the other an older man with a long beard.

The PRC had shot them both as they drove down the dirt track. After being shot multiple times in the leg and chest, the younger man was already dead, with a pool of blood under him. The older man had a gunshot wound in his upper leg that had severed his femoral artery, along with multiple gunshot wounds in his chest. I knew it was too late.

He looked at me, and we made eye contact as he took his last breath, a look of defeat and acceptance as he stopped moving and the blood drained from his face—his gaze still fixed on mine. Either way, I have always wondered what that man was thinking as he lay there dying. Not in a million years would he ever have presumed he would be looking into an Australian commando's face in his last moments.

I quizzed the PRC through the terp, and they said the men had had radios and grenades, but the PRC had already stripped them.

FE-A was leaving TK before us, so we would pick up their primary role of targeting critical Taliban leadership inside Uruzgan with the PRC. As each week went by, Camp Russell shrank, and now even the gym was gone.

When assets got a fix on a target, we would roll out in RW or by vehicle and provide a cordon while the PRC made entry and arrested the target. We conducted half a dozen of these operations in our final weeks, with varying levels of success.

One evening, we got a ping from a Taliban commander at TK in the centre of town, down the road from the base. We grabbed the PRC and Bushmasters and drove up to the house, providing an immediate cordon while the PRC made the arrest. This part of TK was very built up, looking more like Kabul than Uruzgan, and it was the only time I ever conducted an operation in the TK township.

The targeting operations we took over from FE-A differed from the warfighting we had done for years, and most of us would rather have been out of the TK area getting into gunfights. Still, the evolution of the war meant those days were essentially over.

As Camp Russell was being torn apart, we eventually came to our last night in TK, which we all celebrated with a few drinks.

Walking out to the awaiting aircraft was bittersweet. Commandos don't generally talk about how they feel to each other, but I could sense the mood had changed, and I knew most of the operators of my generation were feeling the same way.

The piece of dust TF66 had called home for so long had created a new SF unit. From being continually admonished, minimised and criticised, we had grown into a core of experienced and hardened fighters who had shared fear, friendship, sadness and excitement. The ground around Camp Russell was where Cameron Baird VC, MG, had had his last night's sleep, where Brett Wood MG, DSM, had walked down the main road to board his helicopter for the last time, and where hundreds of operators had spent their days in Australia's longest war. For me, this was almost sacred ground. No Australian SF would live and fight out of Camp Russell ever again.

CHAPTER 31

WHEN THE WAR IS OVER

We thought the first year the unit wasn't committed to a war would be a time to slow the tempo down a bit. How wrong we were. But each year after the last SOTG rotation, the pace and commitments of the regiment seemed to increase, not decrease. As one sergeant in the regiment, Nick, said, 'Every day at work is like trying to drink from a fire hose.'

Afghanistan had been our guiding purpose for so long, and there was an air of uncertainty about what would come next. I remained with Charlie Company as we rotated onto the contingency role or crisis response. Contingency provides the government with a broad, short-notice capability that can be used in multiple environments around the globe, including the recovery of Australians who may be captured or held hostage overseas.

The first year after Afghanistan was a busy one for Charlie Company, and by the end of 2014 our teams had deployed to numerous places around the globe for training and international engagements, to South East Asia and the US, as well as the first rotation of Australia's contribution in the war against the Islamic

State in Iraq. For this role, we would train in numerous vehicles and boats, as well as back 'in the green' or the bush. If we had to deploy to the jungle at short notice, we needed to get out of the Afghanistan mindset and back into grassroots soldiering.

A group of 30 of us flew to Guam, off the Philippines coast, to work with the US Marine Special Operations Command (MARSOC) and a team of US Navy SEALs on maritime recovery operations, and conduct training in shooting and CQB. The scale of the US military arsenal never fails to impress me.

MARSOC, like 2 Cdo Regt a relatively new unit, were gracious hosts, and we developed our relationships over a few too many beers and whisky at the numerous bars on the island. On the other hand, the SEALs did their best to keep to themselves, only interacting with us when they had to for joint training.

Early in the trip, we spent a day at their 'kill house', a live-fire CQB range with a mezzanine level allowing observers a bird's-eye view of room combat training. The TLs got together and decided the best way to assess each unit's tactics, techniques and procedures was for each team to conduct a blank-fire clearance of the facility as the other teams observed. The MARSOC and 2 Cdo Regt teams had very similar tactics, techniques and procedures, and you could see the MARSOC boys had been investing in developing their CQB.

Whenever we worked with US SF who had yet to be exposed to 2 Cdo Regt, they would arrive with an air of arrogance. By the end of the training, though, they were usually humbled by the standard of our teams. Of course, this wasn't the case for all US SF units, but it was certainly my experience during many years of working with them around the globe.

Years later, when the unit held a demonstration for the commander of the US Joint Special Operations Command, his parting comments validated our place in the global SF community, although it was accompanied by a less positive observation on the capabilities of the ADF. 'No argument, you guys are the best assault force on the planet. Too bad you can't get anywhere for us to use you.' How true.

A month after we returned from Guam, we conducted a water parachute jump with the Malaysian SF into the Malacca Strait to train for an offshore water parachute insertion. We seemed to be confined to the inside of the Aussie Hercules for an eternity with our enormous packs, as every time we went to jump, a local fishing vessel would drive through the water drop zone, forcing the drop zone safety officer to chase them off.

Eventually, we got the green light and jumped, following our Zodiac boats out the door. As I got my kit ready to hit the water, piles of rubbish and cigarette butts came floating over, and I landed right in the middle, getting God knows what in my mouth.

I swam over to my boat and began inflating it when the back pontoon completely blew out, leaving the boat in a collapsed mess, like a black bean bag slowly sinking into the water, with litres of petrol spouting out of the cracked fuel canisters. Graham, one of the TLs, who was my team-mate for this boat, overshot the drop zone and took another twenty minutes to swim over to me. Finally, out of breath, he swam over to the half-sunken boat and was furious to find it deflated, while I sat calmly on some floating equipment, eyes red and stinging from the fuel.

'We need to find all the kit from the boat,' he said as he cast around the area and half of it slowly floated away. 'What's that?' He indicated a blue and yellow item floating 40 metres off.

'Fuck knows, mate,' I responded.

'I'll get it,' he said before putting his fins back on and swimming over to rescue the item.

The current must have been stronger than he thought, as he didn't return for 30 minutes. 'How'd you go, Hasselhoff?' I asked, in reference to the main character from *Baywatch*. Tired and red-faced, he threw a blue-and-yellow biscuit tin at me. For the next few years, I would leave blue biscuit tins in Graham's kit everywhere: in his office, pack and car. Graham was a mentor to me as I came through the ranks, and we joke about 'operation biscuit tin' to this day.

We spent a few uneventful weeks with the Malaysians in the jungle, where the highlight, aside from getting a few weekends of downtime in Kuala Lumpur, was 'survival training', where the Malaysians showed us a monkey that they had caught using traps and snares.

I do not recommend eating a monkey arm, and I would skip lizard eggs too—you won't get the taste out of your mouth for a while.

The SOTG campaign in Afghanistan may have finished in 2013, but it continued claiming more casualties. On 1 July 2014, Lance Corporal Todd Chidgey took his life in Kabul while deployed on a long-term PSD tasking. I had known Todd since joining the regiment and always got along with him. Polite, friendly and always smiling—nobody saw this coming.

I was shocked to hear of Todd's death. Deaths in training and environments where you are not prepared for fatalities always hit harder than deaths in combat.

It's always in the back of your mind that you could be deployed somewhere at a moment's notice. Every event on the news comes with the same question: 'What's the chance of us getting a run?' Over the years, 2 Cdo Regt was repeatedly called at short notice to serve around the globe; these deployments keep the operators focused, and serve to retain them in the regiment for a little longer.

On 17 July 2014, a Malaysia Airlines Boeing 777 flying from Amsterdam to Kuala Lumpur, Flight MH17 with 298 people on board, was shot down in Ukrainian airspace at 33,000 feet. Australia joined four other nations to form the Joint Investigative Team. It would deploy investigators from the AFP to work with European authorities in investigating the crash site and recovering human remains.

The following day, MH17 was the topic of discussion as we cleaned our guns, a regular ritual on a Friday after a week of shooting. Rumours were already circulating on the 'digger net' about a possible deployment. We didn't like our chances, but then things moved quickly.

After lunch, we received our warning order and were told to go home and say goodbye to our families, pack some personal possessions, and return to work the following day. The clerks worked furiously, issuing official passports, and checking everyone's deployment status, an essential requirement before any deployment—even a short-notice one.

Our deployment had yet to be released to the press, so we flew a commercial airliner to the UAE and then on to the Netherlands, where we would be based. The recovery task force hurriedly unpacked all the cargo pallets as we settled into our new accommodation at a Dutch air force base near Eindhoven, a few hours from Amsterdam.

As the planning teams worked on possible tasks we could be given, we zeroed our weapons, refreshed ourselves on heavy weapons, and studied the possible weapons and capabilities of what we may be up against, in the event we should go in if the security situation made the task of the investigation and identification of human remains unachievable for the numerous Australian agencies on the ground.

For most of us, it was a non-event as far as operations go, and we never went anywhere near the crash site or Ukraine. On the flip side, we were in Europe with not much to do, so we suggested getting some hire cars and doing some sightseeing—approval for which of course came with the obligatory reminder of the 'no-drinking policy'. We all nodded in agreement, then wholly disregarded the order the moment we left the base.

Like most soldiers, I was a massive fan of the HBO series *Band of Brothers*, based on the book by Stephen E. Ambrose about a company of US paratroopers from the 101st Airborne, and we were only a couple of hours' drive from Bastogne in Belgium, where American forces had had their fierce and protracted battle with the Germans as part of the Battle of the Bulge.

We drove over the border and spent the day touring monuments and museums. A local gave us directions to the Ardennes Forest where the Easy Company foxholes were dug before the assault on the town of Foy, as depicted in the TV series. Even in summer, the forest was bitterly cold, and as we sat in the foxholes, I tried to imagine what it would have been like living in freezing temperatures and being constantly shelled. Over a kilometre of open ground, the Americans assaulted a fortified German-held town. The risk thresholds back then were incomprehensible compared to the wars of today.

On the way back, we also visited the famous Arnhem Bridge over the river Rhine, where a joint US–British airborne invasion had aimed to capture numerous bridges and cross the Rhine, bypassing the German Siegfried Line. The British parachuted near Arnhem and captured the bridge, but they landed too far from their objective and met fierce resistance at the bridge.

The paras managed to hold it as long as they could, but ended up surrendering after significant losses. These events were later depicted in the movie *A Bridge Too Far*, and I relished the opportunity to walk around the bride as I googled key areas and again tried to picture what it must have been like for the men involved.

For me, as a former paratrooper, Arnhem also held a special place in my heart. The whole back wall of the 3 RAR mess at Holsworthy had a large mural depicting an airborne invasion, with the words 'What manner of men are these who wear the maroon beret?', famously quoting Field Marshal Bernard Law Montgomery's comments on the bravery and tenacity of his men during the battle for the bridge.

While we were enjoying a taxpayer-funded battlefield trip in Europe, the eyes of the world were turning back to the Middle East. Defence and politicians were beginning to plan a military response to the meteoric rise of the Islamic State in Iraq, which would see Charlie Company redirected to the first rotation of the SOTG–Iraq.

While our platoon was deployed in Europe, the other assault platoon in Charlie Company was training in Papua New Guinea, starting with a water parachute insertion exercise. As the situation in Iraq deteriorated, the exercise was cancelled, seeing the platoon return to Sydney to prepare for a possible deployment.

We thought we were kissed on the dick partying in Amsterdam while the poor bastards in uniform platoon were sweating their balls off in the jungles of New Guinea. But our attitude suddenly changed when we found out they were heading into the UAE within days to deploy to Iraq—we were gutted.

On 3 October 2014, Prime Minister Tony Abbot announced Australia would deploy forces to support the US effort to counter ISIS, and the Australian task group TG632, SOTG–Iraq was formed, which included Charlie Company. The task group would spend

weeks in the UAE while the governments of Iraq and Australia negotiated the Australian deployment terms. Typically, a status of forces
(SOFA) agreement is negotiated to protect Australian soldiers from
prosecution under the host nation's laws. And there were significant
delays in achieving the SOFA in this case because the Iraqi government had begun to fracture as ISIS claimed more ground around
major cities.[47] Eventually, it was agreed that the task group would
deploy on diplomatic passports, bypassing the requirement for
a SOFA.

Initially, this deployment involved training the Iraqi Counter
Terrorism Service in Baghdad and at Al Assad Airbase to the north.
At Al Assad, while the teams began fortifying their positions and
tried to build some rapport with the Iraqis, they received daily
rocket attacks. Within two years, however, 2 Cdo Regt would play
a pivotal role in a battle, the scale of which had not been seen since
the Second World War.

CHAPTER 32

FATHERHOOD

Sarah and I had been trying for a baby before my 2013 deployment. After months without success, we decided to see a fertility specialist, who informed us we would have to go through IVF if we wanted a family. Sarah's severe endometriosis would make falling pregnant naturally unlikely. I had also frozen my sperm before the trip. If I got my balls blown off, I still wanted to be a dad.

After the trip to Europe, Sarah endured dozens of medical appointments and blood tests. Finally, it was my time to contribute to the IVF process. I walked into the fertility department at Westmead Hospital in Sydney and approached the nurses' desk to tell them my name. I was given a jar and ushered into a small room with a leather couch, a box of tissues and a stack of 1980s *Penthouse* magazines. The nurse asked me if I had any questions, and I replied that I was well prepared—I had been training for this moment since I was twelve years old. She didn't think my comment was as funny or clever as I did.

I casually walked over and handed the nurse my future daughter. Weeks later, we found out the process had been successful, and

I prepared myself for fatherhood, which I found more daunting than anything I had experienced in my life thus far.

To this point, I had been hopeless with money. You would think someone with a humble upbringing would be doing everything he could to secure his financial future, but I spent every dollar I earned. I would have to pull my socks up to ensure my daughter grew up in financial stability.

Knowing nothing about personal finances, I embarked on a learning journey. I had a small brown notebook and would allocate 30 minutes a night to studying online. I started with a search for 'what is equity'. Then the list continued, 'how does interest work', 'what is inflation', 'how does tax work'. I spent every spare minute I had learning as much as possible. This led to a portfolio of investment properties and shares, but I didn't stop there. I even attained a Diploma in Finance and Mortgage Broking and a Certificate IV in Credit Management, so I could make better decisions about investing and borrowing money.

I was sound asleep early one July morning when Sarah grabbed my arm. I had been sleeping lightly for the past few nights, with our hospital bags packed waiting for this moment. I leapt out of bed, grabbed the bags, locked the house, and helped Sarah into the car.

Sarah was taken into the maternity ward as I nervously waited outside until I was allowed to be with her. I walked outside the hospital. It was mid-morning, and I had always said I would quit smoking when I was a father. At 10.30 a.m., I threw my cigarette out. I haven't smoked a cigarette since.

Then it was time to escort Sarah into the operating theatre for her caesarean; I was nervous but tried to put on a brave face for her.

Moments later, I saw a little head covered in fluid, an arm, and some legs. I stood and watched in amazement as this little body came to life and started screaming.

Alice was the most beautiful thing I had ever seen. In that moment, I felt a love I didn't know existed. I was overcome with emotions: she would become the centre of my universe. I felt such an overwhelming sense of responsibility. I knew my sole purpose was to protect my flesh and blood.

I cherished every second I had with Alice, and in time this came to conflict with my other love—being a commando. In the end, the job would lose.

On 16 February 2015, we were rocked by the tragic death of Private Viv Hunt. On returning from Rotation XII in 2010, Viv had a difficult time dealing with the helicopter crash and held onto a lot of guilt—mainly about being unable to save Chucky, despite knowing his injuries were too severe for him to be saved. Viv liked a drink and would turn to the bottle for solace.

Like most operators, Viv kept up a façade to ensure he would deploy again, which he did with Alpha Company's last rotation in July 2012. On return from that rotation, he stopped coming to work, which rang warning bells for his mates.

He began treatment and was placed under full-time observation at the on-base hospital. While Anthony Dimov was working with Mark at the unit's Human Performance Optimisation cell, he would regularly visit Viv, who started gaining a lot of weight from the cocktail of antidepressant medications he was given. Anthony would take him for drives to the shops, and noticed that nothing seemed to help. Some former unit members had created an outdoor 'tough mudder'–style obstacle course business, and Anthony even took Viv to north Queensland to attend one of the events, hoping a change of scenery might benefit him.

Viv regularly spoke about his experiences in Afghanistan, repeating stories of contacts. One day, he turned to Anthony and said, 'I just want to kill people.' The war in Afghanistan was over for Australia, but it wasn't for Viv. He may not have died in combat, but Viv's decline and death can be directly attributed to his combat deployments.

Viv passed away in his home in Perth, his heavy dose of medication exacerbating undiagnosed pneumonia that was affecting his breathing, which was his cause of death. A funeral service was held in Perth, then a traditional Māori ceremony with his extended family in New Zealand. It was a sad ending to a career dedicated to the service of the nation, and another tragic casualty of the war—not the last for the regiment.

As the years went on, the loss of Tim Aplin would continue to severely affect his children. His former wife Jen has told me that Josie was so angry at him for leaving and for dying that she would trash her room. Daniel refused to talk about it, but one day he broke down in the shower, sobbing, which was unusual for him. The impact of Tim's death didn't diminish as Josie and Daniel began their teen years. One night, Jen stood on the front patio, at her wits' end, ready to leave the house, but she managed to hang on. Jen says, 'Over time, Josie began to get more involved, laying wreaths on ANZAC Day, but it was still too hard for Daniel. It was a horrible time, overwhelming, the worst thing anyone could go through.'

However, despite the trauma of the loss of her dad, Josie works to help other veterans and their families. Along with Taylah Langley, the daughter of Sergeant Todd Langley, Josie is an ambassador for the Zero79 Foundation, working actively in the commando community to help other families in their darkest moments.

CHAPTER 33

THE LIONS OF MESOPOTAMIA

The younger operators who had not been to Afghanistan were itching to get to Iraq, where Charlie Company would play a big role in the Battle of Mosul in 2016–17. The fight for this ancient city was sadly one of the few successes in the Middle East for coalition forces in recent times. My role, when I arrived with Charlie Company in November 2016, was to remain in Baghdad to train the Special Tactics Unit (STU) operators from the Iraqi Counter Terrorism Service.

This was the first time I was okay with not being near the action. I was comfortable to stay safely behind the wire, not for myself, but for my daughter. I would picture her standing with Sarah at a ramp ceremony in Richmond, as I had done so many times, and imagine the anguish my death would cause my family. I didn't know this then, but a tiny seed was planted in my mind at this time.

The Baghdad Diplomatic Support Centre (BDSC), my home for the next six months, was a large base opposite Baghdad International Airport. It housed multiple coalition troops, including the US troops, the Italians, the Polish, the British and the Australians. It was run and administered by the US Department of State, which occupied a large compound in the middle of the base, as well as a fleet of US aircraft and their supporting units. Compared to the other locations where 2 Cdo Regt teams were housed during Operation Okra, the name given to the Australian mission, it was a holiday.

BDSC was contained inside the walls of a larger military zone, guarded and patrolled by the Iraqis, and was probably the safest place on the planet, thanks to the thorough security protocols that protected it. To get into BDSC, you had to pass through the main security checkpoints, known as 'air locks'—bunkers with two blast- and ballistic-proof doors—manned by African security contractors. Vehicles would enter a bunker through one gate, and it would shut behind them. Sniffer dogs and security guards would search the vehicle for bombs, then allow it to enter the base through the other ballistic door once cleared.

I chatted with the African guards while they searched my car, and I was shocked to hear some of their stories. Most had been there for years, only going home once a year to see their families. They were only earning a few hundred US dollars a week—a high income by their standards, but minimal compared to what the defence contractors were paid. It was exploitation of migrant workers at the coalface of the military–industrial complex. I felt sorry for them and bought them gifts from the shop on base before I flew home.

The dining facility fed the entire base of diplomats, international coalition forces and civilian contractors. In typical US fashion, the mess was enormous, offering every type of fruit, dessert, snack and meal. Each night there would be a theme for dinner: Mexican night, Indian night and, my favourite, wing night, where you could load up on as many chicken wings as you could eat. We had to train every day, but if we hadn't, we would have left BDSC 10 kilos heavier.

As a qualified sniper supervisor, I was initially tasked with training the snipers from the 1st Special Tactics Unit (1 STU), the

Iraqis' premier SF unit, who had vast combat experience from recent years. Despite being poorly equipped by our standards, the operators were professional, determined and a cut above the conventional Iraqi forces.

On arriving at BDSC, I received my handover, and the role seemed straightforward. As a TL, I had a 2ic, Geoff, who would support the logistics as I delivered a training program for the twenty or so Iraqi snipers. This consisted mainly of shooting coaching and teaching the basics of external ballistics theory, so I wasn't expecting to do much more. Before we began, I wanted a few days to get to know the Iraqi snipers, gauge their skill level, and appreciate how they were typically employed in operations supporting the STU assault platoons.

I was allocated a security-cleared interpreter, as most Iraqis speak little English. Ali, a 32-year-old Baghdad local, was a married father of two who had taught himself English working on coalition bases as a cleaner during the 2003 invasion. He had managed to keep his security clearance, working his way up to being a trusted coalition interpreter. I could be the world's best instructor with a perfect training program, but if there were a disconnect between the interpreter and me, most of it would be lost in translation.

Before we started training, I took time to teach Ali key concepts that I thought would be problematic for the snipers. I told him he wasn't just my interpreter, he was my assistant instructor, which he seemed pleased with, and he approached the training with enthusiasm, feeling more like part of the team than just a conduit.

My first encounter with the Iraqis was a surprise. My experiences with our Afghan partner force had led me to have low expectations. This was different. Three black US Humvees arrived at the range, with all the soldiers in black combat clothing, helmets, NVG, and recon wraps covering their faces. They all carried M4 rifles, had modern ballistic plate carriers and took care with their sniper weapons, having them all in hard-cased protective covers— a sign of a sniper who knows the importance of protecting their most vital instrument.

I introduced myself, gave them my background, and asked them to train as they usually would, as I wanted to gain insight into their level of training and assess their leaders. The snipers lined up their guns, set up some steel plates, and began shooting. After an hour, the platoon commander gave the thumbs up. They were done. Their version of a day's training was very different from mine. As they packed up, I asked them if they could hang around so I could get to know the TLs, and I took Ali to find a quiet spot to chat with them individually.

The TLs had experienced significant combat in the past few years. One of them had fought alongside US SF over the years and told me stories of intense urban combat in Fallujah and Ramadi. He pulled out his phone and showed me a video of his platoon fighting in a hospital in Ramadi that ISIS had taken over. It was a maze of corridors and rooms, and the video showed them in an intense gunfight as they systematically cleared the hospital.

The video showed dead ISIS fighters and numerous Iraqi Special Operations Force casualties in a type of intense urban combat I had never seen before in modern wars. In Afghanistan, the most complex terrain we fought in was bazaars and clusters of compounds, but it paled compared to what I saw in the video. Instantly, I gained respect for them, acknowledging their immense experience fighting in an environment that no Australians had experienced since the Second World War. I wanted to do everything I could to prepare these guys for future combat, and went back to my room to develop a training program.

I gave them a few days off while I decided what the training would entail, consulting the intelligence cell in the SOTG to find out everything I could about the STU's role and how it would most likely be used in future operations. Complicating the training design was the fact that the teams were all operational and were continually called out for real-time jobs.

I included marksmanship, weapon preparation and basic ballistic theory, including assessing the wind and how they could maximise their scopes to improve the chance of a hit—which took a lot of work, as they all had different scopes and different ammunition types. I also included primary navigation, first aid and how to effectively report on their radios in support of an assault force.

Some days would be theory-based in the classroom, others would be at the range outside BDSC. Teaching navigation proved more difficult than I anticipated. The snipers used applications on their phones to navigate, and had difficulty understanding why they had to learn how to read maps and plot grid references.

I explained that the apps were a good tool, but the snipers needed to be able to use a map if their phone battery died. More importantly, they needed to learn map reading to communicate with coalition assets; their phones gave them their location, but they needed to improve in their ability to plan routes and distances.

Classroom days were exhausting. Teaching map reading to Australian soldiers can be challenging, but this was a different level. Most of these guys had less than a secondary education. I soon realised I would have to bring it back to a rudimentary level, explaining to them that the earth has magnetic fields and it spins on an axis, and outlining the difference between true north and magnetic north.

The other Aussie TLs at BDSC would often ask me why I bothered, and tell me to just take them to the range a few times a week, but I was determined to do the best I could with them. As the weeks went by, they began to appreciate the time and effort I was putting in with them, and I saw a significant improvement in their skills.

On my birthday, the Iraqis bought me a large cake and cups of fruit juice to celebrate, with balloons and signs taped up in the class-room. I was moved by their unexpected gesture, which strengthened my motivation to train them. But I was told a week later that I was being removed from training the snipers and was tasked with turning 1 STU into a Baghdad-based HR force. The snipers did not take it well, but they knew it was out of my hands.

Iraqi Special Operations Force had an HR force, but its only mandate was within the confines of the airport. It had therefore requested that 1 STU be trained as a dedicated HR force to respond to hostage situations in Baghdad and surrounding areas. Initially, I was told it would only be a selected group of STU operators, and I met with the Iraqi leadership to find out exactly what they wanted. When I asked the senior officer, who chain-smoked for the entire meeting, what he expected from the training, he showed me a YouTube video of the TAG-E from the early 2000s—the same video I had used years earlier as my inspiration for selection—and said, 'I want them to do this.'

I told him I would do my best and asked how many soldiers he wanted to be trained. 'All of them,' he said. I didn't think I had heard him right and asked him, 'All of them? The whole of 1 STU?' Given that 1 STU comprised three 90-man companies, I wondered how I could train that many Iraqis with just Geoff and me as instructors.

I returned to my room and spent the next few days designing a program on my laptop, but I soon had to accept that it would be impossible for just the two of us to train three companies in the nine-week window. I asked the SOTG to find more instructors to join Geoff and me and warned that otherwise the training would be limited to just one company. They obliged with four more inter-preters, two US Green Berets and two Italian navy SEALs.

Before starting with 1 STU, I organised a week of training with the instructors to review what we would teach and ensure we were all on the same page. The Green Berets were experienced TLs who had arrived, as most US SF do, believing their way was always better. After we spent some time on the range and in the Iraqi 'kill house', however, they soon realised Geoff and I knew what we were talking about and asked many questions about 2 Cdo Regt. The Italians were both senior and despite having different tactics, techniques and procedures from us, they also seemed competent, and I grew in confidence in our ability to provide useful training to the Iraqis.

Our training program had many elements. HR operators require better marksmanship skills than conventional soldiers, to reduce the risk of shooting hostages in complex environments. A conventional soldier can learn to shoot at the 'centre of the seen mass' and still be effective—even if they miss, it will serve the purpose of keeping the enemy's head down. In HR, a miss can still lead to hostages being executed. The other elements are risk and time. In a conventional fight, unnecessary aggression and speed can lead to casualties; the skill of restraint is known esoterically as 'tactical patience'.

Yet for HR, the mission is to save hostages, and the urgency of clearing a building full of hostages means that higher risk thresholds are accepted, depending on the size and complexity of the environment. A four-storey building with terrorists on the fourth floor would require a rapid assault to save hostages—it does not take much time for a terrorist to kill a dozen hostages with a machine gun. If, on the other hand, the locations of the hostages are unknown, a slow, silent assault may be better suited, with the HR force systematically clearing a building to locate them.

I realised it would be futile to spend too much time working on the STU operators' skills unless their leadership understood how to plan and conduct HR assaults. This wasn't easy, as all these guys knew was conventional war—they were used to calling in bombs and shooting everything in sight. These tactics were well suited to clearing ISIS from buildings in Fallujah but not to saving hostages from a shopping centre terrorist attack.

I divided the training blocks into individual and collective training. While the soldiers were at the range, I would take the officers and TLs for planning and tactical considerations. I initially met some resistance, but over the coming weeks, they started to understand how they would have to adapt their thinking if they were planning an HR assault. I continually made the point that there was a possibility they would be rescuing their own families from terrorists, so they couldn't just throw grenades into the room. The following week, that point would be shockingly reinforced.

I was giving a brief to one of the companies when all their phones started ringing. The group's mood changed instantly, and I knew something terrible had happened. One of the TLs began wailing while others ran off, screaming into their phones. I asked Ali what had happened. Looking through texts appearing on his phone, he told me: 'ISIS just blew up a school bus. Most of these guys live in that area and their kids go to that school.'

As I stood there watching that group of hardened Iraqi fighters, I tried to imagine what it would be like if my hometown, ravaged by decades of war, was being constantly attacked by extremists. I tried to imagine an exploding school bus that may have had my daughter on it. My respect for these men grew that afternoon. While most of the men in their country fled as refugees around the globe, these men didn't. They decided to stay and fight, despite the risk their families faced through them doing so.

Once I was happy the commanders understood the basic concepts of planning an HR mission, I ran training scenarios at a nearby training area, formerly one of Saddam's many palaces. I had seen pictures of the palace before the invasion, with its manicured lawns and swimming pools, all of which were now rundown and partially damaged. The gold-plated lifts and elegant architecture still remaining spoke of his wealth.

We started with the single team, then multi-team assaults, followed by sixteen-team, seven-car assaults onto multiple buildings by day and night. I also invited the snipers I had trained to start working with the assaulters, teaching them to build hides and report on what they could see. Seeing how far they had come was satisfying.

During training at night, I noticed how poor their awareness was under night vision, and that they always opted to use white-light torches on their weapons, as most soldiers not used to NVG tend to do. During the insertions, they would trip and fall. They also preferred not to do their helmet straps up properly, which meant any sudden head movements would move the NVGs from their eyes, rendering them useless. No matter how much I told them to do their straps up, they would loosen them again as soon as I turned around.

I always thrive when given autonomy. Where else would a corporal in the regular army be charged with teaching hundreds of Iraqis and leading an international team by himself? I never had anyone supervise me or look over my shoulder. I developed and implemented the training myself. There was complete trust in my ability to deliver it, which only made me work harder.

During a meal break at the range, I was pondering the helmet problem and the question of how to improve their confidence under NVG, when one of the soldiers found a soccer ball and started juggling it. The idea suddenly hit me. It was unorthodox, but it might work. After training, I told them a start time of 7 p.m., gave Ali some cash to buy soccer balls, and then returned to BDSC for dinner.

When they arrived, I broke them into smaller groups and told them to set up some goals, then handed them the soccer ball. I then turned off all the lights on the oval and told them to start. At first, they thought I was joking. I told them I was not, and to begin the game. Operating under NVG is more challenging than it seems in the movies. Getting the focus right to see near and far distances takes practice. Depth perception and hand–eye coordination are reduced, and the goggles need to sit a certain distance away from your eyes to maximise the field of view but minimise the effects of sweat fogging the lens—this is what I hoped playing soccer would teach them.

Within minutes of the game starting, I saw soldiers entirely miss opportunities to kick the ball, then stop to adjust their straps and focus their NVG—exactly what I hoped would happen. By the night's end, they finally knew what I had been harping on about for weeks. Years later, when I asked a 2 Cdo Regt operator how his trip to Iraq had been, he said he had enjoyed the trip but commented, 'I went to watch one of the STU platoons train one night. When I arrived, they weren't at the range but playing soccer under NVG!'

After a much-needed week off partying, or 'forced rest', in Dubai towards the end of the trip, we returned to say goodbye to the men we had been training for six months and wished them the best of luck in their future operations. One of the Iraqi officers presented Geoff and me with a captured ISIS flag they had taken off a dead fighter in one of their recent operations. The five terps brought home-cooked meals for us, and we ate one last meal at the range before departing.

Despite this not having been a combat trip, I thoroughly enjoyed my time training the Iraqi SF units. I left knowing I had done every-thing possible to prepare them for future combat, and had taken immense pride in watching them improve over the months. I must have been doing something right, as I was awarded the ADF Silver Commendation for my efforts, which I brushed off as 'no big deal' but was immensely proud of.

But as much as I enjoyed my deployment, I longed to see my daughter. I had missed key milestones, and for the first time, I started to ask myself if spending this much time away was worth it. So far, I had spent my entire career wishing for deployments—now I was indifferent, almost fearful of deploying again.

After six long months away, I grabbed my bags off the luggage belt at Sydney International Airport and walked out of the arrival gates, petrified that Alice would not remember me. As I walked through the gate, I saw her standing in front of Sarah. When I was a few metres away, she locked eyes with me and came running over to jump into my arms. It is hard to put into words how I felt at that moment. I realised right then that I never wanted to spend that long away from her again, and after that trip to Iraq I never have.

CHAPTER 34

FORAS ADMONITIO

After taking some time off when we returned from Iraq, Charlie Company rotated back onto offshore crisis response, which involved the usual exercises of endless hours preparing boats and vehicles. This time, however, I would have my own team. Unlike in the regular army, promotion to TL doesn't occur quickly or easily in SF. Regardless of your rank outside SOCOMD, non-officer trainees lose their rank and start back at private when they join SF. The average time from a commando private to junior TL (corporal; senior TLs are sergeants), was at least ten to thirteen years.

Having been injured, taken two years off and changed companies, my career path had been a little slower—but I didn't mind as it had given me more time on the tools at the sharp end.

My team's 2ic was again Shaun Taylor, who had left 2 Cdo Regt to pursue a career in the fitness industry and returned a few years later. Shaun was also from 3 RAR and had been my 2ic in Timor in 2006—now here we were, twelve years later, holding the same rank after restarting our careers in SOCOMD.

We spent a few weeks in Thailand training with their SF,

culminating in an HR exercise at Bangkok International Airport. We moved from the Thai base to a holding area close to the airport to begin preparing for the exercise. The scenario had a Thai Airways 747 hijacked by multiple terrorists who had taken dozens of hostages.

At home, this type of training is done in the middle of the night to avoid startling people or giving away any tactics and procedures, as bystanders now record videos and post them on social media. The Thais, however, didn't seem to have a problem with doing it out in the open.

We set up a holding area across the road from Suvarnabhumi Airport and prepared what we thought would be the usual routine of 'standing to' and 'standing down' as the exercise played out—a typical feature of exercises back home. We were using Thai-modified Humvee assault vehicles and set about getting our kit ready when one of the Thai commanders began yelling, 'Get ready—two minutes.' It looked like things were moving quickly. Within minutes, we were stood on the back and sides of the cars and roaring off into the after-noon traffic.

The Thai drivers turned on their lights and sirens to get through the gridlock, and cars swerved out of our way. Standing on the side of the car, in complete assault gear and gas mask, I looked over my shoulder to see two stunned faces looking up at me from a taxi. 'What the fuck? An Aussie,' one of them said, seeing the Aussie flag on my shoulder. Seconds later, we were tearing towards the runway.

As we approached the Thai Airlines aircraft, we drove within 50 metres of a Qantas jet that had just landed. The passengers had their faces pressed against the window, wondering what on earth was happening as we screeched to a stop. We entered the Thai aircraft, in which Thai military were role playing as passengers. Assaulting an aircraft in broad daylight with lights and sirens was a first. Within hours, the aircraft began boarding real passengers.

One of 2 Cdo Regt's roles was to provide close protection to high-ranking military officials and diplomats in declared theatres of ADF operations. I had completed one PSD task as a commando in 2014, as the medic, and was eager to gain more experience.

Ahead of time, a few operators would fly into the locations of the visit to do recon, and prepare for the main arrival. The rest of the team would accompany the VIP and the official party into the country later. Between 2018 and 2020, before the Covid-19 pandemic, Charlie Company completed dozens of PSDs in the Middle East. Some of the company's shooters were among the most experienced PSD operators in the regiment, and I was keen to learn as much as I could from them.

In 2018, I deployed as the recon TL to Afghanistan, where my small team would spend a few weeks planning for Governor-General Sir Peter Cosgrove's upcoming visit. Despite Afghanistan being in a warzone, the risk was relatively low by this time, and the tour was limited to mainly RW flights and vehicle moves in Kabul and Baghdad. Every second of the visit had to be meticulously planned. Every piece of ground he would walk on, every door he would walk through and every move he would make, whether via car or RW, had to be reviewed, and contingency plans put in place in case something went wrong. For road moves, traffic congestion had to be analysed and plans put in place for breakdown, heavy traffic or ambush scenarios. For RW moves, we had to think of what to do if the aircraft crashed or had to land somewhere unexpected due to technical issues. We even conducted a key rehearsal that outlined who had keys for which gate or room, and at which stage they would be handed to the VIP party.

I relished the autonomy and responsibility of the task; nowhere else in the ADF would a mere corporal oversee the planning and execution of a phase of a visit from the governor-general, Australia's commander-in-chief.

For the recon team to be successful, particularly in Kabul, team members were heavily reliant on the personnel and resources of regular ADF elements, in particular the HQ elements in Kabul, located next to Kabul International Airport. But because there was a clash of cultures between SOCOMD and the regular units, it turned out that the most challenging element of the PSD was threats not from bad actors but from a few other Australians. Some people, typically officers and WOs, were what we called 'SF haters'. For whatever reason, they looked at us with disdain and took every opportunity to inhibit our progress. Complicating this was the fact that the highest-ranking person on the PSD recon was a corporal. Some of them simply could not get their heads around a corporal overseeing an entire portion of a PSD, and they took offence at having to work for a *lowly* corporal.

It was even worse for the privates. Once on a PSD job, I tasked a private by the name of George to fly out to an Aussie patrol base to liaise with the company commander to discuss the finer details of the scheduled visit. George sent emails, booked his flight, gave me a back-brief on his plan, and then went off for a few days. I texted the PSD commander back at Camp Baird, Brad, about George's movements, and he replied with a thumbs-up. There was complete trust in me, and I had complete trust in my team member. That's just how it works.

But the patrol base commander George was meeting with, who had just rotated into his role, was shocked when he discovered we had sent a private, and he started pushing back on requests. George called me, understandably frustrated. I urged him to take some time, analyse his interaction so far and find a fix. I wanted him to devise a solution himself, as this was the only way he would learn. So he walked into the commander's office, and apologised for getting off on the wrong foot. He told the commander he hadn't done this before, and that help from an experienced officer like him would be much appreciated.

The commander's tone changed immediately, and he went out of his way to help from that point. George was an experienced operator—he had done more PSDs than I had—but he swallowed his pride and put the mission first. Thinking outside the box and finding novel solutions is not just a hallmark of SF in combat—it has applications in other areas.

Before that PSD, I had given some recommended reading to the boys to enhance their soft skills. One book was Dale Carnegie's *How to Win Friends and Influence People*, which George had read, and he had adopted the strategy 'Make the other person feel important'. You could be the world's best door-kicker, but you wouldn't be suited to PSD work if you couldn't build trust and communicate effectively.

Other times we would get hassled about our weapons. Certain areas were safe and required members only to be in the 'load' condition—a magazine on the weapon but no round chamber in the barrel. On PSD taskings, we had waivers to always be in the 'action' condition, which meant we just needed to flick off the safety catch and start shooting. This included inside buildings, vehicles and aircraft.

On one job, we had a lieutenant colonel on a flight. He walked over to me to let me know my weapon was in action, which was against policy, and said he wanted my name and service number. I could have told him we had a waiver if he had asked me, but because he was a cock, I gave him my details and he took them down in his notebook. I took great pleasure thinking of the time that he would spend drafting angry emails, only to find out we had waivers.

In 2018, as well as the governor-general's visit to Afghanistan, we conducted a PSD for Prime Minister Scott Morrison's visit to Iraq and Afghanistan, where I would be his bodyguard.

I found the PM to be friendly, with a genuine affection for the ADF. We received him at Camp Baird, escorted by the UAE Presidential Guard, and spent some time giving briefs and sizing him up for body armour before flying off to Iraq. The PM's staff fussed around, handing him notes and giving him more briefs to read, and I soon realised just how busy he must be in his day-to-day job. The Department of the Prime Minister and Cabinet staff were excellent, but his travelling media team was more challenging.

They asked me to move away from the PM whenever I got off an aircraft or walked into a venue, as they didn't want to have to edit the footage—as I had a protected identity, I could not have my face shown in the media. I met their requests where I could, but I had a job to do, just as they did. And I did end up on the nightly news walking behind the PM as we stepped off the plane in Baghdad—my face blurred, of course.

As I was in a suit, I had a radio strapped to my lower back with only my earpiece showing and a Glock pistol on my belt. After a few hours, the radio started burning my back, and all I could think about was ripping it off. We met with the Iraqi president at his palace, by which time I was sure I had melted my kidneys.

The trip went on without issues, and we bid the PM and his team farewell at Camp Baird. As we were driving back through the streets of Baghdad from the Iraqi presidential palace, I had to pinch myself. From a kid of Kathmandu to a high-school dropout, then a shitbag digger at 3 RAR, I had become the bodyguard for the prime minister of Australia in a warzone. That was something to be proud of.

In 2020, I rotated back to the TAG-E as a TL. Since my previous time on the TAG-E as a sniper back in 2016, the weapons, equipment, tactics and processes had changed for the better. During Covid, we were classified by the government as an essential service, and we had a good year of training despite the lockdowns. The pandemic allowed us to train in venues we usually could not access. Training offsite allowed the junior members of the team to get a feel for how to adapt CQB techniques outside of the SFTF at work, and tested the TLs on their command and control in complex urban environments.

Despite enjoying my time on the TAG, I knew I had to start making plans for my exit from the regiment. I applied for the University of New South Wales postgraduate program offered by Defence, to give myself the best possible chance of success in my post-army life. As I had left school in Year 10, I didn't like my prospects, but much to my surprise I was accepted into the Master of Business course, fully funded by Defence, to be completed part-time over the next four years.

After a few subjects, I fell into a study rhythm. Some subjects I enjoyed, and used the regiment in my case studies. I struggled with other subjects, such as Accounting for Financial Management, and paid for an online tutor to coach me through accounting theories and formulas. After four long years, I graduated with a Master's degree—the first person in my family to do so.

At this time, Sarah and I decided to leave Sydney for the New South Wales Central Coast. As much as we liked living in Sydney's Hills district, we wanted Alice to spend her weekends at the beach swimming and surfing, not hanging around shopping centres, which was the only thing for kids to do on weekends in the Hills district. Sarah's parents were from the Central Coast, and I loved the summer weekends we would spend at the beach.

The move also coincided with my promotion course for sergeant, which I completed online due to Covid. The combination of study, my promotion courses and planning the move led to some very long days. On my promotion course, I was required to complete a back-brief for an operation to the instructors, which I did in the carpark at a McDonald's restaurant on one of the countless drives with the car packed full of things that we couldn't put in moving boxes. I grabbed a latte and sat in my car to commence my assessment, which I saw purely as a 'box-ticking' activity.

SOCOMD's promotion and progression pathway centred on our core skills, and took more than twelve months to complete. We were still required to complete promotion courses with the regular army though. As I began my brief, the instructor stopped me.

'Corporal Ryder, are you at a McDonald's carpark?' he asked me.

'Yes, I am,' I replied.

'Did anyone say you could do that?' he asked, visibly angry on the video call.

'Well, I was informed this course was to be done remotely. I am doing this remotely,' I said, doing my best to sound sincere.

Despite my utter disregard for the course, he knew I was right. I passed with flying colours.

CHAPTER 35

THE WINDS OF CHANGE

A series of events beginning in 2016 sent shockwaves through the SF community, with long-lasting ramifications for SOCOMD.

In May 2016, in response to rumours of war crimes by Australian SF, Major General Paul Brereton, a NSW Supreme Court judge, was commissioned to lead an inquiry into the conduct of the ADF during the war in Afghanistan between 2005 and 2016. *The Inspector-General of the Australian Defence Force Afghanistan Inquiry report*, commonly known as the Brereton Report, included extensive interviews and thousands of documents.

On 16 March 2020, ABC TV's *Four Corners* aired an episode called 'The Killing Fields' showing an SASR trooper killing an apparently unarmed Afghan male. The audio of the operator showed him asking his TL, 'Do you want me to drop this cunt?' before shooting the man. It gripped the nation and would become headline news worldwide.

Released to the public 19 November 2020, the Brereton Report revealed 23 incidents where SF, predominantly SASR, were allegedly involved in the unlawful killings of 39 Afghan civilians and prisoners, and recommended a criminal investigation into nineteen soldiers. It also revealed a toxic culture in SOCOMD, and rivalry between SASR and commandos.

In response to the Brereton Report, the Office of the Special Investigator was established, and it would interview and conduct searches of the homes of numerous current and former members of SOCOMD.

In November 2020, we all crammed into the briefing room at the TAG and watched the media address by the chief of the defence force, General Angus Campbell, on the findings of the report. We heard him say, 'And to the people of Australia, I am sincerely sorry for any wrongdoing by members of the ADF.'

We are all proud operators, and news of possible crimes committed by our colleagues shocked us. But the chief's language gave us an insight into how this saga might unfold—with those of us at the coalface paying the highest price.

'I'm confused. Wasn't this just supposed to be an initial report? It seems like they have already made their minds up,' a colleague beside me commented. I shared his view. As did Martin Fox, an operator who served most of his time in the regiment with Alpha Company: 'It seemed like they'd already made their minds up, and now were in damage control.'

SASR's 2 Squadron was consequently disbanded, and numerous SASR soldiers were given their notice to show cause, an administrative process allowing ADF members an opportunity to reply to findings. In addition, a reform process began to improve the relationship between the west coast (SASR) and the east coast (commandos). In 2021 and 2022, I took part in countless working groups with SASR to find a way forward with a combined selection course and training cycle. Perth was vehemently against the idea, claiming that the integrity of their unit would be compromised. To be fair, most of us on the east coast didn't want it either.

The entire inquiry impacted the morale and identity of the regiment. From 2020 onwards, there was a drastic increase in discharges from 2 Cdo Regt. For some, it was just their time. For others, the Brereton Report and the ADF's handling of it were enough to make them look for the door.

'I realised I had zero willingness to risk my life for an organisation where officers can abrogate all responsibility, and the junior ranks at the coalface are held culpable, so I left,' said Martin Fox. This view was shared by many.

As the reform process evolved, the mundane tasks imposed on us felt like retribution. This was particularly frustrating for operators who had never been to Afghanistan. 'We joined 2 Cdo Regt as we wanted to be a part of a premier fighting force. Instead, we were being used for floods, fire and Covid assistance, which everyone saw as a punishment from the Afghan inquiry, where the narrative from the brass seemed to be the abolition of a culture of elitism, so I put my discharge in,' said Nick, a senior operator who had never deployed to Afghanistan. Again, this was a view shared by many.

The regiment was used to provide assistance for flood disasters, bushfires and Covid-19, all under an ADF operations banner. Again, the frustration wasn't with the fact that operators were being used to help Australians—that's why commandos exist. The frustration was with *how* the regiment was used. 'We had highly trained water operators filling sandbags, while Australians climbed onto their roofs waiting to be rescued. We could have had our boats and medical teams on the ground in hours providing specialist rescue, but it's like we couldn't do anything that was perceived as "special", as a punishment for alleged war crimes,' said Martin.

Regardless, the regiment was still putting operators in harm's way. 'I was sitting in Iraq, away from my family, under rocket fire every night, while back home they watched SF being called murderers on the nightly news,' said one senior operator with whom I did selection, who didn't wish to be named. 'I thought to myself, "Why am I here?" It was a key reason for me to put my discharge in when I got back.'

During my year on the TAG-E in 2020, my body started failing me. Years of lugging around a heavy pack had caught up with me, and standing around in my body armour and helmet was causing serious pain in my lower back and neck, so I asked for a posting to the ADFSSO training wing as an instructor. The posting would give me time to study for my degree, and I could remain up to speed on the tools by teaching core commando skills to the reo.

I knew I was in the final years of my army service. And if I couldn't hang around for another decade, I wanted to make sure the next generation could benefit from the lessons I had learned in my career. By becoming an instructor, I could also develop my management and administration skills to help me in my next career, whatever that might be.

I was promoted to sergeant before posting to the school, and for the first year understudied a colleague of mine who was the senior instructor there. At the same time, I filled the role of course manager for the demolitions and breaching course. I embraced the new role and, for the first time, enjoyed being behind a desk, planning and developing the administration and logistics elements of the course.

The small team of training wing instructors worked hard to ensure that the next generation of commandos taking up positions in the regiment teams were prepared for the vast array of tasks that the government requires of our unit. While our courses were on, we worked long hours, sometimes up to sixteen-hour days, for weeks on end. But when we weren't running courses, we had a lot of flexibility with our hours, which suited me well with university and the constant driving up and down the coast to see my family.

My career started at the school and would now finish at the school. As always, my imposter syndrome set in before I began teaching, and I had to remind myself that I was an experienced member of the regiment, and that despite how I felt, I now had an opportunity to give back to the future generations of operators.

In my second year at the school, I took over as the senior instructor for the demolitions course and the SF weapons and precision strike direct action and recovery continuum courses for the Royal Australian Navy clearance drivers who form the water platoon in the TAG. I thoroughly enjoyed seeing months of planning coming to fruition.

CHAPTER 36

ZERO REGRETS

I was on three months' leave, and just before Christmas I got a phone call from the RSM of 2 Cdo Regt asking me if I wished to deploy back to Iraq early the following year. I would work with a small team of Australians and US Navy SEALs. For many, this would have been a dream opportunity. But I still had zero desire to spend six months away from home, and I politely declined. There were plenty of other lads who could fill the spot.

I tried to imagine my life not being a commando, and spent many sleepless nights reflecting on this. Ultimately, I decided it was time for me to move on. I was approaching 40 and had spent 22 years in the army. If I left now, I could start another career, but if I stayed another five or six years, my prospects for another career would be limited by my age.

During my time off, I realised how nice it was to be home. I could see Sarah and Alice every day and be present for once, not having my mind race, constantly thinking about work. And yet. Despite having given the regiment the better part of my adult life, I felt like I was letting it down. I thought about all the boys I had trained at the school and felt as if, should they deploy, I should be there to guide and mentor them, as my previous team commander had done for me. I imagined what it would be like if I turned on the news and saw commandos gunfighting in some foreign land, while I sat at home and watched, now an outsider. Even worse, how would I feel if a commando had been killed, and I sat at home helpless, unable to attend the ramp ceremony as their casket draped with the Australian flag was carried off?

For so long, I was the commando—it wasn't just a job, it had become my identity. Once I left, who was I? I had always dreaded being just a 'normal' person, and I had spent more than two decades looking down on civilians. I judged everyone and everything through the lens of a commando, having unrealistically high expectations of everyone around me, as well as of myself.

During my time off, I received the news that a friend from high school had passed away, and I attended her funeral and then the wake at a pub. As the beers started to flow, I talked to people I hadn't seen in years, who all had questions about life in the army as a commando, and about my time in Afghanistan. I will admit I relished the attention. For someone who wanted nothing more than to be accepted and fit in as a kid at school, I was now the person with the stories everyone wanted to hear. I was the guy they all talked about. In some strange way, I felt like I was finally validated.

Then it dawned on me—my family and the people who loved and cared about me the most couldn't care less if I was a commando, a plumber or a florist. They wanted the best for me, and mainly they just wanted me around.

I had been staying in the army because I was petrified about who I was on the outside. At 39, I was embarking on a journey of self-discovery that most people go through in their late teens or early twenties.

I am out of the army now, and the world on the outside is different but not as scary as I imagined. I have come to terms with the fact that although I may no longer be in uniform, I will always be a commando—that will never change. Weapons, technology and tactics will change, but the one thing that won't change is that people will be sent into harm's way, and SF will again bear most of the deaths and injuries.

War is an extension of politics, and mistakes and poor decisions are made. We can spend a lifetime blaming politicians and military commanders for committing Australians to wars in faraway lands, and view the veterans as victims of these decisions. I can't speak for those with other jobs in the ADF, but I can tell you that no single commando regretted being deployed to Afghanistan or any other part of the globe.

Yes, the war did take many casualties, in body and spirit, but if our bodies were up to it and a similar war broke out, I know there would still be dozens of us lining up again, ready to throw on our body armour and get back into the fight. We are not victims and nor are we survivors. We are special operators who all knew the risks when we signed up. Like most former operators of the regiment, if I had my time again, I wouldn't change a thing—I have zero regrets.

COMMANDO ROLL OF HONOUR (2007-2023)

1. Private Luke James Worsley: serving with the SOTG in Uruzgan province in southern Afghanistan when killed in a deliberate operation against Taliban leadership on 23 November 2007.
2. Lance Corporal Jason Paul Marks: serving with the SOTG when killed during deliberate operations against a Taliban safe haven on 27 April 2008 in Afghanistan.
3. Lieutenant Michael Housdan Fussell: serving with the SOTG when killed by an improvised explosive device while conducting a dismounted patrol in Uruzgan province, Afghanistan, on 27 November 2008.
4. Private Gregory Michael Sher: serving with the SOTG in Uruzgan province in southern Afghanistan when killed in a rocket attack on 4 January 2009.
5. Lance Corporal Mason Kerrin Edwards: serving with the Sydney-based 2nd Commando Regiment when killed in an operational training accident at Cultana Range, South Australia, on 20 October 2009.

6. Private Timothy James Aplin: serving with the SOTG when he tragically lost his life in a helicopter crash in Afghanistan on 21 June 2010, during his second tour of Afghanistan.

7. Private Benjamin Adam Chuck: serving with the SOTG when he tragically lost his life in a helicopter crash in Afghanistan on 21 June 2010.

8. Private Scott Travis Palmer: serving with the SOTG when he tragically lost his life in a helicopter crash in Afghanistan on 21 June 2010.

9. Sergeant Brett Mathew Wood, MG, DSM: serving with the SOTG when he was tragically killed by an explosive device in the conduct of operations within a Taliban safe haven in Afghanistan on 23 May 2011.

10. Sergeant Todd Mathew Langley: serving with the SOTG when he was killed during deliberate operations against a Taliban safe haven on 4 July 2011 in Afghanistan.

11. Private Nathanael John Aubrey Galagher: serving with the SOTG in Afghanistan when tragically killed in a helicopter crash on 30 August 2012 while on his second tour of Afghanistan.

12. Lance Corporal Mervyn John McDonald: serving with the SOTG in Afghanistan when tragically killed in a helicopter crash on 30 August 2012 while on his sixth tour of Afghanistan.

13. Corporal Cameron Steward Baird VC, MG: killed on operations during a battle in Afghanistan on 22 June 2013. Corporal Baird VC, MG would be posthumously awarded Australia's 100th Victoria Cross.

14. Lance Corporal Todd John Chidgey: serving with a protective security detachment, which provided protection for a senior Australian officer at Headquarters International Security Assistance Force Joint Command in Kabul, Afghanistan.

15. Sergeant Gary Frankie Francis: A former British Royal Marine and an expert in cold weather operations from the Sydney-based 2nd Commando Regiment, died during a training activity on Mount Cook in New Zealand on 16 July 2014.

16. Sergeant Peter Cafe: Sergeant Peter Cafe was one of the founding members of the TAG-E and completed numerous tours of Afghanistan. Sergeant Cafe took his own life on 6 February 2017.

17. Corporal Ian Turner: Corporal Ian Turner deployed eight times to Timor-Leste, Afghanistan and Iraq, but succumbed to combat-induced PTSD and took his own life on 15 July 2017.

ENDNOTES

1   The butts: The name given to a rifle range's dug-in target area. Older ranges require someone to raise and lower the target frame for firers to engage from varying distances.

2   Karen Middleton, *An Unwinnable War: Australia in Afghanistan*, Melbourne: Melbourne University Press, 2011.

3   James Kerr, *Legacy: What the All Blacks Teach Us about the Business of Life*, London: Constable, 2015.

4   Middleton, *An Unwinnable War*.

5   Chris Masters, *No Front Line: Australia's Special Forces at War in Afghanistan*, Sydney: Allen & Unwin, 2017, p. 77.

6   Geoffrey Robinson, *'If You Leave Us Here, We Will Die': How Genocide Was Stopped in East Timor*, Princeton: Princeton University Press, 2010.

7   Auscam: Australian camouflage pattern unique to Australian soldiers.

8   Face ripping: Army slang term for being reprimanded by a higher rank.

9   Matthew Morris, 'Nick Hill Australian Army Special Forces, 2nd Commando Regiment Warrant Officer', episode 91, *Zero Limits Podcast*, 16 March 2023, www.zerolimitspodcast.com/ep-91-nick-hill-australian-army-special-forces-2nd-commando-regiment-warrant-officer.

10 Dan Box, *Carry Me Home: The Life and Death of Private Jake Kovco*, Sydney: Allen & Unwin, 2008.

11 'Kovco's brother accuses military of destroying evidence', *ABC News*, 4 September 2006, https://www.abc.net.au/news/2006-09-04/kovcos-brother-accuses-military-of-destroying/1255180.

12   Brendan Nicholson & Sarah Smiles, 'Kovco debacle inquiry', *The Age*, 18 May 2006, www.theage.com.au/national/kovco-debacle-inquiry-20060518-ge2c4x.html.

13   Dry hole: An abandoned or empty compound.

14   The two main fighting units in the SOTG were the SASR's Force Element Alpha (FE-A), and the commandos' Force Element Bravo (FE-B).

15   Middleton, *An Unwinnable War*, p. 199.

16   ISR platforms: Or drones. Either manned or unmanned aircraft in support of ground troops.

17   Conga line: Slang for walking in single file to minimise the chance of stepping on an IED.

18   Aeromedical evacuation (AME): Typically, US military medical evacuation aircraft carrying specialist medical teams, usually located at larger coalition bases in southern Afghanistan.

19   Cat A: IEDs are given categories depending on their size. Cat A is the highest, usually denoting many explosives. IEDs typically held between 5 and 25 kilograms of home-made explosives.

20   Masters, *No Front Line*.

21   Dushka: Soviet-era 12.7mm .50-calibre heavy machine gun, pre-dating the Second World War.

22   'Sarbi', Australian War Memorial, www.awm.gov.au/learn/memorial-boxes/2/case-studies/sarbi.

23   *Allahu akbar*: Arabic phrase meaning 'God is most great'.

24   Masters, *No Front Line*.

25   Supersonic rounds: Bullets that travel faster than the speed of sound; subsonic rounds do not. Aurally, the two can be distinguished by the 'cracking' sound the supersonic bullet makes as it breaks the sound barrier.

26   Weapon rack: Swivel mount on the frame of the bike for the MAG58 and ammunition liners.

27   CH-47 Chinook: Tandem rotor heavy lift helicopter.

28   SR98 sniper rifle: Accuracy International, 7.63mm bolt-action rifle used in SOCOMD for the SF sniper course.

29   Bullet drop: The effect of gravity on a round once it leaves the gun barrel.

30   Surface pressure: The atmospheric pressure at a given point on the earth's surface.

31   Truing: The process of calculating the ballistic shooting algorithm for a bullet's flight path in specified environmental conditions.

32   Magnus effect: An observable phenomenon associated with a spinning object, where the path is deflected in a manner not present when the object is not spinning.

33   Anthony 'Harry' Moffit, *Eleven Bats: A story of combat, cricket and the SAS*, Sydney: Allen & Unwin, 2017.

34   Angles: The distance an operator can engage a target in proximity to another operator. Advanced SF training allows operators to shoot at reduced angles, which replicates real-time combat conditions.

35   Masters, *No Front Line*.

36   Kestrel weather station: Handheld, multifunction weather meter and data logger.

37   Masters, *No Front Line*.

38   Inquiry Officer's report into the deaths of Private T.J. Aplin, Private B.A. Chuck, and Private S.J. Palmer in Afghanistan on 21 June 2010 and 28 October 2010. Author's name redacted.

39   Whiteout: A term used to describe loss of vision through night-vision tubes when looking at a bright light.

40   Fallen Angel: A coalition-wide term used to communicate a downed aircraft.

41   Chris Masters, 'Australian war hero court drama', *Daily Telegraph*, 28 February 2011, www.dailytelegraph.com.au/australian-war-hero-court-trauma-/news-story/509ab812f303a873462b1f561409fcfa.

42   Masters, *No Front Line*.

43   Dan Pronk, *The Combat Doctor*, Sydney: Pan Macmillan, 2022.

44   Tier Units: The US classifies its special operations units in tiers, depending on the capability they provide. These units sit under the US Joint Special Operations Command, which comprises units from numerous services.

45   Middleton, *An Unwinnable War*.

46   Light assault order: An order for a short-duration task—less than 24 hours—with minimal equipment.

47   Ben McKelvey, *Mosul: Australia's Secret War Inside the ISIS Caliphate*, Sydney: Hachette Australia, 2020.

REFERENCES

Armitage, Rebecca & Lucia Stein, 'A royal massacre: 20 years ago, a lovesick Nepalese prince murdered his family', ABC News, 1 May 2023, www.abc.net.au/news/2021-05-01/how-a-lovesick-prince-wiped-out-nepals-royal-family/100056562

Blaxland, John, 'Operation Astute in Timor-Leste, 2006 and beyond', in *The Australian Army from Whitlam to Howard*, Melbourne: Cambridge University Press, 2015

Box, Dan, *Carry Me Home: The Life and Death of Private Jacob Kovco*, Sydney: Allen & Unwin, 2008

Calder, Simon, 'Malaysia Airlines Flight 17 crash: everything we know about the gunning down of a passenger plane', *The Independent*, 17 November 2022, www.independent.co.uk/travel/news-and-advice/mh17-crash-malaysia-airlines-ukraine-russia-what-happened-a9007826.html

'Complaint against parachute regiment', *Sydney Morning Herald*, 9 May 2002, www.smh.com.au/national/complaint-against-parachute-regiment-20020509-gdf9j3.html

Gregson, Jonathan, *Massacre in the Palace: The Doomed Royal Destiny of Nepal*, New York: Miramax, 2002

Joint Standing Committee on Foreign Affairs, Defence and Trade, *Rough Justice? An Investigation into Allegations of Brutality in the Army's Parachute Battalion*, Canberra: Commonwealth of Australia, 2001, www.aph.gov.au/Parliamentary_Business/Committees/Joint/Completed_Inquiries/jfadt/DOD_Rept/MJindex

Kerr, James, *Legacy: What the All Blacks Teach Us about the Business of Life*, London: Constable, 2015

McKelvey, Ben, *The Commando: The Life and Death of Cameron Baird VC, MG*, Sydney: Hachette Australia, 2017

McKelvey, Ben, *Mosul: Australia's Secret War Inside the ISIS Caliphate*, Sydney: Hachette Australia, 2020

Masters, Chris, *No Front Line: Australia's Special Forces at War in Afghanistan*, Sydney: Allen & Unwin, 2017

Masters, Chris, *Uncommon Soldier*, Sydney: Allen & Unwin, 2012

Middleton, Karen, *An Unwinnable War: Australia in Afghanistan*, Melbourne: Melbourne University Press, 2011

Moffit, Anthony 'Harry', *Eleven Balls: A story of combat, cricket and the SAS*, Sydney: Allen & Unwin, 2017

Morris, Matthew, 'Nick Hill Australian Army Special Forces, 2nd Commando Regiment Warrant Officer', *Zero Limits Podcast*, episode 91, 16 March 2023, www.zerolimitspodcast.com/ep-91-nick-hill-australian-army-special-forces-2nd-commando-regiment-warrant-officer

Nicholson, Brendan & Sarah Smiles, 'Kovco debacle inquiry', *The Age*, 18 May 2006, www.theage.com.au/national/kovco-debacle-inquiry-20060518-ge2c4x.html

Pronk, Dan. *The Combat Doctor: A Story of Battlefield Medicine and Resilience*, Sydney: Pan Macmillan, 2022

Robinson, Geoffrey, *'If You Leave Us Here, We Will Die': How genocide was stopped in East Timor*, Princeton: Princeton University Press, 2010

Witty, David, *The Iraqi Counter Terrorism Service*, Washington, DC: Brookings Institution, 2016, www.brookings.edu/wp-content/uploads/2016/06/David-Witty-Paper_Final_Web.pdf

ACKNOWLEDGEMENTS

Taking on the challenge of telling my story and that of the 2nd Commando Regiment during my time there came with many hurdles, mainly ones I created myself. I became fanatical about ensuring I did the regiment justice—I continually had to evaluate how much to reveal in the book, careful not to divulge so much that I would draw criticism from our community. I wanted to ensure this was not written in isolation but, as much as possible, collaboratively with the operators in the regiment, taking them on the journey with me. I hope I have been able to achieve that.

Thank you to all the current and former operators and their families who took the time to share their stories with me over numerous phone calls and Zoom recordings. I know it was challenging for some of you. Thank you for your kind words and encouragement and for entrusting me with your stories. Numerous stories of operators and their families didn't make the final version of the book. This is a memoir, not a historical account of the regiment; therefore, the publishers omitted most of the sections that I was not directly involved in. All your stories matter;

despite not being in this book, I hope they will be published someday.

The first years after separating from the defence forces are risky. This book became a way to close that chapter of my career, metaphorically and literally. The eight months it took to transform this from a journal and collection of stories into something resembling a book came at the cost of being present with my family. I was physically there, but my spirit was lost in the pages of this book—everything that wasn't writing became a distraction, a hindrance, something to be endured until I could return to writing. Thank you to my family for giving me the space and time to write.

Thank you to Sarah, who has been with me throughout this journey. Despite the stress and anxiety you were put through from the crash and the agonising recovery, you knew how much I needed to get my job back, and you pushed me to fight. I know the thirteen years I served after the crash, including multiple deployments, weren't easy for you, and I am eternally grateful for your love and support.

I called Chris Masters in early 2023 and shared with him that I had been doing some writing. I asked him to have a look, give me his thoughts and be brutally honest. Should this be a journal for me to keep a record of my career that would only be read by my family? Or would it be worth approaching publishers? I didn't want to waste my time if my writing was subpar. I sent him my manuscript, and he invited me to lunch a few weeks later. To my surprise, he told me I could write and should consider publishing. Aside from surprising me completely, Chris's words gave me the confidence to finish the project, energised and with a new focus. This was going to be a book.

Chris then introduced me to Elizabeth Weiss from Allen & Unwin, and a lunch meeting was arranged. I left the meeting unconvinced that Allen & Unwin would take it on. Weeks later, I received a letter and a contract to publish. It is safe to say that without Chris, my words would never have seen the light of day. For this, I am very grateful. Thank you for your mentorship and friendship.

To Elizabeth Weiss, Greer Gamble and the entire team at Allen & Unwin, thank you for embracing my vision and helping me transform my words into a book worthy of bearing the logo of the 2nd Commando Regiment on the cover. Thank you for your guidance, mentorship and professionalism throughout this process. I am humbled and proud to have Allen & Unwin's name on my book.

Finally, I want to acknowledge the families of all the fallen. The stories of the loss of your loved ones and the unit they belonged to deserve to be told. I am sorry I could not cover every single fallen commando. I hope a better understanding of the regiment in which they served can shed some light on their sacrifice and your pain.

THE ZERO79 FOUNDATION

The Zero79 Foundation's mission is to provide niche support to current and former commando operators and their families. Visit the website to donate or for more information.

zero79foundation.com